The Book of Bond, James Bond

by Hoyt L. Barber and Harry L. Barber

Dedication:
In loving memory of Peggy Barber
who generously gave us years of inspiration, guidance and support.
She will be forever in our Hearts and Minds.

Special thanks to:
Bryan Krofchok, Editor of *Shaken, Not Stirred,* a publication of the Ian Fleming Foundation, for his invaluable contribution to this work.

Kitty Kladstrup for her contribution and support.

Tifani Fulmer and Kim Terminel for their many long hours on the preparation of the manuscript.

The Book of Bond, James Bond
By Hoyt L. Barber and Harry L. Barber

Library of Congress Catalog Number: 99-62909

ISBN #1-890723-20-7

Library of Congress Cataloging-in-Publication Data
Hoyt L. Barber and Harry L. Barber

   The Book of Bond, James Bond

   1. The Book of Bond, James Bond
I. Title

Published by Cyclone Books, 420 Pablo Lane, Nipomo, CA 93444
Visit our website at http://cyclone.8m.com
Email us at info@cyclone.8m.com

Designed and edited by Melany Shapiro
Cover design by Tony Hubert of Trubeat Media   http://www.trubeat.com

First Printing 1999

Printed in the USA

INTRODUCTION

Not since the 1930's when author Robert J. Hogan described the daring exploits of America's flying spy "G-8" and his battle aces, Nippy Weston and Bull Martin, who flew their Spads over the Western Front in WWI, have we witnessed anyone comparable in stature to James Bond.

"G-8" and his comrades not only swept the Fokker D-7's from the skies, but oftentimes, as prisoners behind the German lines, they also had to do battle with a fiendish new plan or a machine of the German High Command in order to save the Allies from total destruction. Sound familiar? Oh yes, they were wonderful stories indeed!

Such stirring adventures contained the same ingredients as the future assignments of James Bond.

On Tuesday, January 15, 1952, Ian Fleming sat down before his twenty-year-old Imperial portable typewriter and, for the first time, placed the words "James Bond" to paper. In doing so, he changed the lives of thousands and provided pure enjoyment to millions more throughout the world.

Since that time, millions of words have been written about James Bond and Ian Fleming and millions of books have been sold detailing the exploits of the world's most famous secret agent.

However, for the avid Bond reader, film enthusiast, and/or memorabilia collector, there seemed to be a void; the lack of a quick and easy reference to "all things Bond". So many assignments, villians, and women over the years. And what about the automobiles, the weapons, and the continuous parade of characters that have passed across the Bond stage? After forty-seven years, recollections were beginning to fade.

Until now, there has never been an all-inclusive reference work on James Bond, nor one compiled in the "encyclopedia/almanac" format. The answer of course is *The Book of Bond, James Bond*. This is not a picture book nor a book of trivia, but rather a true encyclopedia and complete reference work.

When you read the Table of Contents you will realize that *The Book of Bond, James Bond* does indeed afford the reader quick, easy access to "all things Bond" – the most comprehensive work of its kind – together with information never before available to Bond enthusiasts. You will also note the ease and amplitude afforded by the encyclopedic plan, with the innumerable references easily found in the *alphabetic* format throughout the book.

Every attempt has been made to insure accuracy of the subject matter by going directly to the source. Hopefully *The Book of Bond, James Bond* will answer all the questions you may have regarding this fascinating and legendary figure of our time.

Hoyt L. Barber & Harry L. Barber

ACKNOWLEDGEMENTS

We would particularly like to thank the following individuals for their additional contributions to the manuscript and for making themselves accessible to us for further research questions.

Reg Abbiss, Rolls-Royce Motor Cars, Lyndhurst, New Jersey
Eric Barass, Rolls-Royce Enthusiasts Club, Tunbridge Wells, England
British Consulate General, Los Angeles, CA
Ralph Cole, Beretta USA Corp. Accokeek, Maryland
Sherry A Collins, Smith & Wesson, Springfield, MA
Patrick Curran and Sandy Stefaniak of the Wisconsin Center for Film and Theater Research, Madison, Wisconsin
Julianne Dalena, Venice Simplon-Orient Express, New York, NY
Linda M. DeProfio, Sturm, Ruger and Co., Southport, CT
Jean Diamond, London Management, London, England
The Lord Fairhaven DL, Anglesey Abbey, Cambridge, England
Ron Foster, Lotus Cars USA, Inc., Lawrenceville, Georgia
Patrick Giles, Royal Ordnance, Nottingham, England
Alex Glanville, National Motor Museum, Beaulieu, England
Steve Hoechster, Geltzer & Co., New York, NY
Peter Hoffman, Carl Walther, Ulm, West Germany
Per Janson, AB Bofors, Bofors, Sweden
Kathy L. Johnson, Aston Martin Lagonda, Stanford, CT
Gary S. Krampf, Sotheby's, New York.
Jacqueline G. Leggo, St. James's Management, Thames Ditton, England
Len Lonnegran and Jim Ventrilio, Saab Scandia of America, Orange, CT
John A. McGerty, Timberline-Hawk Co., Inc., Costa Mesa, CA
Jan C. Mladek, Colt Industries, Hartford, CT
Colleen E. Mueller, Piper Aircraft Corp., Vero Beach, Florida
Luigi Pellissier, Lancia, Torino, Italy
Pat Perilli and Sue Wilson, British Film Institute, London, England
Hardy Price, The Scottsdale Progress, Scottsdale, AZ
J.C. Proute, The Gleaner Company, Ltd., Kingston, Jamaica, WI
Charles Musse, Rex USA, Ltd., New York, NY
Richard F. Sailer, Goodyear Tire & Rubber Co., Akron, OH
Fred Sconberg, Snap Photo Imaging, Roseville, CA
George Walker, Glastron Boats, New Braunfels, TX
A. Werner, Heckler & Koch, Oberbdorf, West Germany
Wing Commander Kenneth H. Wallis, R.A.F. Retired, Wallis Autogyros, Reymerston Hall, Norfolk, England

For permission to reprint portions of the article "James Bond Collectibles" as requested, credit is given Lightner Publishing Corporation, Antiques & Collecting Hobbies Magazine, and authors Jon Heitland and Doug Redenius.

Table of Contents

The Book of Bond, James Bond is structured in encyclopedic format, with entries accessible through alphabetic reference, from A through Z. For quick reference, see Table of Contents.

ACADEMY AWARDS

1964 .... **GOLDFINGER**. Norman Wanstall, for best achievement in sound effects.
1965 .... **THUNDERBALL**. John Stears, for special effects.
1982 .... Albert R. Broccoli, the Irving G. Thalberg Award.[1]

ACADEMY AWARD NOMINATIONS

1971 .... **DIAMONDS ARE FOREVER**. Gordon McCallum, John Mitchell, Alfred J. Overton, for sound.
1973 .... **LIVE & LET DIE**. Paul McCartney & Wings for title song.
1977 .... **THE SPY WHO LOVED ME**. Ken Adams and Peter Lamont, for production design. For set direction, Hugh Scaife. Marvin Hamlisch and Carole Bayer, for best song and best score, "Nobody Does It Better."
1979 .... **MOONRAKER**. Derek Meddings, Paul Wilson and John Evons, for visual special effects.
1981 .... **FOR YOUR EYES ONLY**. Michael Leeson, Bill Conti and Sheena Easton for title song, "For Your Eyes Only".

[1] Has also been awarded the order of the British Empire (OBE) by Queen Elizabeth and the French Commandeur des Arts et des Lettres.

ACTORS AND ACTRESSES, BIOGRAPHIES

ADAMS, MAUDE. Actress. Born Maud Wikstrom in Lulea, Sweden February 12, 1945. Beautiful, striking, leading lady of films of the 70s and 80s. Portrayed Andrea in *The Man With The Golden Gun,* 1974 and the title role in *Octopussy,* 1983.

ANDRESS, URSULA. Actress. Born March 19, 1936 in Bern, Switzerland. Voluptuous beauty of quickie Italian films in the 50s. Portrayed Honey Ryder in the first Bond film *Dr. No* 1962 and Vesper Lynd in *Casino Royale,* 1967.

ARMENDARIZ, PEDRO. Actor. Born May 9, 1912 in Churnbusco, Mexico. Died 1963 of a self-inflicted gunshot wound after learning he had cancer. Portrayed Kermin Bey in *From Russia With Love,* 1963.

AUGER, CLAUDINE. Actress. Born April 26, 1942 in Paris. Former Miss France. An accomplished swimmer and skindiver. Studied at the Dramatic Conservatory. Star of French and international films since 1960. Portrayed Domino in *Thunderball,* 1965.

BAKER, GEORGE. Actor. Born April 1, 1931 in Varna, Bulgaria. Handsome leading man. On the stage from age 15. In films since 1953. Portrayed Sir Hilary Bray in *On Her Majesty's Secret Service,* 1969 and Captain Benson in *The Spy Who Loved Me,* 1977.

BAKER, JOE DON. Actor. Born February 12, 1936 in Goesbeck, Texas. Leading man of American Films. Best remembered for the film *Walking Tall.* Portrayed Witaker in *The Living Daylights,* 1987. Portrayed Jack Wade in *Goldeneye,* 1995, and *Tomorrow Never Dies,* 1997.

BARNES, PRISCILLA. Actress. Born in Ft. Dix, New Jersey December 7, 1956. Best known for her role as the dumb blonde in the TV series "Three's Company." Portrayed Della Churchill in *License to Kill,* 1989.

BASINGER, KIM. Actress. Born December 8, 1953 in Athens, Georgia. Beautiful, blonde blue-eyed leading lady of films of the 80's and 90's. Former Eileen Ford fashion model. Academy award, 1998. Portrayed Domino in *Never Say Never Again,* 1983.

BASS, ALFIE. Actor. Born April 8, 1921 in London. British character actor of stage, screen. In films since 1945. Portrayed the "Consumptive Italian" in *Moonraker,* 1979.

BECKWITH, REGINALD. Actor. Born November 2, 1908 in Houghton, England. Died in 1965. Character actor of British stage, TV, screen. A war correspondent for the BBC during WWII. Portrayed Kenniston in the film *Thunderball,* 1965.

BENNETT, JILL. Actress. Born December 24, 1931 in Penang, British Malaya. Died 1990. In films since 1952, mostly second-lead roles. Portrayed Jacoba Brink in *For Your Eyes Only,* 1981.

BESWICK, MARTINE. Actress. Born 1941 in Jamaica. Former Miss Jamaica. Portrayed Zora in *From Russia With Love,* 1963 and Paula in *Thunderball,* 1965.

BIANCHI, DANIELA. Actress. Born in Rome, Italy, 1942. Lovely leading lady of Italian and European action films. A student of classical ballet. Former Miss Italy and runner-up in the 1960 Miss Universe contest. Portrayed Tatiana Romanova in *From Russia With Love,* 1963.

BLACKMAN, HONOR. Actress. Born in 1926 in London. Leading lady of British films since 1947. Best known as Cathy Gale in the TV series, "The Avengers" and as Pussy Galore in *Goldfinger,* 1964.

BLISS, CAROLINE. Actress. Born in 1961 in England. Granddaughter of composer Sir Arthur Bliss, Master of the Queen's Music. Trained for the theatre at the Bristol Old Vic School. A member of the National Theatre Company. Portrayed Miss Moneypenny in *The Living Daylights,* 1987 and *License To Kill,* 1989.

BRANDAUER, KLAUS MARIA. Actor. Born 1944 in the Austrian province of Styria. A leading player of the Burgtheatre in Vienna. Made his film debut in 1971. Became an international star with his performance in the title role of "Mephisto" which won the 1981 Academy Award for best foreign language film. Portrayed Largo in *Never Say Never Again,* 1983.

BROSNAN, PIERCE. James Bond Number Five. See separate biography under Brosnan.

BROWN, ROBERT. Actor. Portrays 'M' in the Bond films. See separate biography under Brown.

CABOT, BRUCE. Actor. Born Jacques Etienne de Bujac April 20, 1904 in Carlsbad, New Mexico. Died in 1972. Grandson of the French Ambassador to the U.S. Most memorable role as that of the hero who saved Fay Wray from King Kong. Portrayed Saxby in *Diamonds Are Forever,* 1971.

CARRERA, BARBARA. Actress. Born 1945 in Managua, Nicaragua. Educated in the U.S. A former fashion model. Made her film debut in 1975 in *The Master Gunfighter.* Portrayed Fatima Blush in *Never Say Never Again,* 1983.

CASEY, BERNIE. Actor. Born in West Virginia. Master of Fine Arts from Bowling Green University. Accomplished painter and published poet. Made his screen debut in *Guns of the Magnificent Seven.* Portrayed Felix Leiter in *Never Say Never Again,* 1983.

CELI, ADOLFO. Actor. Born July 27, 1922 in Sicily. Died 1986. In films since the 40's, often times as the heavy. Films of note: *Von Ryan's Express, Murders in the Rue Morgue, Ten Little Indians, Hitler: The Last Ten Days.* Portrayed Largo in *Thunderball,* 1965.

CONNERY, SEAN. Actor. James Bond Number one. See separate biography under Connery.

CULVER, ROLAND. Actor. Born August 31, 1900 in London. Died 1984. A fighter pilot with the RAF in WWI. Made his film debut in 1931 playing character parts as a British gentleman. Portrayed the Home Secretary in *Thunderball,* 1965.

DALTON, TIMOTHY. Actor. James Bond Number Four. See separate biography under Dalton.

EATON, SHIRLEY. Actress. Born 1937 in London. Beautiful blonde of British comedy films. Best known to audiences as the girl painted in gold in *Goldfinger* and featured on a Life Magazine cover on November 6, 1964. Portrayed Jill Masterson in *Goldfinger,* 1964.

EKLAND, BRITT. Actress. Born Britt-Marie Eklund in 1942 in Stockholm, Sweden. Leading lady of international films since the 60s and formerly married to Peter Sellers. Portrayed Mary Goodnight in *The Man With The Golden Gun,* 1974.

FERZETTI, GABRIELE. Actor. Born Pasquale Ferzetti March 3, 1925 in Rome, Italy. Leading man of the Italian stage and international films. Portrayed Draco in *On Her Majesty's Secret Service,* 1969.

FOX, EDWARD. Actor. Born April 15, 1937 in London. British leading man. Films of note: *Edward & Mrs. Simpson, The Day of the Jackal, A Bridge Too Far, Force Ten From Navarone, Gandhi.* Winner of three British Academy Awards. Portrayed Sir Miles Messervy ('M') in *Never Say Never Again,* 1983.

FROBE, GERT. Actor. Born Gert Frober December 25, 1912 in Planitz, Zwickau, Germany. Died 1988. Made his film debut in 1948, often times as a heavy. Films of note: *Those Magnificent Men in Their Flying Machines, Chitty Chitty Bang Bang, Is Paris Burning?, The Longest Day.* He is best remembered in the title role of the *Goldfinger,* 1964.

GRAY, CHARLES. Actor. Born 1928 in England. Made his screen debut in *The Entertainer.* Other films of note: *The Secret War of Harry Frigg, The Seven Percent Solution, Silver Bears.* Portrayed Henderson in *You Only Live Twice,* 1967 and "Blofeld" in *Diamonds Are Forever,* 1971.

HEDISON, DAVID. Actor. Born Ara Heditson in Providence, Rhode Island May 20, 1929. Educated at Brown University. Made his film debut in *The Enemy Below.* Best known for his role as Captain Lee Crane in the TV series "Voyage To The Bottom of the Sea." Portrayed Felix Leiter in *Live & Let Die,* 1973 and *License to Kill,* 1989.

HUTTON, ROBERT. Actor. Born Robert Bruce Winne, June 11, 1920 in Kingston, N.Y. Leading man of American films. Became a screenwriter in the 70s. Portrayed the role of the "Leader's Aide" in the film *You Only Live Twice*, 1967.

JAMES, CLIFTON. Actor. Born May 29, 1921. Educated at Oregon University. Films of note: *The Last Mile, Cool Hand Luke, The Rievers, Silver Streak, Superman II.* Portrayed Sheriff J.W. Pepper in *Live & Let Die*, 1973 and *The Man With The Golden Gun*, 1974.

JURGENS, CURT. Actor. Born December 13, 1912 in Munich, Germany. Died 1982. Veteran of over 100 films. His autobiography was titled *Sixty & Not Yet Wise*. In 1944 he was sent to a concentration camp by direct order of Dr. Goebbels. Portrayed Karl Stromberg in *The Spy Who Loved Me*, 1977.

KEEN, GEOFFREY. Actor. Portrays Sir Freddie Gray, Minister of Defense in the Bond series. See separate biography under Keen.

KIEL, RICHARD. Actor. Born in Redford, Michigan. Memorable as the villain Jaws in *The Spy Who Loved Me*, 1977 and *Moonraker*, 1979.

KITZMILLER, JOHN. Actor. Born December 4, 1913 in Battle Creek, Michigan. Died 1965. An American serviceman who stayed in Europe at the close of WWII to act in European films. Portrayed Quarrel in *Dr. No*, 1962.

KNOX, ALEXANDER. Actor. Born January 16, 1907 in Strathroy, Ontario, Canada. A leading actor for over thirty years. Nominated for an Academy Award for his performance as Wilson in the film *Wilson*, 1944. Portrayed role of "American Leader" in the film *You Only Live Twice*, 1967.

KOTTO, YAPHET. Actor. Born November 15, 1937 in New York City. A leading American actor. Films of note: *The Thomas Crown Affair, Brubaker, Raid on Entebbe, Report to The Commissioner.* Portrayed Dr. Kananga/Mr. Big in *Live & Let Die*, 1973.

LAWRENCE, MARC. Actor. Born February 17, 1910 in New York City. A film actor since 1933. In over one hundred films, mostly as a heavy. Portrayed a gangster in Diamonds Are Forever, 1971 and *The Man With The Golden Gun*, 1974.

LAZENBY, GEORGE. Actor. James Bond Number Two. See separate biography under LAZENBY.

LEE, BERNARD. Actor. Portrayed Admiral Sir Miles Messervy ('M') in the James Bond series. Died 1981. See separate biography under Lee.

LEE, CHRISTOPHER. Actor. Born May 27, 1922 in London. In films since 1947 and star of dozens of horror films. Over one hundred films to his credit. Portrayed Scanamanga in *The Man With The Golden Gun*, 1974.

LENYA, LOTTE. Actress. Born Karoline Blamauer on October 18, 1900 in Hitzing, Austria. Died 1981. Noted European singer and former star of German theatre. Played role of Jenny Diver on stage/screen in *The Three Penny Opera*. Portrayed Rosa Klebb in *From Russia With Love*, 1963.

LINDER, CEC. Actor. Born 1921 in Canada. Noted character actor of screen & TV. Made his debut in *The Flaming Frontier*. Others of note: *A Touch of Class, Atlantic City.* TV credits include *Armstrong Circle Theatre, It Takes A Thief* and *The New Avengers.* Portrayed Felix Leiter in *Goldfinger*, 1964.

LLEWELYN, DESMOND. Actor. Portrays 'Q' in the James Bond series. See separate biography under Llewelyn.

LONSDALE, MICHAEL. Actor. Born in 1931 in Paris. A noted character actor of French and international films. Portrayed the villain Drax in *Moonraker*, 1979.

LORD, JACK. Actor. Born John Joseph Ryan on December 30, 1928 in New York City. Died 1998. Given his big film break by Gary Cooper in *The Court Martial of Billy Mitchell*. Most noted for his role as McGarrett on the TV series "Hawaii Five-0." Portrayed CIA agent Felix Leiter in *Dr. No*, 1962.

LOVE, BESSIE. Actress. Born Juanita Horton September 10, 1898 in Midland, Texas. Died 1986. Featured as a leading lady in over 85 films opposite such stars as William S. Hart and Douglas Fairbanks. Portrayed an "American guest" at the casino in *On Her Majesty's Secret Service*, 1969.

MACNEE, PATRICK. Actor. Born in London February 6, 1922. Educated at Summerfields, Oxford, England. Royal Navy 1942-1946. Best known for his portrayal of "Steed" in the TV series "The Avengers," 1960-1970 and "The New Avengers," 1976-1979. Portrayed Sir Godfrey Tibbett in *A View To A Kill*, 1985.

MAXWELL, LOIS. Actress. Portrayed Miss Moneypenny in the James Bond series through *A View To A Kill*. See separate biography under Maxwell.

MCCOWEN, ALEC. Actor. Born in Tunbridge Wells, England May 26, 1925. One of the great English stage actors. Won the London Critic's Best Actor Award for his performance in *Hadrian VII*. Appeared in many "West End" and N.Y. stage productions with the likes of Laurence Olivier, Vivien Leigh and Ruth Gordon. Portrayed 'Q' in *Never Say Never Again*, 1983.

MOORE, ROGER. Actor. James Bond Number Three. See separate biography under Moore.

NAISMITH, LAWRENCE. Actor. Born Lawrence Johnson in Thames Ditton, Surrey, England, December 14, 1908. Died 1992. Served in the British Royal Artillery during WWII. Films of note: *Mogambo*, *Lust For Life*, *Boy On A Dolphin*, *Sink The Bismark*, *The World Of Suzie Wong*, *Cleopatra*, *Young Winston*. Portrayed Sir Donald Munger in *Diamonds Are Forever*, 1971.

NEWTON, WAYNE. Singer, Actor. Born in Norfolk, Virginia April 3, 1942. A leading entertainer primarily in Las Vegas hotels. In his film debut, Newton portrayed Joe Butcher in *License To Kill*, 1989.

PALUZZI, LUCIANA. Actress. Born in 1931 in Italy. A beautiful redhead and leading lady in over forty films beginning with *Three Coins In The Fountain*. TV credits include "Have Gun, Will Travel," "Burke's Law," "The Man From Uncle," "Twelve O'Clock High," "Hawaii Five-0." Portrayed Fiona Volpe in *Thunderball*, 1965.

PLEASANCE, DONALD. Actor. Born October 5, 1919 in Worksop, Nottingham, England. Prominent character actor of British and international stage and screen. With the RAF in WWII and former POW. Made his stage debut in 1939 and films in 1954. Portrayed Blofeld in *You Only Live Twice*, 1967.

RIGG, DIANA. Actress. Portrayed "Tracy" in *On Her Majesty's Secret Service*, 1969. The only wife of James Bond. See separate biography under Rigg.

SAKATA, HAROLD. Actor. Born 1920. Died 1982. A Hawaiian wrestler known as the Great Togo. Former Olympic Silver Medal winner in weightlifting. A Judo and Karate expert. Appeared as a TV villain in "Hawaii Five-0," "Sarge," and "Highcliffe Manor." Portrayed Oddjob in *Goldfinger*, 1964.

SALEM, PAMELA. Actress. Born in England. Leading roles in British TV productions "The Buccaneer," "Into The Labyrinth." Her film credits include *The Great Train Robbery*, among others. Portrayed Miss Moneypenny in *Never Say Never Again*, 1983.

ST. JOHN, JILL. Actress. Born Jill Oppenheim on August 19, 1940 in Los Angeles. Leading lady of films of the 60s. Films of note: *The Roman Spring of Mrs. Stone*, *Tender is the Night*, *Tony Rome*, *Banning*, *Brenda Starr*. Also numerous TV productions. Portrayed Tiffany Case in *Diamonds Are Forever*, 1971.

SAVALAS, TELLY. Actor. Born Aristotle Savalas on January 21, 1925 in Garden City, New York. Died 1994. A Purple Heart veteran of WWII. Former news director for ABC news. A Peabody Award winner for ABC documentary. Started in films in the 50's. Portrayed Blofeld in *On Her Majesty's Secret Service*, 1969.

SEYMOUR, JANE. Actress. Born Joyce Frankenberg on February 15, 1951 in Hillingdon, England. Trained in the Kirov Ballet, she then switched to acting. A leading lady of British and international films and TV. Portrayed Solitaire in *Live & Let Die*, 1973.

SHAW, ROBERT. Actor, author, playright. Born August 9, 1927 in West Houghton, England. Died in 1978. Mainly a character actor, he became a highly paid star of major films during the 70's. Portrayed Red Grant in *From Russia With Love*, 1963.

STROUD, DON. Actor. Born in Hawaii in 1937. Rugged supporting actor in mostly "tough guy" roles. Started his film career in the film *Games* in 1967. Portrayed Heller in *License To Kill*, 1989.

SYDOW, MAX VON. Actor. Born Carl Adolf von Sydow on April 10, 1929 in Lund, Sweden. Trained at Stockholm's Royal Dramatic Theater School. Screen debut in 1949. Today an international film star. Portrayed the villain Blofeld in *Never Say Never Again*, 1983.

TOPOL. Actor. Born Haym Topol September 9, 1935 in Tel Aviv. Played Tevye on the London stage in *Fiddler On The Roof*. Repeated the same role in the film production. Nominated for an Oscar. Portrayed Columbo in *For Your Eyes Only*, 1981.

VILLECHAIZE, HERVE. Actor. Born in Paris, April 23, 1943. Died 1993. Performed mime in NYC opera productions. Numerous film credits. Was a regular on the TV series "Fantasy Island." Portrayed Nick Nack in *The Man With The Golden Gun*, 1974.

WALKEN, CHRISTOPHER. Actor. Born March 31, 1943 in Astoria, Queens, New York. Lead and supporting player of the American stage and screen. Won New York Film Critics Award and Oscar as best supporting actor in *The Deer Hunter*. Portrayed Max Zorin in *A View To A Kill*, 1985.

WISEMAN, JOSEPH. Actor. Born May 15, 1918 in Montreal. On the American stage from the mid-thirties and in films since the 50s. Oftentimes the villain. A long time player with the Lincoln Center Repertory theatre. Portrayed *Dr. No*, 1962.

BOX OFFICE STARS (ANNUAL TOP TEN)

	RANK	YEAR
Sean Connery	1	1965
Sean Connery	2	1966
Sean Connery	5	1967
Sean Connery	9	1971
Roger Moore	9	1979

FEWEST WORDS SPOKEN

Harold Sakata who portrayed "Odd Job" in *Goldfinger* never spoke a single word in the entire film.

Richard Kiel who portrayed "Jaws" in *The Spy Who Loved Me* and *Moonraker* spoke one line of dialog in the entire two films. In *Moonraker* he said at the very end, "Well, here's to us."

FREQUENCY OF APPEARANCES IN BOND FILMS (TWO OR MORE)

ADAMS, MAUDE (2)
The Man With The Golden Gun .... Andrea
Octopussy .... Octopussy

ANDRESS, URSULA (2)
Dr. No. .... Honey Ryder
Casino Royale .... Vesper Lynd

ASHBY, CAROL (2)
Octopussy...................................... Octopussy girl
A View To A Kill............................... Whistling girl

BAKER, GEORGE (2)
On Her Majesty's Secret Service.................. Sir Hilary Bray
The Spy Who Loved Me .... Captain Benson

BAUER, DAVID (2)
You Only Live Twice .... Uncredited Role
Diamonds Are Forever .... Mr. Slumber

BESWICK, MARTINE (2)
From Russia With Love .... Zora
Thunderball .... Paula

BISHOP, ED (2)
You Only Live Twice .... Hawaii Radar man
Diamonds Are Forever .... Hergescheimer

BLISS, CAROLINE (As Miss Moneypenny) (2)
The Living Daylights   *License To Kill*

BROWN, ROBERT (5)
The Spy Who Loved Me .... Admiral Hargreaves
Octopussy .... 'M'
A View To A Kill .... 'M'
The Living Daylights .... 'M'
License To Kill .... 'M'

BULLOCK, JEREMY (2)
For Your Eyes Only .... Aide to 'Q'
Octopussy .... Zec

CHIN, ANTHONY (2)
You Only Live Twice .... Uncredited role
A View To A Kill .... Taiwanese Tycoon

CONNERY, SEAN (As James Bond) (7)
Dr. No   *From Russia With Love*
Goldfinger   *Thunderball*
You Only Live Twice   *Diamonds Are Forever*
Never Say Never Again

DALTON, TIMOTHY (As James Bond) (2)
The Living Daylights   *License To Kill*

DAWSON, ANTHONY (2)
Dr. No .... Professor Dent
From Russia With Love (back only).............. Blofeld

DENCH, JUDI (As 'M') (2)
Goldeneye   *Tomorrow Never Dies*

FORTUNE, KIM (2)
The Spy Who Loved Me .... HMS Ranger crewman
Moonraker .... RAF Officer

GAYSON, EUNICE (As Sylvia Trench) (2)
Dr. No   *From Russia With Love*

GOTELL, WALTER (7)
From Russia With Love .... Morzeny
The Spy Who Loved Me .... General Gogol
Moonraker .... General Gogol
For Your Eyes Only .... General Gogol
Octopussy .... General Gogol
A View To A Kill .... General Gogol
The Living Daylights .... General Gogol

GRAY, CHARLES (2)
You Only Live Twice .... Henderson
Diamonds Are Forever .... Blofeld

GRAYDON, RICHARD (3)
You Only Live Twice .... Russian Cosmonaut
On Her Majesty's Secret Service .... Driver
Octopussy .... Francisco the Fearless

HEDISON, DAVID (As Felix Leiter) (2)
Live & Let Die   *License To Kill*

JAMES, CLIFTON (As Sheriff J.W. Pepper) (2)
Live & Let Die
The Man With The Golden Gun

KEEN, GEOFFREY (as Minister of Defense) (6)
The Spy Who Loved Me	*Moonraker*
For Your Eyes Only	*Octopussy*
A View To A Kill	*The Living Daylights*

KIEL, RICHARD (As Jaws) (2)
The Spy Who Loved Me   *Moonraker*

KWOUK, BERT (2)
Goldfinger... Mr. Ling
You Only Live Twice .... S.P.E.C.T.R.E. 3

LAWRENCE, MARC (2)
Diamonds Are Forever .... Gangster
The Man with the Golden Gun .... Rodney

LEE, BERNARD (As 'M') (11)
Dr. No	*From Russia With Love*
Goldfinger	*Thunderball*
You Only Live Twice	*On Her Majesty's Secret Service*
Diamonds Are Forever	*Live & Let Die*
The Man With The Golden Gun	*The Spy Who Loved Me*
Moonraker	

LEON, VALERIE (2)
The Spy Who Loved Me .... Hotel receptionist
Never Say Never Again .... Nassau pickup

LLEWELYN, DESMOND (As Major Boothroyd, 'Q') (16)
From Russia With Love	*Goldfinger*
Thunderball	*You Only Live Twice*
On Her Majesty's Secret Service	*Diamonds Are Forever*
The Man With The Golden Gun	*The Spy Who Loved Me*

Moonraker	*For Your Eyes Only*
Octopussy	*A View To A Kill*
The Living Daylights	*License To Kill*
Goldeneye	*Tomorrow Never Dies*

MAXWELL, LOIS (As Miss Moneypenny) (14)

Dr. No	*From Russia With Love*
Goldfinger	*Thunderball*
You Only Live Twice	*On Her Majesty's Secret Service*
Diamonds Are Forever	*Live & Let Die*
The Man With The Golden Gun	*The Spy Who Loved Me*
Moonraker	*For Your Eyes Only*
Octopussy	*A View To A Kill*

MOORE, ROGER (As James Bond) (7)

Live & Let Die	*The Man With The Golden Gun*
The Spy Who Loved Me	*Moonraker*
For Your Eyes Only	*Octopussy*
A View To A Kill	

MOSES, ALBERT (2)

| *The Spy Who Loved Me* | Barman |
| *Octopussy* | Sadruddin |

MUNRO, CAROLINE (2)

| *The Spy Who Loved Me* | Naomi |
| *Casino Royale* | Un-named |

PORTEOUS, PETER (2)

| *Octopussy* | Lenkin |
| *Living Daylights* | Gaswork's supervisor |

REDWOOD, MANNING (2)

| *Never Say Never Again* | General Miller |
| *A View To A Kill* | Bob Conley |

REGIN, NADJA (2)

| *From Russia With Love* | Kerim's girl |
| *Goldfinger* | Bonita the flamenco dancer |

REID, MILTON (3)

Casino Royale	Indian attendant
The Spy Who Loved Me	Sandor, the assassin
Dr. No	guard

RIETTY, ROBERT (2)

| *On Her Majesty's Secret Service* | Chef de Jen |
| *Never Say Never Again* | Italian Minister |

RIMMER, SHANE (3)
You Only Live Twice .... Hawaii Control
Diamonds Are Forever .... Tom
The Spy Who Loved Me .... Captain Carter

RUEBER-STAIER, EVA (As Rublevich) (3)
For Your Eyes Only   *Octopussy*
The Spy Who Loved Me

SCOULAR, ANGELA (2)
On Her Majesty's Secret Service .... Ruby Bartlett
Casino Royale .... Agent Buttercup

SHEYBAL, VLADEK (2)
From Russia With Love .... Kronsteen assassin
Casino Royale .... LeChiffre's representative

STAVIN, MARY (2)
Octopussy .... Octopussy girl
A View To A Kill .... Kimberly Jones

WARVILLE, LIZZIE (2)
Moonraker .... Russian girl
For Your Eyes Only .... Girl by the pool

*Eric Pohlmann is the voice of Blofeld in both *From Russia With Love* and *Thunderball*.

ACTORS/ACTRESSES WHO HAVE APPEARED IN BOTH BOND FILMS AND THE AVENGERS TV SERIES

DIANA RIGG:
From Emma Peel in "The Avengers" to Tracy in *On Her Majesty's Secret Service*.

PATRICK MCNEE:
From John Steed in "The Avengers" to Sir Godfrey Tibbett in *A View To A Kill*.

HONOR BLACKMAN:
From Cathy Gale in "The Avengers" to Pussy Galore in *Goldfinger*.

JOANNA LUMLEY:
From the English girl in *On Her Majesty's Secret Service* to Purdy in "The New Avengers."

CEC LINDER:
From Felix Leiter in *Goldfinger* to "The New Avengers."

GUY DOLEMAN:
From Count Lippe in *Thunderball* to "The New Avengers."

Other major actors who appeared in both Bond and The Avengers: Edward Fox, Robert Brown, Julian Glover, Douglas Wilmer, James Velliers, Christopher Lee, Roland Culver.

IN BOND FILMS WHO ARE RELATED

Identical Twin Brothers:
David and Tony Meyer (Twins 1 & 2) .... *Octopussy*

Father and Son:
Pedro Armendariz (Father) .... Kerim Bey, *From Russia With Love*
Pedro Armendariz (Son) .... Hector Lopez, *License To Kill*

SHORTEST ACTOR IN A BOND FILM

Herve Villechaize who portrayed Nick Nack in *The Man With Golden Gun* was 3' 9" tall.

TALLEST ACTOR IN A BOND FILM

Richard Kiel who portrayed Jaws in *The Spy Who Loved Me* and *Moonraker* is 7' 4" tall.

MAJOR ACTORS/ACTRESSES OF BOND FILMS TRAINED AT THE ROYAL ACADEMY OF DRAMATIC ART (RADA)

Sean Bean   Desmond Llewelyn   Jonathan Pryce
Roland Culver   Lois Maxwell   Robert Shaw
Timothy Dalton   Alec McCowen   Bernard Lee
Edward Fox   Roger Moore   Diana Rigg
Geoffrey Keen   John Rhys-Davies

Goodyear Airship Europa shown over London. Big Ben is just to the right of her nose. (Goodyear Tire and Rubber)

It was high above Geneva, Switzerland where Bond battled with S.P.E.C.T.R.E. Chief, Colonel Rehani, in the cockpit of Europa when on assignment in *Role of Honor*. (Goodyear Tire and Rubber)

AIRCRAFT

BEDE ACROSTAR

At the time of filming it was the world's smallest jet. Length 12', height 5' 8", weight 450 lbs, wing span 17', engine: Micro - turbo TRS - 18, service ceiling 30,000', rate of climb 2800 fpm, 30,000 ft. in less than 11 minutes, cruising speed 160 mph, top speed 310 mph, seats one, number produced two. Bond flew this jet in "Octopussy." The one shown in the film is owned and was flown by "Corky" Fornof of Louisiana.

PIPER CUB

Maximum speed 100 mph. Stall speed 25 mph. Bond commandeered this aircraft to escape Mr. Big's henchmen. The student, Mrs. Bell, was quite chagrined when Bond sheared the wings off this plane in *Live & Let Die*.

BEECHCRAFT SUPER H18

The Beechcraft Model 18 had the longest production run in aviation history; 33 years (1937-1970). The final version of this Twin Beech was the Super H18. This plane was flown by Kamal Khan while trying to escape from Bond in *Octopussy*.

Engines .... Dual 450 hp Pratt & Whitney radial air-cooled.
Rate of climb .... 1400 fpm
Maximum load weight .... 9900 lbs.
Service ceiling .... 21, 400' with two engines, 9400' with one engine.
Length .... 35' 2.5"
Height .... 9' 4"
Wingspan .... 49' 8"
Accomodates .... 9 passengers, two pilots. Contains toilet and
baggage compartment.
Propellers .... 3-blade, full feathered.
Top Speed .... 235 mph, high cruise speed: 220 mph.
Range .... 1500 miles
List Price .... $179,500.

PIPER CHEROKEE 140

This is the aircraft that Pussy Galore and her flying circus flew in *Goldfinger* when supposedly they were going to spray Ft. Knox with the deadly Delta Nine gas. Fortunately Pussy switched sides at the last minute so that what she sprayed proved harmless!

List price: .... $9,600.
Engine: .... Lycoming 0-320, 150 hp, 4-cylinder, dual ignition.
Fuel capacity: .... 50 gallons
Accomodates: .... One pilot, three passengers.

GOODYEAR AIRSHIP EUROPA

High above Geneva, Switzerland, Bond battles with S.P.E.C.T.R.E. Chief, Colonel Rahani. Gunfire erupts and men die as events build to climax in *Role of Honor*.

The Piper Cherokee 140: Pussy Galore and her flying circus flew this aircraft in *Goldfinger* when supposedly they were going to spray Ft. Knox with the deadly Delta nine gas. (Piper Aircraft Corporation)

The Beechcraft Super H18. This plane was flown by Kamal Khan while trying to escape from Bond in the film *Octopussy*. (Beech Aircraft Corporation)

The Goodyear Airship Europa was built in 1972 of a new and larger design. Europa's giant envelope is made of two-ply Neoprene-coated Dacron and is filled with helium which is inert and non-flammable. This airship was taken out of service but Goodyear now has a new airship in the skies over Europe.

OVERALL DIMENSIONS

Length .... 192'
Height .... 59'
Width .... 50'
Volume .... 202, 700 cubic feet

CAR DIMENSIONS

Length .... 23'
Height .... 8'

OPERATIONAL LIMITS

Normal Altitude .... 1-3,000'
Maximum Altitude .... 8,500'
Range .... 500 miles

ENVELOPE FABRIC

Material (2-ply) .... Rubber coated Polyester fabric.

WEIGHT & LIFT

Maximum Gross weight .... 12,230 lbs.
Maximum lift .... 3,281 lbs.
No. of passengers .... Six plus pilot

POWER

Twin Continental engines
(6 cylinder, pusher type) .... 210 hp. each
Cruising speed .... 35 mph
Maximum speed .... 50 mph

WALLIS WA-116 (XR - 943) AUTOGYRO "LITTLE NELLIE"

Bond flew "Little Nellie" on assignment in *You Only Live Twice*, shooting down four Spectre helicopters which had attacked him. For Bond's battle with Spectre, "Little Nellie" was equipped with twin .30 calibre machine guns & 100 rounds of ammunition, air to air heat seeking missiles, air mines, 1.75" free-flight rockets, and two flame throwers.

However, in actuality, the fixed, forward-firing machine guns fired sixty electrically-initiated blanks. Nevertheless, the multiple rocket pack actually fired "Icarus" parachute flare rockets; the rockets being substituted by dummy warheads. The two "infrared" guided rockets were also fired a number of times for cameras, and the weighted "parachute grenades" were dropped. The weapon firing was filmed in Spain as the Japanese would not allow it in the volcano area of Kyushu where most of the filming occurred.[1]

Wing Commander Kenneth A. Wallis, R.A.F. retired, flew "Little Nellie" throughout the film *You Only Live Twice*. (Kenneth Wallis Collection)

The short sequence seen on the film screen involved 85 flights and 46 hours airborne, many flights at about 6000 feet above the volcanos in Kyushu. Wing Commander Kenneth H. Wallis, R.A.F. Retired, flew "Little Nellie" throughout the film.[2]

[1] It is only in the early shots that the aircraft is seen with her full "weapons system" including the smoke & flame-throwers on the tail. Wing Commander Wallis asked that these should be used first in the aerial combat sequence since they were rather cumbersome on the tail. They were jettisoned after use and this was filmed as they fell away, streaming smoke, into a canyon. However, that shot was never used. Further, after the combat sequence, as "007" flies away, the smoke and flame-throwers have somehow got back on the aircraft.

[2] Wing Commander Wallis flew 36 missions over Germany and Italy during WWII as the pilot of a Wellington bomber. He retired from the RAF in 1964 and devotes his time to Wallis Autogyros in Reymerston Hall, Norfolk, England. In 1974 he received the Breguet Trophy from Prince Phillip for his achievements in aviation.

"Little Nellie" was one of three military Type WA - 116's built in 1962. Wallis also builds additional models of autogyros. The Wallis autogyros, until recently, held for the United Kingdom all eighteen official World Records for autogyro speed, altitude, range and duration.[3]

SPECIFICATIONS
Level speed .... 14-130 mph
Weight .... 260 lbs. (less the Bond weapon system)
Service ceiling .... 18,500'
Rotors .... 20'-2" overall
Fuselage .... 11' (nose to tail)

"Little Nellie" was shipped to Japan and Spain in four large suitcases and assembled in thirty minutes. Four Japanese stunt pilots flew the four S.P.E.C.T.R.E. helicopters.

[3] In April 1998, the Altitude Records for autogyros were regained for the U.S. by Dr. Bill Clem of Denver, Colorado, using a turbo-charged engine. However, Wallis did set a new World Record for Time-to-Climb to 3,000 metres, on the 19th of March, 1998. This was achieved in seven (7) minutes, twenty (20) seconds.

Wallis flew "Little Nellie" doubling for Bond. During the filming of these sequences, second unit cameraman John Jordan lost one foot. The remainder of the helicopter sequences were filmed over Torremolinos, Spain with French pilots. Tony Brown replaced John Jordan as unit photographer. However, after losing his entire leg three months later, Jordan eventually came back to film action sequences for *On Her Majesty's Secret Service*. Unfortunately, he was killed later the same year while filming "Catch-22."

Wing Commander Kenneth H. Wallis explains how "Little Nellie" got her name. "In case you may wonder how the little autogyro became "Little Nellie", I should explain that in the late thirties, or the war-time years, if your name was 'Wallis', or 'Wallace', your nickname was 'Nellie', since Nellie Wallace was a famous music-hall star. Group Captian Hamish Mahaddie, a much-decorated member of the R.A.F. 'Pathfinders' during the war, was the Aviation Consultant to Eon Productions and had heard me speaking on the radio concerning a film I was to make for an Italian company, Film-Studio Roma, in Brazil. In the interview I was asked if I would like to have a fight with a helicopter with one of my autogyros. I said I would."

"This led to Hamish Mahaddie, who I knew from our R.A.F. days, inviting me to bring one of my autogyros to Pinewood Studios, just before I was to leave for Brazil. I took G-ARZB and demonstrated it in flight from the studios for 'Cubby' Brocolli, etc., and was immediately booked for *You Only Live Twice*, with the aircraft, "with cosmetics on," as Cubby described the weapons. It was named "Little Nellie" by Gp Capt. Hamish Mahaddie from the Wallis nickname."

ANIMALS, FOWL & MARINE LIFE

FEATURED IN BOND FILMS

Goldfinger	Horses
Dr. No	Fish, octopus, giant tarantulas
Thunderball	Manta ray, sharks, cat
Diamonds Are Forever	Rat, scorpion, cat, fish, elephant, gorilla
You Only Live Twice	Piranha fish, cat
Live & Let Die	Sharks, alligators, snakes, crocodiles
The Spy Who Loved Me	Fish, camels, horses, turtles, sharks
Moonraker	Dogs, pheasants, snakes, horses
For Your Eyes Only	Turtle, parrot, sharks
Octopussy	Camels, horses, octopus, circus animals, spiders, snakes, birds, elephant
Never Say Never Again	Sharks, horses, snake
A View To A Kill	Horses, bird, cat, rats, butterflies
The Living Daylights	Horses, camels, parrots, monkeys
License To Kill	Sharks, iguana, squid
From Russia With Love	Cat, fish, rats
On Her Majesty's Secret Service	Horses, bears, bulls

FEATURED IN BOND BOOKS

For Special Services	Giant Python snakes
Nobody Lives Forever	Sharks
Scorpius	Sand pipers, pelicans, snakes
From A View To A Kill	Birds
For Your Eyes Only	Dog, deer, chipmunks, beaver, birds
Hildebrand Rarity	Fish
Octopussy	Fish, octopus
License To Kill	Sharks, iguana
Broken Claw	Wolves
Death Is Forever	Fiddle Back Spiders
Sea Fire	Dogs
Tomorrow Never Dies	Fish

Wing Commander Wallis flew 36 missions over Germany and Italy during WWII as pilot of a Wellington bomber. He retired from the RAF in 1964 and devotes his time to Wallis Autogyros in Reymerston Hall, Norfolk, England. In 1974 he received the Breguet trophy from Prince Phillip for achievements in aviation.

ARTISTS, ILLUSTRATORS, MODELS & SCRIPTWRITERS

James Bond 007 Logo:
Joseph Caroff, Davis Chasmon, Mitchell Hooks.

Illustrators of Bond Poster Art & Photo Compositions:
Design concepts supervised by Donald Smolen.
Robert Brownjohn, Daniel Gouzee, Douglas Kirkland, Frank C. McCarthy, Robert McGinnis, Robert Peak.

Illustrators of Comic Strip Art:
Robert Brown, Gual, Yaroslav Horak, John McLusky, Harry North, Robb Sarompas.

Scriptwriters of Comic Strip Art:
O'Donnell, Henry Gammidge, James Lawrence.

Other Bond Artists & Illustrators:
Chuck Austin, Richard Chopping, Mick Dolby, Mike Grell, Sam Peffer, Stan Woch, Tom Yeates.

Models:
Dick Orme. Model whose face was featured as that of Bond on the early Pan book covers.

ARTWORK BOND HAS VIEWED ON ASSIGNMENT (BOOK)

Dr. No	Botticelli's Venus, Degas ballet sketches, The Duke Of Wellington by Goya.
Thunderball	Mona Lisa.
Hildebrand Rarity	Girl in black & white striped blouse by Renoir, Sailing Ship by Montague Dawson.
License Renewed	Admiral Jervis fleet triumphing over the Spanish off Cape St. Vincent in 1797 by Cooper, Pink Nude by Matisse, Two Picasso's from his Blue Period, Hockney & Bratby.
Nobody Lives Forever	Original Hockney, Piper, Sutherland, Bonnard and Gross.
No Deals Mr. Bond	Kurosaki woodblock print, dark Victorian German prints of mountain scenes with clouds gathering between valleys.
Scorpius	Hockney's The Panama Hat etching, The Spinning Man VII by Frink.
Role of Honor	The Green Lady (print).
For Special Services	Hograth prints. Set of six titled: "The Lady's Progress" (forgeries), four rare Holbeins, signed color print by Baxter, set of original Bewicks (from General History of Quadrupeds), large canvas reproduction of San Creek Massacre by Robert Lindneux and Harper's Weekly engraving of the Fetterman battle, a reproduction.
Moonraker	Lawrence of Beau Brummel, Romney's unfinished, full-length portrait of Mrs. Fragonard's Jue de Cartes.
From Russia With Love	Reproduction of the Annigoni portrait of the Queen. Beaton's wartime photograph of Winston Churchill.
Win, Lose or Die	Old naval prints, three paintings of various garden views, one in the style of Hockney.
A View To A Kill	The Duke of Wellington by Goya.
Broken Claw	Chinese & American Indian art, Museum Poster Eyuind advertising da Vinci exhibition, vivid Easle oil painting, large watercolor of lakes & mountains, large engraving of the River Thomas.
Death is Forever	Lovejoy Fecit, Jackson Pollack, Chagalls, Picasso, photos of U.S. Presidents.
The Man From Barbarossa	Landscape oil by R. Abel.
Coldfall	Picasso, Matisse, Schonberg.
Goldeneye	Framed portrait of KGB Headquarters.
Zero Minus Ten	Original paintings by George Chinnery, Original Kandinsky, In Bond's office: watercolor of the Royal St. George Clubhouse, black and white photo on desk of Bond with Felix Leiter.

AUTOMOBILES BOND HAS DRIVEN (FILM)

Dr No .... 57 Chevrolet convertible
Sunbean Talbot convertible

From Russia With Love .... Truck

Goldfinger .... Aston Martin DB5

Thunderball .... Aston Martin DB5, 65 Lincoln Continental

You Only Live Twice .... None

On Her Majesty's Secret Service .... Aston Martin DB6, salon

Diamonds Are Forever .... Aston Martin DB6, 1971 Red Mustang,
ATV Moon Buggy

Live & Let Die .... Leyland R.T. Double-Decker bus,
1995 Chevrolet Caprice

The Man With The Golden Gun .... American Motors Hornet Hatchback[1]

The Spy Who Loved Me .... Lotus Esprit

Moonraker .... None

[1] Bond drove this machine off the showroom floor and through a plate glass window

For Your Eyes Only .... Lotus Esprit, Citroen 2CV.

Never Say Never Again .... BSA Motor Bike, Vintage Bentley

Octopussy .... Mercedes Benz

A View To A Kill .... Citroen Paris Taxi cab, snowmobile, San Francisco
fire truck

The Living Daylights .... Aston Martin Volante, Aston Martin Vantage,
Audi 200 Quattro, Audi 200 Avant, Susuki 4x4.

License To Kill .... Continental Mark VII, Kenworth W900B trucks

Goldeneye .... BMW Z3 convertible roadster, T-55 Tank, Aston
Martin DB5

Tomorrow Never Dies .... BMW 750 IL, BMW R 1200 C motorcycle

AUTOMOBILES BOND HAS DRIVEN (BOOKS)

Casino Royale .... 1933 Bentley Convertible, 4 cylinder, 4.5 liter with
Amherst Villiers supercharger

Live & Let Die .... Same

Moonraker .... Same[1]

Diamonds Are Forever .... None

From Russia With Love .... 1954 Bentley Continental

Dr. No .... Austin A30, Sunbeam Talbot, Hillman Minx

Goldfinger .... Aston Martin DB3

Thunderball .... 1954 Bentley Continental

The Spy Who Loved Me .... Dark gray, 2-seater Thunderbird with soft cream top

On Her Majesty's Secret Service .... 1954 Bentley Continental with the "R" type chassis,
big 6 engine, 13:40 back axle ratio

You Only Live Twice .... Same

The Man With The Golden Gun .... Sunbeam Alpine

Colonel Sun	1954 Bentley Continental
License Renewed	Saab 900 Turbo
For Special Services	Same
Icebreaker	Same plus Yamaha snow scooter
Role Of Honor	Bentley Mulsanne Turbo
Nobody Lives Forever	Same
No Deals Mr. Bond	Same
Scorpius	Same
License To Kill	Maserati sports car, Kenworth truck
Win, Lose Or Die	BMW 520i, Lanica, Fiat
Broken Claw	Rental car
The Man From Barbarossa	Gray van
Death Is Forever	Rental car
Never Send Flowers	Saab 9000, rental BMW
Seafire	Triumph Daytona motorcycle, Saab 9000, VW Corrado
Coldfall	Ford Taurus rental car
Goldeneye	Aston Martin DB5, BMWZ3 convertible roadster
Tomorrow Never Dies	BMW 750 Sedan
Zero Minus Ten	Toyota Crown Motors, taxicab, 1995 Suzuki Vitara Wagon, four wheel drive
The Facts of Death	Jaguar XK8 Coupe, Bentley Turbo R

[1]This machine was crushed by a 1400 pound roll of newsprint as Bond was in pursuit of Sir Hugo Drax.

AUTOMOBILES BOND HAS DRIVEN (SHORT STORIES)

From A View To A Kill	BSA motor bike
For Your Eyes Only	None
Quantum Of Solace	None
Risico	None
The Hildebrand Rarity	None
Octopussy	None
The Living Daylights	Mark II Bentley Continental

OTHER AUTOMOBILES FEATURED (BOOK & FILM)

1968 LANCIA FLAMINA ZAGATO SPYDER

A custom built convertible owned and driven in the novel *On Her Majesty's Secret Service* by Bond's wife, the former Teresa di Vicenzo. This was the machine in which she was murdered by Ernest Blofeld as she and Bond were driving to their honeymoon.

Also, a 1969 Mercury Cougar was driven by Tracy (Film).

From A View to a Kill	Black Peugeot 403 driven by Mary Ann Russell Citroen taxi driven by Bond

Goldfinger	Lincoln Continental driven by Oddjob, Dove-gray Triumph TR3 driven by Tilly Masterson, White Mustang driven by Tilly Masterson, Rolls Royce driven by Oddjob
Thunderball	1965 Thunderbird, BSA motorbike driven by Fiona Volpe, Sapphire blue 2-seater MG driven by Domino, Powder blue Mustang driven by Domino, 1965 Lincoln Continental
You Only Live Twice	Toyota 2000 sports car driven by Aki
On Her Majesty's Secret Service	Red Maserati driven by Ernst Blofeld
The Man With the Golden Gun	Red Thunderbird driven by Scaramanga
Nobody Lives Forever	White Alfa Romeo Sprint driven by Sukie Tempesta
The Spy Who Loved Me	Vespa motor bike driven by Viviene Michele
Role of Honor	Percy Proud drives a little blue Dodge 600ES
License to Kill	Rolls-Royce driven by 'Q'
Goldeneye	Bright yellow Ferrari F355 driven Xenia Onatopp; the color is red in the film
The Facts of Death	Black Ferrari, 73556TS
Diamonds Are Forever	Ford Van
From Russia With Love	Citroen Sedan

BOND'S PERSONAL AUTOMOBILES

1933 Bentley Convertible

4 cylinder, 4.5 liter with Amherst Villiers supercharger. Bond owned this car for 22 years, keeping it in careful storage throughout WWII, but in *Moonraker* (1955), it was "totaled-out" in a chase with the villain Hugo Drax when it collided with a 1400 pound roll of newsprint.

1954 Bentley Mark II Continental

Battleship gray. Bond bought this machine wrecked, paying 1500 pounds, and had it refitted with a Mark IV engine with 9.5 compression ratio. "R" type chassis, big 6 engine, 13:40 back-axle ratio, Arnott supercharger and body by Mulliner coach builders. Bond last drove it in *On Her Majesty's Secret Service*.

1981 Saab 900 Turbo

Silver. Bond drove this car for several years and like the Aston Martin DBSV from motor pool, had it outfitted with both offensive and defensive weapons and sophisticated electronic gear. The Saab had a digital instrument display, cruise control system, fire detection and extinguisher system, bullet-proof glass, steel-reinforced ram bumpers, heavy-duty self-sealing tires and an easy conversion from gasoline to gasahol should fuel prices sky rocket. Studded tires, telephone, bright lights on front and rear bumpers, tear gas ducts located at each wheel, sensor activated alarms. Bond drove this machine through *License Renewed, For Special Services* and *Icebreaker*.

Engine	4-cylinder, in-line, water-cooled turbocharger with APC charge pressure control, intercooler
Horsepower @ rpm	160 @ 5500
Displacement, cc	1985

Curb weight 2956
Wheelbase 56.3
Length 184.3
Height 56.1

BENTLEY MULSANNE TURBO. 1984

Built by Rolls-Royce engineers to Rolls-Royce standards of quality of finish. Bond had received a substantial inheritance from his uncle, Bruce Bond, and subsequently paid cash for his machine which he began driving in *Role of Honor*. He chose British racing green with a magnolia interior décor. He had no special technology built into the car other than a small weapon compartment and a long-range telephone.

Engine .... 6.75 litre V-8
Acceleration, 0-60 .... 6.7 seconds
Top Speed 140mph
Total displacement .... 412 cubic inches
Wheelbase 120. 5
Overall length 207. 4
Overall width 79.0
Curb weight 5270

Bond gave up the Bentley due to high fuel costs and switched to the Saab 900, which he began driving on assignment in *Never Send Flowers*.

Bond drove both the Aston Martin Vantage and the Volante (hardtop and convertible) on assignment in *The Living Daylights*.
(Aston Martin Lagonda)

Goldfinger 1937 Rolls-Royce Phantom III. Originally owned by the Rt. Honorable Lord Fairhaven, Anglesey Abbey, Cambridge, England (Sotheby's NY)

Later, he sold the Saab and purchased the Aston-Martin DB5 he drove on assignment in *Goldfinger*. M16 recovered this machine and had it repaired. Bond also owns an aging but reliable Bentley Turbo R which he drove on assignment in *The Facts of Death.*

GOLDFINGER'S ROLLS-ROYCE (BOOK)

1925 SILVER GHOST

Primrose yellow with black top. Weight: three tons, including one ton of armor plating and armor plate glass. Silver radiator, aluminum engine cowling, luggage rack of polished brass. Heavy coach-built limousine body with two Lucas 'King of the Road' headlamps of polished brass and bulb horn. Originally built for a South American president who died before taking delivery.

TECHNICAL DATA

Electric lighting and starting apparatus. 3. 1 litre ohv, 6-cylinder twenty with three-speed unit gearbox, and servo four-wheel brakes.

1937 ROLLS-ROYCE PHANTOM III (FILM)

Custom body by Parker & Company, Ltd. of London, England. Twelve cylinder, dual ignition, 7.4f litre engine, finished in yellow and black. Weight: 7000 lbs. This car was custom built for the Rt. Honorable Lord Fairhaven, Anglesey Abbey, Cambridge, England. It was on the folding desk in the rear seat that Goldfinger wrote out the check to Bond for $10,000 after their memorable golf match. Later in the film the car featured prominently in chase scenes through the Swiss Alps.

KNOWN GENEALOGY OF THE GOLDFINGER ROLLS

1937 to 1962 .... Rt. Hon. Lord Fairhaven. Cambridge, England

1962 .... Eon Productions

1962 to 1986 .... Richard Losee, Provo, Utah

1986 to present .... Steven Greenberg, co-owner of the New York Palladium, purchased this
machine at Sotheby's auction June 28, 1986 in NYC for $121,000

AUTOMOBILES FROM MI-6 MOTOR POOL

LOTUS ESPRIT (FILM)

British made sports car provided by 'Q' armory. Bond drove this machine in *The Spy Who Loved Me* and *For Your Eyes Only*. In the *The Spy Who Loved Me* this machine was modified to be submersible and operate under water by a two-man team wearing wet suits and breathing apparatus.

The car could turn, dive, and climb. Modification was completed by Perry Oceanographies of Florida. Other modifications for the surface to air missile launcher, mine laying panel, and underwater rockets were completed on other shells of the car at Pinewood Studio in England.

THE CONVENTIONAL LOTUS ESPRIT: Technical Data

Engine .... 4 cylinder, in-line

Displacement, cc .... 2174, 228 bhp @ 6500 rpm

Curb weight 2820

Top speed 155.6

Acceleration 0-60 .... 5.22 seconds

0-100 .... 12.65 seconds

Length 170. 5

Width 73.2

Height 45.3

Aston Martin DB5. This machine was driven by James Bond on assignment in *Goldfinger.* (See detail genealogy) (Sotheby's NY)

When James Bond received an inheritance in 1984, he purchased this new Bentley Turbo R and began driving it on assignment in *Role of Honor.* (Reg Abbiss, Rolls Royce)

ASTON MARTIN DB3S (BOOK)

From British Secret Service motor pool. Battleship grey. Outfitted with reinforced steel bumpers and hidden compartment for a .45 calibre Colt long-barrel revolver together with a homing device that enabled Bond to follow Goldfinger from long distances in the novel *Goldfinger*. Radio pickup was tuned to receive a homer. Switches allowed Bond to alter the type and color of his front and rear lights if being followed.

List price, approx. .... $10,000.
Number of cylinders & type .... 6-cyl, in-line, dohc
Displacement, cc 2922
Bhp @ rpm .... 210 @ 6000
Curb weight 2250
Top speed 129

ASTON MARTIN DB6 SALON

From motor pool. Battleship grey. This machine was outfitted identical to the DB5 with the exception that 'Q' replaced the .50 calibre machine guns with heat-seeking rockets. It was featured in the films *On Her Majesty's Secret Service* and *Diamonds Are Forever*.

List price $15,400
Engine .... 6-cyl, dohc, 3995 cc, 325bhp
Curb weight 3410
Top speed 135
Acceleration, 0-60 mph, seconds. 8.4
50-70 mph (3rd gear) 5.2

ASTON MARTIN 1963 DBV

Designer .... Lionel Martin
First competition success .... Aston Hill near Aston Clinton
DB .... David Bruce
1963 DBV .... Introduced at Earl's Court Motor Show, London

MACHINE NO. I: 1963 ASTON MARTIN DBVGT (BMT 216-A)

This machine was used only for close-ups. Bond drove this machine in the films *Goldfinger* and *Thunderball*.[1]

[1] Roger Moore also drove this machine in *The Cannon Ball Run*.

It was equipped with twin. 50 calibre Browning machine guns, front and rear bumper over-riders which extend as ramming devices, tire slashers which extend from the rear wheels, front and rear license plates which revolve to show British (BMT-216-A), French (4711-EA-62), and Swiss (LU6789) registration numbers, a special radio telephone, a weapons compartment under the front seat, concealing a folding Armalite rifle with telescopic sight, Mauser automatic pistol with separate silencer, hand grenade and throwing knife. The car also features a radar screen, smoke screen generator, oil and tack dispensers, retractable bulletproof shield in back, bulletproof windows and doors, and ejector seat. This machine was exhibited throughout the United States and Europe. It highlighted the charity premiere of *Goldfinger* in New York, was displayed at the New York World's Fair, was featured on a Jonathan Winters TV spectacular, the Paris Motor Show and again for Thunderball. During an 18 month period it traveled around the world twice.

SPECIFICATIONS

Weight .... two tons
Speed .... 140-150 mph
0-60 mph .... 6 second range

Bond drove this machine on two assignments: *The Spy Who Loved Me* and *For Your Eyes Only*. In the first of these assignments, the machine is modified to be submersible and operate under water. (Lotus Cars, USA)

When Bond gave up the Bentley because of high fuel costs he switched to the Saab 900 on assignment in *Never Send Flowers*. Later he moved to the Saab 9000. (Saab Scandia of America)

Chassis No. .... #DP 216/1 (Development Project)
Engine No. .... #400/P/4 (a special prototype)
Color .... Birch/silver

Five speed gearbox, 6 cylinder twin overhead camshaft, 4 litre engine, grey leather interior. This machine was auctioned at Sotheby's NY on June 28, 1986 for $275,000. Original cost $45,000.

GENEALOGY OF THE DBVGT (BMT 216-A)

1963 – 1968 .... Aston Martin Lagonda. Original registration BMT 216-A
1968 – 1971 .... Gavin Keyzar. Chislehurst, Kent, England
1971 – 1986 .... Richard D. Losee, Provo, Utah
1986 – 1997 .... Anthony V. Pugliese III, Florida

In the early morning hours of June 20, 1997, thieves broke into a locked hangar and secure area of the Boca Raton airport. They escaped with the Aston Martin and it has never been recovered!

MACHINE NO. 2 (DB / 1486 / R)

This machine was used for "long shots" in the filming of *Goldfinger* and *Thunderball*. Jerry Lee of Philadelphia, Pa. purchased this machine from Aston Martin. It is now displayed in a special-built wing of the Lee home. It is complete with all of its original equipment.

THE REPLICAS (TWO) (DB5 / 2008 / R AND DB5 / 2017 / R)

1969 .... Both of these machines were purchased from Eon Productions for a total of 1500 pounds by Anthony Bamford of the UK.
1969 .... DB5 / 2008 / R was sold to the Smokey Mountain Car Museum in Tennessee. Bruce Atchley, owner. It has been on display there for the past 34 years.

DB/2017/R

1969 – 1992 .... During this period, nine separate individuals owned this machine in the U.K., Canada, and the U.S.

1992 – 1999 .... Owned and on display at the Dutch National Motor Museum,* Steurweg 8, 4941 VR Raamsdonksveer, Netherlands.

*1993 – 1998 .... On loan and displayed at the National Motor Museum, Beaulieu, England.

1999 .... Dutch National Motor Museum.

ASTON MARTIN VANTAGE

This machine was driven by Bond in *The Living Daylights* and 'Q' equipped the Vantage with 80s technology. It featured Laser beam cutter, rocket jet propulsion unit, automatic missiles and rockets, head-up display, automatic protruding skis from sills, studded tires, and the usual bullet-proof glass and rotating license plates.

Most sources credit the Volante in this film but aside from a "short take" of the Volante being "winterized" and being driven to the "safe" house, the film crew actually used both the Volante and the Vantage. It is the Vantage that Bond actually drives and eventually destroys.

Engine	dohc V-8
Displacement, cc	5340
Bhp @ rpm, net	est 300 @ 5600
Curb weight	4330
Top speed, mph	175
Wheelbase, in.	102.8
Length	189.5
Height	54.0

JAGUAR XK8 COUPE 1998

The first V-8 engine designed by Jaguar. Major Boothroyd commissioned Jaguar's Special Vehicle Operations Unit to improve the car's power to do 400 b.h.p. The car was equipped with a Z5HP24 automatic transmission, which offered five forward gear ratios to optimize performance. First through fourth gears were selected for sharp response and effortless acceleratoin, while fifth was on overdrive ration for fuel economy. The transmission's versatility began with two driver-selected gear modes, Sport and Normal. Switching into Sport mode timed the gear changes for peak response.

The car is coated with chobam armor, which is impenetrable. 'Q' used it with reactive skins that explode when they are hit. This deflects the bullets. The metal is self-healing. On being pierced, the skin can heal itself by virtue of viscous fluid.

Certain paints have also been used that have electrically sensitive pigments which will change color. Used in conjuction with the electonically controlled standard interchangeable license plate, the car can change identity a number of times.

The Jaguar is fitted with an intelligent automatic gearbox, and gears are changed by means of a combined manual and automatic five-speed adaptive system through a "J" gate mechanism when one wishes to use the manual system.

Bond drove this machine on assignment in *The Facts of Death* and *High Time to Kill*.

BEAUTY QUEENS IN BOND FILMS

Claudine Auger .... *Thunderball*. Former Miss France, 1958.

Martine Beswick .... *From Russia With Love* and *Thunderball*. Former Miss Jamaica.

Daniela Bianchi .... *From Russia With Love*. Former Miss Italy and runner-up to the 1960 Miss Universe.

Julie Ege .... *On Her Majesty's Secret Service*. Former Miss Norway.

Aliza Gur .... *From Russia With Love*. Former Miss Israel.

Sylvana Henriques .... *On Her Majesty's Secret Service*. Former Miss Jamaica.

Margaret Lewors .... *Dr. No*. Miss Jamaica 1961.

Carolyn Seward .... *Octopussy*. Former Miss England and runner-up to Miss Universe.

Mary Stavin .... *Octopussy* and *A View To A Kill*. Former Miss Sweden and Miss World.

Michelle Yeoh .... *Tomorrow Never Dies*. Former Miss Malaysia.

BLADES PRIVATE CLUB, LONDON

The most exclusive club in London, established 1778.[1]

MEMBERSHIP

Restricted to 200. Confined to those who behave like gentlemen and can show 100,000 pounds in cash or securities. Every member is required to win or lose 50 pounds a year on the club premises or pay an annual fine of 250 pounds.

FACILITIES

Elegant smoking, dining, and gambling rooms. Twelve "member bedrooms" for overnight guests.

[1] It was here that Bond won 15,000 pounds in a game of bridge against Sir Hugo Drax.

SOCIAL AMENITIES

1) Only new currency notes and silver are paid out on the premise.
2) Overnight guests are given new money in the morning with their tea and the London Times.
3) No newspaper comes to the reading room before it has been ironed.
4) Floris soaps and lotions in all lavatories and bedrooms.
5) Direct wire to Ladbrokes.
6) Finest tents and boxes at Wimbledon.
7) Members traveling abroad have automatic membership in leading clubs in every foreign capitol in the world.

STAFF
1) Lord Basildon, Chairman of Blades
2) Brevett, Guardian of Blades
3) Headwaiter, Porterfield[2]
4) Headwaitress, Lily
5) Wine Steward, Grimley
6) Six waitresses for personal service

[2] Retired British naval Chief Petty Officer who served under 'M' in his last command.

BOND, JAMES: PERSONA

Bond is an avid golfer, skier[1], and swimmer. He enjoys mountain climbing and card games and is a judo expert. He boxed as a lightweight in school. He loves to drive fast cars and his favorite golf course is the Royal St. Mark's at Sandwich, England. Coincidentally, this was also Ian Fleming's favorite course. Bond is an all-around athlete; expert pistol shot and knife thrower. Other golf courses Bond likes to play close to London are Huntercombe, Swinly, Sunningdale, and the Berkshire. His handicap is nine. In cards, he never loses at Chemin de fer.

[1] Bond learned to ski in his teens from his friend Hannes Oberhauser in Europe prior to WWII. Oberhauser was murdered at the end of the war by Major Dexter Smythe of the British Royal Marines. Smythe's story is told in *Octopussy*.

AIRLINES (COMMERCIAL) FLOWN BY BOND (BOOK & FILM)

Live and Let Die	BOAC Stratocruiser, Pan Am London to New York
Diamonds Are Forever	BOAC Monarch, London to New York
	Lufthansa, Amsterdam to Los Angeles
From Russia With Love	BEA, Pan Am, London to Istanbul
Dr. No	Super Constellation, Pan Am, London to Jamaica
Goldfinger	Transamerica Constellation, Caracas to Miami
	BOAC Monarch, New York / Crashed
	British United Air Ferries, England to France
On Her Majesty's Secret Service	Swissair, London to Zurich, Zurich to London, London to Zurich
You Only Live Twice	Japan Airlines, London to Tokyo
The Man With the Golden Gun	BWI, Trinidad to Jamaica
For Your Eyes Only	Olympic, Greece to London
	BOAC Comet, London to Montreal
Moonraker	Apollo, Africa to London
	Air France Concorde, Italy to S. America
The Living Daylights	BEA Charter, London to Berlin
For Special Services	Bristish Airways, Singapore to London
Icebreaker	Finnair, Helsinki to London
	TAP, London to Lisbon to Funchal
	TAP, Funchal to Lisbon
	KLM, Lisbon to Amsterdam
	Finnair, Amsterdam to Helsinki

Nobody Lives Forever .... Pan Am, Zurich to Miami
No Deals Mr. Bond .... Aer Lingus, London to Dublin
Cathay Pacific, Paris to Hong Kong
Scorpius .... Piedmont, London to Charolette, N.C.
License to Kill .... Pan Am, London to Keywest
Win, Lose or Die .... None
Broken Claw .... Horizon Air, Alaska, Vancouver to San Francisco
The Man From Barbarossa .... Military, England to Russia
Death is Forever .... British Airways, London to Germany
Air France, France to Italy
Never Send Flowers .... SIS CO. Jet. Hawker-Siddley, London to Bern
Commercial (no name), Bern to London
Commercial (no name), London to Bonn
Commercial (no name), Bonn to Milan
Commercial (no name), Milan to London
Seafire .... British Airways, Spain to Israel
Lufthhansa, Germany to Puerto Rico, Delta
Coldfall .... Alitalia, New York to Rome
Goldeneye .... Not named
Tomorrow Never Dies .... British Airways, London to Hamburg
Zero Minus Ten .... British Airways, London to Hong Kong
The Facts of Death .... American Airlines, London to Dallas
Olympic Airways, Akrotiri to Athens

AIRCRAFT BOND HAS FLOWN HIMSELF (BOOK & FILM)[1]

Goldfinger .... B.O.A.C. Monarch commercial airliner
You Only Live Twice .... Wallis Autogyro. Aero Commander monoplane
Live & Let Die .... Hang-glider
The Man With the Golden Gun .... Seaplane
Moonraker .... Hang-glider
For Your Eyes Only .... Helicopter
Octopussy .... Bede Acro-Star
The Living Daylights .... C-130 Hercules cargo plane
License to Kill .... Cessna 185 Seaplane
Win, Lose or Die .... British Sea Harrier V/ STOL fighter
Coldfall .... AH-1W COBRA helicopter
Goldeneye .... Piper Archer, Russian Torch
Tomorrow Never Dies .... Russian M26 Fighter
Zero Minus Ten .... Cessna Grand Caravan
Single-engine Turboprop

[1] Bond is fully licensed for helicopter, fixed wing, multi-engine, and jet aircraft.

APPEARANCE

Height: 6'2", Weight: 167 lbs. Slim build, blue eyes, black hair, scar down right cheek. Plastic surgery on back of right hand. Straight nose, cruel mouth, firm jawline, flecks of grey hair, tanned.

AWARDS

- Presented with a silver plated .38 calibre Smith & Wesson Police Positive revolver from the President of the United States.
- Awarded the Jamaican Police Medal for gallant and meritorius services to the Independent State of Jamaica.
- Recommended to Queen Elizabeth for knighthood for which Bond declined the honor.
- Bond has been awarded the Order of Lenin twice by the Kremlin.
- Awarded French Croix de Guerre.

BANK ACCOUNT

Barclay Bank, Oxford Street. Box 700. James Boldman. Similar boxes in Paris, Rome, Vienna, Madrid, Berlin, and Copenhagen.

BASIC NEEDS

Good food, drink, clothes, fast cars, a gun, beautiful women, money and general luxury.

BIOGRAPHY, BOND, JAMES: COMMANDER, G. MG., R.N.V.R.

Father .... Andrew Bond, Glencoe, Scotland. Foreign representative of Vickers Armaments firm.

Mother .... Swiss. Monique Delacroix from Canton de Vaud.

Both of Bond's parents were killed in a climbing accident when he was eleven years old. He was raised by an aunt, Miss Charmian Bond, in the village of Pett Bottom, near Canterbury, in Kent. His only other known relative was an uncle, Bruce Bond, living in Australia, now deceased.

CLOTHES

Bond wears the following clothes for business and leisure. He prefers dark-blue serge suits, single-breasted, lightweight. Navy blue tropical worsted trousers. Black knitted ties, four in hand knot. Sea Island shirts in cotton. Shoes without laces, soft leather or moccasins, black "Ted Lapidus" cords, black cotton turtleneck sweater, light suede jacket, silk traveling "Hoppi-Coat, " gray "Oscar Jacobson Alccantara" jacket, gray "Cardin" suit, navy and white spotted "Cardin" tie, light blue shirt by "Hilditch & Key" of Jermy Street, London. Hong Kong tailor; Bel Homme. Light blue and red track suit, "Damart thermal long-johns, padded ski pants and jacket. Dunhill slacks and blazer. Bathrobe or dressing gown with the initials JB. Heavy rollneck sweater, "Mukluk" boots, thermal hood, scarf, woolen hat and goggles, "Damart" thermal-lined gloves, gray gabardine suit, plain blue "Coles" shirt, "Jacques Faith" knitted tie, "Crombie British" warm blue padded cold-weather jacket, single-breasted dinner jacket, "Saxone" golf shoes, black windbreaker, white linen swim trunks, blue sandals, old black and white hound's tooth tweed jacket, "Adidas" sport shoes.

CODE NAME

Predator

COST OF BOND'S LUXURIES

Bond's stainless steel Rolex Oyster Perpetual Chronometer wristwatch would today cost Bond $15,000. His Dom Perignon, $125.00, Beluga caviar, 30 grams $55.90, 50 grams $109.00 and his Hennessy's cognac, $97.95.

CREDIT CARD

Platinum American Express

EDUCATION

Bond is an educated man. Born into the comfortably well-off upper middle class. Entered Eton at age 12. Transferred to Fettes University of Geneva. Also, the Hermes-Schneider School at St. Anton Arlberg. Graduated with a "first" in Oriental Languages from Cambridge (*You Only Live Twice*). Speaks fluent French and German.

EMPLOYMENT

Bond entered the Ministry of Defense as a Lieutenant in a Special Branch of the Royal Volunteer Reserves. Ended WWII with rank of Commander. His naval serial number: CH4539876. After the war he joined the British Secret Service. In 1954 he was appointed a Companion to the Order of St. Michael and St. George for duties performed with outstanding bravery and distinction. Universal Export, aka: Transworld Consortium, aka: Special Section, is a front for the British Secret Service. Bond was the senior of three men initially to earn the double-o number, with license to kill. Bond was awarded the "double-0" number for two assignments in the service. Bond wears two rows of ribbons on his Commander's uniform.[1]

[1] Bond was promoted to Captain RN on assignment in Win, Lose, or Die in 1989.

EXERCISE

Bond begins his day with 20 slow push-ups and leg lifts, followed by 20 toe touches plus breathing exercises. These are followed by a very hot shower, immediately followed by a very cold one.

FAMILY MOTTO

"The World is Not Enough."

FAN CLUBS & BOND / FLEMING ORGANIZATIONS

The James Bond Int'l Fan Club
P.O. Box 007
Addlestone, Weybridge,
Surrey KT15 IDY
England
(http://www.thejamesbondfanclub.com)

The Bondmanian Society
15 Crathie Place
Wrexham, CLWYD, North Wales
LL112HB Great Britain
(http://www.geocities.com/hollywood/studio/3496)

Club James Bond 007
42, reu Rovelle
75015 Paris, France
(http://jamesbond007.net)

The Ian Fleming Foundation
P.O. Box 1850
Burbank, California, USA
(http://www.ianfleming.org)

FAVORITE CIGARETTES

Bond originally smoked a special Balkan and Turkish blend made for him by Morelands of 83 Grosvenor Street, London, WI. He smoked 60-70 cigarettes a day. Each cigarette carried three gold bands. Later, Bond switched to low tar cigarettes made for him by H. Simmons of Burlington Arcade and reduced his intake to 20-25 a day.* His gunmetal cigarette case holds 50. He lights each one with a black oxidized Ronson lighter. When in a foreign country, he smokes the following:

Jamaica	Royal Blend
Canada	Senior Service
Greece	Xanthi
U.S.A.	Chesterfields, Moreland specials
Turkey	Diplomates
Japan	Shinsei
France	Laurens jaune

* Bond has since reduced his intake to five or six a day.

FAVORITE DRINKS

Beer	Lowenbrau, Miller, Red Stripe.
Bourbon	Old Grandad, I.W. Harper, Walker Deluxe, Jack Daniels, Canadian Club, all preferably on the rocks.
Brandy	Hennessy Three Star with soda or ginger ale, cognac.
Champagne[1]	Don Perignon 46, 53, 55, 69, Taittinger Blanc de Blanc 45, Clicquot, Krug, Pommery, Bollinger, Mouton Rothchild, Pol Roger (various years).
Cocktails	Old-fashioned, martini, Vesper, Negroni, Americano.
Gin	Beefeater, House of Lords, Gordon's, with tonic, fresh limes, Angostura bitters.
Liquers	A ten year old Calvados, Stinger.
Saki[2]	No brand specified
Scotch	Dimple & Haig. Preferably with soda.
Vodka	Stolichnaya, Wolfschmidt (ice-cold w/ tonic in hot weather).
Wine	A ten year old claret, Rose d' Anjou, red Chianti, red Bardolin.

[1] Bond says champagne must never be drunk above a temperature of 38 degrees Fahrenheit.

[2] According to Bond, Saki must always be drunk at a temperature of 98.4 degrees Fahrenheit.

Recipe for the famous Bond martini, shaken but not stirred[1]

3 measures of Gordon's gin
1 measure of vodka
½ measure of Kina Lillet (a white aperitif)[2]
Shake well until ice-cold. Add a large slice of lemon peel. Serve in a deep champagne goblet, straight up.

Bond's recipe for an Old Fashioned:

2 teaspoons water
Add one small sugar cube
Add dash of bitters
1 ½ ounces of bourbon
Add ice cubes
Add sliced oranges

Bond's recipe for the Stinger:

1 ½ ounces of Vodka
1 ounce white Crème de Menthe

[1] Bond named this drink the "Vesper" after Vesper Lynd in *Casino Royale*. The "Vesper" originally served to Fleming in Jamaica consisted of frozen rum, with fruit and herbs.

[2] Kina is a brand name and Lillet (pronounced LIL-LAY) is a type of French aperitif wine. Lillet is available in red (awful taste) and white (absolutely delightful taste). Most connoisseurs conclude that Fleming "goofed" when he called out a "Kina Lillet" as it is flavored with quinine. A simple Lillet would have been appropriate.

On the continent, Bond may order an Americano:

1 measure of Campari
1 measure of Martini & Rossi sweet vermouth
A splash of Perrier
Garnish with a slice of orange

In Rome he drinks a Negroni:

2 ounces of gin
1 ounce of Italian sweet vermouth
1 ounce of Campari
Generous slice of orange

When in Japan, Bond drinks Saki. In Greece, Ouzo with an ice water chaser. In Turkey, Anise flavored raki. In England he likes Black Velvet, half and half stout and champagne in a tankard. Also Guiness Stout.

WHAT BOND DRINKS (FILM)

Dr. No	Vodka Martini, Dom Perignon ('55).
From Russia With Love	Taittinger, Blanc de Blanc.
Goldfinger	Dom Perignon ('53), Mouton Rothschild ('47).
	Vodka martini, Mint Julep, brandy.
Thunderball	Dom Perignon ('55), Rum Collins.

You Only Live Twice .... Dom Perignon ('59), Saki, Siamese vodka, Russian vodka.

On Her Majesty's Secret Service .... Martini, Dom Perignon ('57), malt whiskey.

Diamonds Are Forever .... Mouton Rothschild ('55), Solero sherry.

Live And Let Die .... Bollinger, Chianti, bourbon & water.

The Man With the Golden Gun .... Mouton Rothschild ('34), Moet Champagne Phuyuk ('74), Dom Perignon ('69).

The Spy Who Loved Me .... Dom Perignon ('52), vodka martini.

Moonraker .... Dom Perignon ('46), Bollinger ('69).

For Your Eyes Only .... Ouzo, champagne.

Octopussy .... Champagne, martini.

A View to a Kill .... Stolichnaya vodka, Bollinger ('75).

Never Say Never Again .... Vodka martini, Absolut vodka.

The Living Daylights .... Vodka martini, Bollinger, red wine.

License to Kill .... Budweiser beer, Bolliger RD, martini.

Goldeneye .... Vodka Martini.

Tomorrow Never Dies .... Vodka Martini.

WHAT BOND DRINKS (BOOK)

Casino Royale .... Veuve Clicquot Americano, vodka martini. Brut Blanc de Blanc ('43).

Live & Let Die .... House of Lords Gin, Haig & Haig scotch, Old Fashioned's with Old Grandad bourbon, Liebfraumilch.

Moonraker .... White Bordeaux wine, vodka martini rocks, Black & White whiskey with soda.

Diamonds Are Forever .... Brandy & Soda, Black Velvet, Irish Whiskey, martini, Clicquot Rose, Stinger, Old Fashioned.

From Russia With Love .... Americano, ouzo, martini, Calvet Claret, saki, vodka & tonic, Chianti, anise-flavored raki, Broglio, Kavaklidere, a Balkan burgundy.

Dr. No .... Double gin & tonic, Red Stripe beer, Royal Blend, Canadian Club blended rye.

Goldfinger .... Double bourbons, Pommery ('50) pink champagne, vodka martini with lemon peel, Piesporter Goldtopfchen ('53) moselle, Mouton Rothchild ('47), Rose d'Anjou, Hennessy's three-star, Enzian, Lowenbrau, Fondant wine.

Thunderball .... Chianti wine, vodka & tonic, double dry martini. Cliquot Rose.

The Spy Who Loved Me .... None.

On Her Majesty's Secret Service .... Taittinger Blanc de Blanc, Pouilly-Fuisse, Mouton Rothchild ('53) Krug, Calvados, I.W. Harper, double vodka & tonic, brandy & ginger ale, vodka martini with lemon peel, bourbon / rocks, Jack Daniels sour mash, Steinlager.

You Only Live Twice	Brandy & ginger ale, sake, Suntory whiskey, Jack Daniels.
The Man With the Golden Gun	Red Stripe beer, champagne cocktails, Walker's deluxe bourbon/ rocks, Beefeater's gin & bitters.
Colonel Sun	Carafe of cheap wine, ouzo & ice, Retsina white wine, Bell scotch, Namas Retsina, Anjou Rose, Votris Greek brandy.
License Renewed	Dom Perignon ('55), Perrier, Talisker, fine malt whisky, port, red Bordolino ('79).
For Special Services	Dom Perignon ('69), martinis, Mint Juleps, brandy
Icebreaker	Champagne, vodka.
Role of Honor	Retsina, champagne cocktails, vodka & tonic.
Nobody Lives Forever	Gordon's vodka with lillet, Campari & soda, Frecciarossa Bianco, Calypso dacquiris, Tattinger ('73).
No Deals Mr. Bond	Vodka & tonic, brandy, Krug chablis ('78), white burgundy, Hine (1914).
Scorpius	Whiskey, Chablis Grand Cru.
License to Kill	Remy Martin Brandy, virgin colada, martini, champagne.
Win, Lose or Die	Vin Gran Caruso red wine.
Broken Claw	Champagne, martini, brandy.
The Man From Barbarossa	Champagne cocktail, brandy.
Death is Forever	Red Chianti wine, white cartese de Goui 85 & Red Gottinara '83, brandy, Riesling Spatlese, a Kreuznacher '73.
Never Send Flowers	Vodka martini, Beaujalais wine, Schloss Drache, port wine.
Seafire	Dom Perignon, martini.
Coldfall	Red Dog Beer, Beoune.
Goldeneye	Bourbon.
Tomorrow Never Dies	Scotch, champagne.
Zero Minus Ten	Vodka martini, plum wine, brandy, beer.
The Facts of Death	Ambelida white wine, vodka martini, tequila, whiskey, Bourbon Margaritas, Taitinger champagne, ouzo, the Macallan, Chatzimichali red wine, Villitsa white wine.

WHAT BOND DRINKS: SHORT STORIES

From A View to a Kill	Americano, bitter Campari, Cinzano, a large slice of lemon peel in Perrier.
Quantum of Solace	Brandy.
Risico	Negroni with Gordon's gin, chianti, whisky & soda.
Hildebrand Rarity	Pink champagne.
The Living Daylights	Dimple Haig whiskey, Molle mit Korn, Lowenbrau.
The Property of a Lady	None.

FOOD

Bond's favorite meal of the day is breakfast. He likes scrambled eggs, a double portion with bacon, toast and marmalade. Also,very hot, black coffee, no sugar. Bond also enjoys soft-boiled brown eggs, 3 ½ minutes. He prefers two slices of whole wheat toast with Jersey butter, Tiptree "LittleScarlet" strawberry jam from Fortum & Mason, Cooper's vintage oxford marmalade And Norwegian heather honey on two slices of whole-wheat toast. Bond's soft-boiled egg cup is dark blue with a gold ring around the top. Minton China and Queen Anne silver.

His lunch might consist of any combination of the following: Grilled sole, cold roast beef with potato salad, escalope of veal, steaks, french fries, ham sandwiches, meat pies, fruit salad, green salad, sausage, bread butter, Perrier, and ½ litre of wine.

Here is Bond's recipe for salad dressing:
½ teaspoon ground pepper
½ teaspoon salt
½ teaspoon sugar
2 ½ teaspoons powdered mustard.
Mix well, crush and add:
3 tablespoons oil
1 tablespoon white wine vinegar, plus a few drops of water
Stir well and pour over salad

FAVORITE FOODS

Bond's dinner might consist of the following: Smoked salmon, lamb cutlets, peas, new potatoes, asparagus with Bernaise sauce, pineapple slices, green salad, lobster. One of Bond's favorite puddings is Scottish cream-crowdie (toasted oatmeal folded into a thick whipped cream). Bond's housekeeper, May, purchases his coffee from DeBry in New Oxford street and brews it in an American Chemix coffee maker.

FAVORITE RESTAURANTS

Bond's favorite restaurant is Scott's, Coventry Street, London. The following are some selected restaurants Bond has frequented while on assignment:

Hotel de Paris	Monte Carlo
Hermitage	Royale-les-Eaux
St. Regis, Ritz, Le Perigord, The Plaza,	
Voisins, 21 Club, Lutece, Oyster Bar,	
Grand Central Station.	New York
Blades, Trattoo, Compana,	
Veeraswamy's	London
Café Royal	Dover
Granville	St. Margaret's Bay
Sagamore	Sarasota Springs, NY
Tiara Hotel	Las Vegas
Joy Boat	Kingston

Bill's On The Beach .... Miami
Channel Packet .... Ramsgate
L'Oasis .... La Napoule
Negresco .... Nice
La Reserve .... Beauliew
Le Galion .... Garavan
Le chateau .... Dublin
Malmaison .... Glasgow
Au Savarin .... Helsinki
Fouquets, Café de la Paix, Rotande .... Paris
Columba d'Oro, Cochon d'Or .... Rome
Harry's Bar, Florians .... Venice
Café Martinique, the Wharf,
The Bahamian .... Nassau
Lucien's .... Brighton
Hotel de la Gare, Pouilly-Fuisse .... Orleans
Maison Rouge .... Strasbourg
The Pier House .... Key West
Gulf Winds Bar .... Florida
Terminus Nord .... Paris
Café Royal .... London
Willy's Wolf's Lair .... Coeur d'Alene, Idaho
Jo & Mo's .... Washington, D.C.
Grande Bretagne Hotel .... Athens, Greece

Bond was a member of the Playboy Club prior to their closing. His membership number was 40401.

FIRST MOVIE THEATRE APPEARANCE

London. October 6, 1962. *Dr. No*

FIRST TV SCREEN APPEARANCE

Climax Mystery Theatre. CBS: *Casino Royale* October 21, 1954
Producer .... Bretaigne Windust
Presenter .... William Lundigan
James Bond .... Barry Nelson
Le Chiffre .... Peter Lorre
Valerie Mathis .... Linda Christian
Clarence Leiter .... Michael Pate
Chef de partie .... Eugene Borden
Croupier .... Jean De Val
Le Chiffre's hoods .... Gene Roth and Kurt Katch
Directed by .... William H. Brown
Associate Producer .... Elliot Lewis
Art Directors .... Robert Tyler and James De Val
Writers .... Anthony Ellis and Charles Bennett
CBS purchased the TV rights in 1954 for $1000.

HOTELS WHERE BOND HAS BEEN A GUEST

Casino Royale .... Hotel Splendide, Royale-les-Eaux, two story inn near Les Nectambieles, France. Hotel Tropicale.

Live & Let Die .... St. Regis, New York; Everglades Cabanas, St. Petersburg, Florida; San Monique, (island).

Diamonds Are Forever .... Ritz Hotel, London; Plaza Hotel, New York; Sagamore Hotel, Sarasota Springs, New York; Tiara Hotel, Tropicana Hotel, Las Vegas.

From Russia With Love .... Kristal Blas, Istanbul.

Dr. No .... Blue Hills, Kingston, Jamaica.

Goldfinger .... Floridiana Hotel, Miami; Fountainbleu, Miami; Channel Packet Hotel, Ramsgate, England; Hotel de la Gare, Orleans, France; Hotel des Bergues, France.

Thunderball .... Shrublands Health Clinic, Sussex, England; Royal Bahamian Hotel, Nassau.

The Spy Who Loved Me .... Dreamy Pines Motor Court, Hotel Cala Di Volpe, Sardinia.

On Her Majesty's Secret Service .... Hotel Splendide, Royale-les-Eaux, France; Hotel Maison Rouge, Strasbourg Hotel; Vier Jahreszeiten, Munich, Germany.

You Only Live Twice .... O'Kura Hotel, Tokyo; Miyako Hotel, Kyoto; Hilton Hotel, Tokyo.

The Man With the Golden Gun .... Morgan's Harbour, Kingston; Thunderbird Hotel near Savannah La Mar.

From a View to a Kill .... Hotel Gare du Nord, Paris.

For Your Eyes Only .... KO-ZEE Motor Court, Montreal, Mira Monte, Cortina, Italy.

Quantum of Solace .... British Colonial Hotel, Nassau.

Risico .... Hotel Nazionale, Rome; Gritti Palace, Venice; Hotel Albergo Danieli, Venice.

Colonel Sun .... Grande Bretagne, Athens.

License Renewed .... Central Hotel, Glasgow; Negresco Hotel, Nice, France.

For Special Services .... Loew's Drake Hotel, New York; unnamed motel, Washington, D.C.; small motel, Springfield, Missouri; small, obscure motel, Amarillo, Texas; Maison de Ville Hotel, New Orleans, Louisiana.

Icebreaker .... Inter-continental Hotel, Helsinki; Reid's Hotel, Funchal, Madeira; Hilton International, Amsterdam; Hesperia Hotel, Helsinki; Revontuli Hotel, Salla, Finland; Ovnasvaara Polor, Rovaniemi, Finland.

Role of Honor .... Hotel de Paris, Monte Carlo, Monaco; The Bull at the Cross, Nun's Cross, England; Villa Medici, Rome; unnamed hotel, Athens; small bungalow Hotel, Corfu, Greece.

Nobody Lives Forever	Hotel Sofitel, Place Saint-Pierre-le-Jeune, France; Mirto Du Lac, Lacarno, Switzerland; the Golden Hirsch, Salzburg, Austria; The Pier House, Key West, Florida.
No Deals Mr. Bond	Mayfair & International Hotels, Dublin; the Newpark Hotel, Kilkenny; Mandarin Hotel, Hong Kong, China.
The Living Daylights	Hotel Im Palois, Schwarzenkerg.
License to Kill	The Pier House & Casa Marina Hotel, Key West, Florida. El Presidente Hotel, Isthmus City.
Win, Lose or Die	Feathers Hotel, Woodstock, England; Villa Capricciani, Island of Ischia, Italy.
Broken Claw	Empress, Victoria, B.C; Fairmont, San Francisco.
The Man From Barbarossa	Hotel de la Justice.
Death Is Forever	Hotel Bristol Kempinski, Berlin; Crillon & Amber Hotel Paris; Cipriani, Venice, Italy.
Never Send Flowers	Falcon Hotel, Thun, Switzerland; Palace Hotel, Milan, Italy; Hotel Victoria, Jung Frace, Germany; Hilton, Athens, Greece; Villa om Rheuil, Ondernach, Germany.
Seafire	University Arms Hotel, Cambridge, United Kingdom; King David Hotel, Jerusalem, Israel; Paulanerstubese, Wasserburg, Germany; Gran Hotel, El Convento, Puerto Rico; Splendid Hotel-Munich.
007 In New York	The Plaza Hotel, Astor Hotel.
Coldfall	The Rock, Gibralter; Hotel du Rhone, Geneva; Unnamed hotel in Washington D.C., Dulles Airport
Goldeneye	Grand Hotel Europe, St. Petersburg, Russia
Tomorrow Never Dies	The Kempiinski Hotel Atlantic, Hamburg, Germany.
Zero Minus Ten	Mandarin Oriental, Hong Kong; Star & Garter, Kalgoorlie, Australia.
The Facts of Death	Grande Bretagne, Athens; Porto Fira, Santorini.
Octopussy	Shianivas Hotel, Udoipur, India.

LIKES & DISLIKES

BOND LOVES:

Golf	Gambling
Swimming	Exercise
Women	Freedom
Vodka Martinis	Food
Fast Cars	Conflict
Custom-Made Cigarettes	Specific Books
Floris Bath Essence	King & Queen

BOND HATES:

Office Work	Tea
Social Parties	Shoe Laces
Buttons	Port
Villains	Boredom

BOND IS:

Healthy, detached, disengaged, occassionally cruel, tough, ruthless, sensual, hedonistic, courageous, patriotic, a bit of a bastard, a professional killer, self-indulgent, egotistic, sadistic, amoral, savage, virile, lean, arrogant, lustful, hard, strong, quiet, sardonic, fatalistic, and capable of great tenderness.

LOCATION OF BOND'S LOVEMAKING (FILM)

DR. NO:
Sylvia Trench	Bond's apt., London
Miss Taro	Her flat, Kingston
Honey Ryder	Small boat off Crab Key

FROM RUSSIA WITH LOVE:
Sylvia Trench	Small Boat on the Thames
Tatiana Romanova	Kristal Blas Hotel, Orient Express

GOLDFINGER:
Jill Masterson	Bond's room, Fountainbleau Hotel
Pussy Galore	Underneath a parachute / island

THUNDERBALL:
Patricia Fearing	Shrublands Health Clinic
Fiona Volpe	Bond's hotel room, Nassau
Domino	On the beach

YOU ONLY LIVE TWICE:
Akiko Wakabayashi	Bond's bedroom, Tanaka's house
Helga Brandt	Cabin on board the Ning-Po
Kissy Suzuki	Small boat

ON HER MAJESTY'S SECRET SERVICE:
Ruby Windsor	Ruby's room, Piz Gloria Clinic
Tracy di Vicenzo	Bond's hotel room; barn

DIAMONDS ARE FOREVER:
Tiffany Case	Tropicana Hotel room; Queen Elizabeth ocean liner

LIVE & LET DIE:
Rosie Carver	Bond's room, San Monique Hotel
Solitaire	Her room, train compartment

THE MAN WITH THE GOLDEN GUN:
Mary Goodnight .... Bond's hotel room, Chinese junk
Andrea Anders .... Bond's hotel room

THE SPY WHO LOVED ME:
Major Anya Amasova .... Bond's hotel room; train compartment;
                                            Stromberg's escape bell
Unnamed girl .... Austrian mountain cabin

MOONRAKER:
Corrine Dufour .... Bond's bedroom, Drax estate
Holly Goodhead .... In space ship

FOR YOUR EYES ONLY:
Countess Lisl .... Her place
Melina Havelock .... Havelock's yacht "Triana"

OCTOPUSSY:
Magda .... Bond's hotel room
Octopussy .... Her palace, her boat

NEVER SAY NEVER AGAIN:
Fatima .... Fishing boat
Lady in the Bahamas .... Her hotel room
Domino .... Their hotel room

A VIEW TO A KILL:
Girl in a boat .... Boat
Mayday .... Bond's bedroom, Zorin's chateau
Stacey Sutton .... Her place

THE LIVING DAYLIGHTS:
Kara Milovy .... Their hotel rooms

LICENSE TO KILL:
Pam Bouvier .... El Presidente Hotel
Lupe Lamora .... Sanchez house

CASINO ROYALE:
Vesper Lynd .... French Inn

LIVE & LET DIE:
Solitaire .... House in Jamaica

DIAMONDS ARE FOREVER:
Tiffany Case .... Queen Elizabeth Ocean Liner

FROM RUSSIA WITH LOVE:
Tatiana Romanova .... Kristal Blas Hotel; Orient Express

GOLDFINGER:

Jill Masterson.................................. Silver Meteor train

Pussy Galore .... Weathership in Atlantic Ocean

VIEW TO A KILL:

Mary Ann Russell .... In the woods

FOR YOUR EYES ONLY:

Judy Havelock .... KO-Zee Motor Court

RISICO:

Lisl Baum .... Albergo Danieli Hotel, Venice

THE SPY WHO LOVED ME:

Vivienne Michel .... Dreamy Pines Motor Court

THUNDERBALL:

Patricia Fearing .... Shrublands Health Clinic

Domino Vitali .... Hut on the beach

ON HER MAJESTY'S SECRET SERVICE:

Tracy .... Hotel Splendide & Vior Jahreszeiten

Ruby Windsor .... Piz Gloria Clinic

YOU ONLY LIVE TWICE:

Kissy Suzuki .... Her place, Kuro Island

THE MAN WITH THE GOLDEN GUN:

Mary Goodnight............................ Morgan's Harbour Hotel; her place

COLONEL SUN:

Ariadne Alexandrou .... Hotel Grande Bretagne, Athens

LICENSE RENEWED:

Qute .... Her place, London

Lavender Peacock .... Her place, Murik Castle, Negresco Hotel, French Riviera

FOR SPECIAL SERVICES:

Qute .... Her place in London

Nena Bismaquer .... Her place in Louisiana & Bismaquer ranch, Texas

ICEBREAKER:

Rivke Ingber .... Hotel Revontuli, Finland

Paula Vacker .... Her place, Hotel Revontuli

ROLE OF HONOR:

Percy Proud................................... Villa Medici, unnamed Athens hotel, small bungalow hotel, Corfu, Greece

Lady Freddie Fortune .... Bond's room, Bull at the Cross

Cindy Chambers .... Nun's Cross, her room

NOBODY LIVES FOREVER:
Suki Tempesta & Nannie Norwich .... The Pier House, Key West, Florida

NO DEALS MR. BOND
Ebbie Heritage .... Apartment in Paris; Newpark Hotel Dublin

SCORPIUS:
Harriet Horner .... Ten Pines, Hilton Head, North Carolina

LICENSE TO KILL:
Pat .... The Pier House, Key West, Florida
Pam Bouvier .... El Presidente Hotel, Isthmus City
Lupe Lamora .... Sanchez mansion

WIN, LOSE OR DIE:
Beatrice Maria da Ricci .... Villa Capricciani, Island of Ischia
Nikola Ratnikov .... Bond's stateroom aboard HMS Invincible

BROKEN CLAW:
Sue Chi-Ho .... Her apartment, San Francisco

THE MAN FROM BARBAROSSA:
Nina Bibkova .... Russia
Asore Rampart .... Paris

DEATH IS FOREVER:
Easy St. John.. OST-West Express. Berlin to Paris
Praxi Simeon .... Wolfgang Weisen's apartment in Venice

NEVER SEND FLOWERS:
Fredericka Von Grusse .... Falcon Hotel, Thun, Switzerland; Palace Hotel,
                                                                            Milan, Italy; Victoria Hotel, Jungfrav, Germany;
                                                                            Hilton Hotel Athens, Greece; Villa Am Rheine,
                                                                            Andernach, Germany

SEAFIRE:
Fredericka Von Grusse .... University Arms, Cambridge, UK; King David Hotel,
                                                                            Jerusalem; Gran Hotel El Convento, Puerto Rico

COLDFALL:
Sukie Tempesta .... Unnamed hotel, Dulles International Airport,
                                                                            Quantico, Virginia
Beatrice da Ricci .... Hotel du Rhone, Geneva, Switzerland

GOLDENEYE:
Natalye .... Beach House, Puerto Rico; River bank, Russia

TOMORROW NEVER DIES:
Paris Carver .... Atlantic Hotel, Hamburg, Germany
Wai Lin .... Boat and raft, Southeast Asia

ZERO MINUS TEN:

Sunni Pei .... M.I.6 Safe House, Hong Kong; Star & Garter, Kalgoorlie, Australia

THE FACTS OF DEATH:

Heri Volopoulos .... Her Athens apartment

Niki Mirakos .... Bond's Jaguar XK8; Grande Bretagne, Athens; Hotel Porto Fira, Santorini; Bond's barracks bunk bed

Dr. Ashely Anderson .... Repro Care Exam Room, Austin, Texas

MARITAL STATUS

Single. Bond was married briefly in 1962 to Teresa (Tracy) Contessa di Vicenzo, the only daughter of Marc-Ange Draco of Marseille, France. No children. Bond and Tracy were married at 10:30 AM, New Year's day in the British Consul General's drawing room in Munich, Germany. The best man was Commander Savage, head of Station 'M' in Munich. The weather was clear and warm. Unfortunately, Tracy was accidentally killed by gunfire from Blofeld's mistress who had intended the bullet for Bond.

NUMBER OF MEN BOND HAS KILLED (BOOK)[1]

Casino Royale 0

Live & Let Die 4

Moonraker 0

Diamonds Are Forever 6

From Russia With Love 3

Dr. No 6

Goldfinger 1

Thunderball 3

The Spy Who Loved Me .... 3 [2]

On Her Majesty's Secret Service 6

You Only Live Twice 2

The Man With the Golden Gun 2

License Renewed 4

For Special Services 3

Icebreaker 2

Role of Honor 4

Nobody Lives Forever 5

No Deals Mr. Bond 7

Scorpius 2

Colonel Sun 5

License to Kill 11

Win, Lose or Die 3

Broken Claw 1

The Man From Barbarossa .... 3 [3]

Death is Forever .... 12 [4]

Never Send Flowers 2

Seafire .... 6 (5 men, 1 woman)
Coldfall 3
Goldeneye 6
Tomorrow Never Dies (Book and Film) .... 21 [5]
Zero Minus Ten 14
The Facts of Death 21

[1] Bond killed a Japanese cipher expert in New York and a Norwegian double agent in Stockholm prior to Casino Royale and being awarded the 00, the license to kill. These two are included in the count.

[2] Bond killed S.P.E.C.T.R.E. agent Horst Uhlmann in Toronto, Canada, just prior to this assignment. Included in count.

[3] On this assignment Bond recalled killing a man by running his car off the road in Hollywood Hills. Included in count.

[4] On this assignment Bond recalled killing two Smersh agents years before at the Louvre in Paris, among the Egyptian antiquities. One of them was a woman. Included in count.

[5] Included in the count are four women.

NUMBER OF MEN BOND HAS KILLED (SHORT STORIES)

Quantum of Solace 0
For Your Eyes Only 3
From a View to a Kill 1
The Hildebrand Rarity 0
Risico 0
Octopussy 0
The Living Daylights 0
The Property of a Lady 0

NUMBER OF MEN BOND HAS KILLED (FILM)

Dr. No 3
From Russia With Love 13
Goldfinger 2
Thunderball 21
You Only Live Twice 13
On Her Majesty's Secret Service 4
Diamonds Are Forever 5
Live & Let Die 7
The Man With the Golden Gun 1
The Spy Who Loved Me 14
Moonraker 4
For Your Eyes Only 9
Octopussy 15
Never Say Never Again 3
A View to a Kill 5
The Living Daylights 3
License to Kill 10
Goldeneye 6
Tomorrow Never Dies 21

OFFICE[1]

The office of James Bond is on the fifth floor of M.I.6 building overlooking Regents Park, London. Bond has three telephones on his desk; 1) black, for outside calls, 2) green, for internal office, 3) red, a direct line to 'M'.

[1] M.I.6 has since moved its headquarters. It is now located on the bank of the river Thames at Vauxhall, and Bond's office is now on the fourth floor.

ORIGIN OF THE NAME BOND

Fleming took the name of Bond from a book he owned titled *Birds of the West Indies* by ornithologist James Bond. James Bond was a curator of ornithology with the Academy of Natural Sciences in Philadelphia and the world's leading authority of birds of the West Indies. In recognition of his discovery that some Caribbean birds were of North American origin, the geographic line dividing Caribbean birds from South American birds has been called the "Bond Line."

The real James Bond was a native of Philadelphia and held degrees from Cambridge University in England. He died February 14, 1989.

PASSPORT (BRITISH)

James Bond has three passports he uses on assignment. They are:

J.B. Boldman, Company Director	Number 0094567
David Barlow	Number 391354
John Hunter	Not Given

PSEUDONYMS USED BY BOND: BOOK & FILM

Octopussy	Col. Luis Toro, Argentine Army Officer
	Charles Morton, manufacture's rep.
The Spy Who Loved Me	Robert Sterling, marine biologist
You Only Live Twice	Mr. Fisher, Empire Chemicals
A View to a Kill	James St. John-Smythe, horse buyer
	James Stock, London Financial News
No Deals Mr. Bond	J. Boldman
Nobody Lives Forever	James Boldman
For Your Eyes Only	Mr. James
For Special Services	Prof. Joseph Penbrunner, art expert
Scorpius	J.B. Boldman
Live & Let Die	Mr. Bryce
Diamonds Are Forever	Sergeant James, Peter Franks and Mr. Jones.
Risico	James Bond, writer of adventure stories
From Russia With Love	Prof. David Somerset, Company Director
Dr. No	John Bryce
You Only Live Twice	Taro Todoroki, Japanese coal miner
For Special Services	General James A. Banker
The Man With the Golden Gun	Mark Hazard, Transworld Consortium
	Frank Westmacott, Company Director

On Her Majesty's Secret Service	Sir Hilary Bray
Brokenclaw	Peter Abelord
	Peter Argentbright
The Man From Barbarossa	James Boldman; Dr. James Betteridge
Death is Forever	James Boldman; James Bates; John E. Bunyan
Seafire	James Boldman; Mr. and Mrs. James Bushy
James Bond in New York	David Baslow (Short Story)
Coldfall	James Boldman
Zero Minus Ten	James Pickard
	John Hunter
The Facts of Death	John Bryce

PSEUDONYMS USED IN BOND NOVELS / FLEMING & FRIENDS

Hilary Bray	Sir Hilary Bray in *On Her Majesty's Secret Service*
Ivar Bryce	John Bryce in *Dr. No*, and *Live & Let Die*
Aubyn Cousins	Quarrel in *Dr. No*
Ernie Cuneo	Benie Cureo in *Diamonds Are Forever*
Ian Fleming	James Bond
Mrs. Valentine Fleming	'M'
Red Grant	Red Grant in *From Russia With Love*
Tommy Leiter	Felix Leiter in numerous books & films
May Maxwell	"May", the housekeeper in Bond's flat
Hon. John Fox-Strangways	Commander Strangways in *Live & Let Die* and *Dr. No*
Albert Whiting	Albert Blacking in *Goldfinger*
Honeychile Wilder:	Honeychile Rider in *Dr. No.*
Lord Arron: (nickname "Boofy")	Mr. Kidd in *Diamonds Are Forever* is nicknamed "Boofy"

READING MATERIAL (ON BOND'S BOOKSHELF)

The Craft of Intelligence	Allen Dulles
Modern Fundamentals of Golf	Ben Hogan
Scarne on Cards	Scarne
The Travelers Tree	Patrick Leigh-Fermor
The Mask of Dimitrios	Eric Ambler
Profiles in Courage	John F. Kennedy
Periodicals:	London Times, The Daily Express, Country Life, Evening Standard, The Daily Gleaner
Scarnes Complete Guide To Gambling	Scarne
How To Play Your Best Golf All The Time	Tommy Armour
The Skills, Arts, & Secrets Of The Dip-Cut Purse	
The Books of Dornford Yates	
Chesterfield's Letters	

The Bible Designed To Be Read As Literature. Contains a Walther PPK, 7.65mm pistol and holster. Bond is also familiar with the works of Poe, Le Fanu, Brom Stoker and Ambrose Pierce.

RESIDENCE

Bond owns a small, comfortable flat in Chelsea, in a tree-lined square just off the King's Road. More recently, he purchased a small country retreat five miles out of Haslemere. Bond's housekeeper "May" is an elderly Scotswoman with iron-gray hair and a handsome, closed face. She is originally from Glen Orchy, Scotland. She refers to her employer as "Mister James."

TO CONTACT BOND

Letter or cable, but not telephone: c/o Ministry of Defense, Storey's Gate, London, S.W.1.

TOILETRIES

Safety Razor:	Old fashion Gillette or his new Hoffritz.
Shampoo:	Pinaud Elixir.
Soap:	Guerlain's *Fleur des Alpes*.
Cologne:	Guerlain's Imperial.
After-Shave Lotion:	Lentheric lotion, *Floris Lime* bath essence for men.

TRAINS BOND HAS RIDDEN ON ASSIGNMENT

Live & Let Die:	Seaboard Air Line Railroad. Silver Phantom, car 245, compartment H, New York / Florida.
Diamonds Are Forever:	The Cannonball. Private train of mobster Spang. Nevada.
From Russia With Love:	Simplon Orient Express, compartments 7 & 8, Istanbul to Paris.
Goldfinger:	Silver Meteor. Miami to New York. Special private train. New York to Kentucky.
You Only Live Twice:	Express. Tokyo to Gamagori. Private underground train of T. Tanaka.
The Man With the Golden Gun:	The Belle. Thunderbird Hotel to Green Island.
Risico:	Laguna Express. Rome to Venice.
For Special Services:	Private turbine monorail to Bismaquer ranch, Texas.
Death is Forever:	OST-West Express. Berlin to Paris.
Goldeneye:	Private Train

WOMEN KILLED

During the course of his assignments Bond has intentionally killed seven women. (See Women Who Died a Violent Death.)

BOOKS AND SHORT STORIES: CASTS & SYNOPSES

Books (Ian Fleming)

Casino Royale 1953
Live & Let Die 1954
Moonraker 1955
Diamonds Are Forever 1956
From Russia With Love 1957
Dr. No 1958
Goldfinger 1959
Thunderball 1961
The Spy Who Loved Me 1962
On Her Majesty's Secret Service .... 1963 [1]
You Only Live Twice .... 1964 [2]
The Man With The Golden Gun .... 1965 [3]

Short Stories (Ian Fleming)

For Your Eyes Only .... 1960 [4]
From A View To A Kill .... [4a]
For Your Eyes Only ....
Quantum of Solace .... [5]
Risico ....
The Hildebrand Rarity .... [6]
Octopussy .... 1966 [7]
The Living Daylights .... [8]
The Property Of A Lady .... [9]

The Simplon-Orient Express. Bond, Tatiana Romanova and Kerim Bey board this train in Istanbul. Later, Smersh agent Red Grant joins them. (Venice Simplon-Orient Express)

Books (Robert Markham) [10]

Colonel Sun 1968

Books (John Gardner)

License Renewed 1981
For Special Services 1982
Icebreaker 1983
Role of Honor 1984
Nobody Lives Forever 1986
No Deals Mr. Bond 1987
Scorpius 1988
License to Kill 1989
Win, Lose or Die 1989
Brokenclaw 1990
The Man From Barbarossa 1991
Death is Forever 1992
Never Send Flowers 1993
Seafire 1994
Goldeneye 1995
Cold Fall 1996

Books (Raymond Benson)

Tomorrow Never Dies 1997
Zero Minus Ten 1997
The Facts of Death 1998
High Time to Kill .... Release date 6/99

[1] Initially published a limited edition of 250 copies, each numbered and signed by Fleming and including a reproduction of a Fleming portrait by Amherst Villiers.

[2] A brief version of this novel originally appeared in Playboy Magazine. Originally titled "You Only Die Twice."

[3] Published posthumously.

[4] Published in one volume. Derived from stories Fleming originally wrote for a proposed CBS television series titled "James Bond, Secret Agent."

[4a] Previously appeared in the London Daily News titled "Murder Before Breakfast."

[5] Originally appeared in *Cosmopolitan* magazine.

[6] Originally appeared in *Playboy* magazine.

[7] Originally appeared in *Playboy* magazine.

[8] Originally appeared in *Argosy* magazine under the title "Berlin Escape."

[9] Originally published in a book titled *The Ivory Hammer: The Year at Sotheby's.* Sotheby's commissioned Fleming to a story of an auction. It later appeared in *Playboy* magazine.

[10] Pseudonym for Kingsley Amis.

CASINO ROYALE

Le Chiffre, treasurer and paymaster of a French communist trade union used 50 million union francs to purchase a chain of brothels. Not long after, the French Government closed all brothels, putting Le Chiffre out of business. If the shortfall was discovered by Smersh, he would be executed. British[1] intelligence learned of Le Chiffre's plan to replace the money by hopefully winning it back at Casino Royale in Royale-les-Eaux. 'M' sends Bond to play against Le Chiffre in hopes of beating him so that he is discredited and disposed of by Smersh. The British also send Vesper Lynd to support Bond. Felix Leiter of the CIA and Mathis of the French Deuxieme are also sent to lend him support. After arrival an unsuccessful attempt is made on Bond's life by Le Chiffre hoods.

In the casino Bond plays Baccarat against Le Chiffre and wins 70 million francs, leaving Le Chiffre penniless. That night Le Chiffre and his thugs kidnap Vesper Lynd. When Bond pursues them, he too is captured and brutally tortured by Le Chiffre to learn where the money is hidden. Abruptly he and his hoods are murdered by a Smersh agent, who in turn spare the life of James Bond. Bond regains consciousness in the hospital and eventually his health. He and Vesper go to a small inn to spend time together but unbeknownst to Bond, Vesper is a double agent and Smersh has sent someone to eliminate her. Before they can do so, however, she commits suicide.

CAST

James Bond	007
M	Chief, M.I.6
Bill Tanner	Chief of Staff
Moneypenny	M's secretary
Mathis	Head, French Deuxieme
Le Chiffre	Treasurer, communist trade union
Fawcett	Picture desk, Daily Gleaner
Vesper Lynd	Double Agent
Madame Muntz	Le Chiffre employee
Monsieur Muntz	Le Chiffre employee
Felix Leiter	CIA agent
Gibson	Nurse
"The Corsican"	Hood
"The Thinman"	Hood
French doctor	Deuxieme Bureau
Head of S	Unnamed
Monsieur Versoix	Inn proprietor
Madame Versoix	Inn proprietor
Adolph Gettler	Soviet agent

LIVE & LET DIE

'M' sends Bond on assignment to New York to investigate Mr. Big, a gangster and Smersh agent, and to determine the source of ancient gold coins which keep turning up by the thousands in New York City. They are believed to be part of Bloody Morgan's treasure from Jamaica. Bond and Leiter go to Harlem where Bond is confronted by Mr. Big and meets Solitaire. Bond manages to escape, killing three of Mr. Big's hoods.

Later, he and Solitaire travel to St. Petersburg , Florida where they meet Leiter who loses an arm and a leg to Mr. Big's sharks. Solitaire is recaptured by Mr. Big and Bond flies to Jamaica to await their arrival aboard Mr. Big's private yacht "Secatur." Bond and Quarrel establish a base of operations and when Secatur arrives Bond swims to it underwater and attaches a limpet mine on the hull.

Eventually Bond is captured and he and Solitaire are to be dragged over the coral reefs behind the ship until dead. However, as the Secatur is leaving the harbor dragging Bond and Solitaire behind it to certain death, it blows up and Mr. Big is eaten by sharks.

'M' grants Bond a fortnight's leave which he intends to spend with Solitaire.

CAST

James Bond	007
M	Chief, M.I.6
Moneypenny	M's secretary
Halloran	U.S. Dept. of Justice
Captain Dexter	FBI
Bill Tanner	Chief of Staff
Commander Damon	Head of Station "A"
Mr. Big	Smersh Agent
Lt. Binswanger	New York homicide
Tee-Hee Johnson	Hood
Sam Miami	Hood
Blabbermouth	Hood
The Fannel (McThing)	Hood
Samuel D. Baldwin	Pullman attendent
Solitare (Simone Latrelle)	Mr. Big's ward
Baron Samedi	Voodoo-Spirit of Death
Poxy	Cab driver
'The Robber'	Mr. Big hood
Mrs. Stuyvesant	Manager
Captain Franks	Detective
Strangeways	Head of Station "C"
Quarrel	Cayman Islander

MOONRAKER

At the request of 'M', Bond plays bridge with Sir Hugo Drax at Blades Club and discovers that he is cheating. To prevent a club scandal, Bond beats him at his own game. The following day, a British Security Agent is murdered and Bond is sent to investigate.

Wealthy Sir Hugo Drax has invested 10 million pounds to build the rocket "Moonraker"as a defense measure for Great Britain and is knighted by the Queen. Working on the Moonraker base with Gala Brand, Bond discovers that Drax's true intention is to bomb London with a nuclear device atop Moonraker. Although captured by Drax, they free themselves and reset the rocket gyros so it will land in the North Sea. Drax and his men who are fleeing on a submarine are ultimely destroyed by the Moonraker and London is saved! 'M' sends Bond on a well-earned month-long holiday.

CAST

James Bond	007
Firing Range Instructor	BSS
Loelia Ponsonby	Bond's secretary
Moneypenny	M's secretary
Sir Hugo Drax	Millionaire industrialist
Graf Hugo Von der Drache	Sir Hugo Drax
Lord Basildon	Chairman of Blades
Meyer	Drax card partner
Gala Brand	Scotland Yard
Vallance	Scotland Yard
Professor Train	Ministry of Supply
Major Tallon	Ministry of Supply
Dr. Walter	Drax assistant
Egan Bartsch	Electronics expert
Group Captain Tandy	Ministry of Supply
Peter Trimble	Naval security
Detective / Inspector Vivian	Gala Brand's boyfriend

DIAMONDS ARE FOREVER

'M' assigns Bond to investigate the smuggling of industrial diamonds from Africa to America, via Great Britain. M.I.6 arrests Peter Franks, a known diamond courier and Bond assumes his identity. The trail leads him to Tiffany Case in London, then on to New York and Las Vegas. Bond is captured in Nevada and brutally beaten but he and Tiffany manage to escape and kill their pursuers. They in turn are rescued by Felix Leiter and managed to board the Queen Elizabeth in New York, bound for England. On board are Kidd and Wint of the Spangled Mob who kidnap Tiffany. Bond breaks into their cabin, killing both men. With Tiffany safe in Bond's flat in London, he returns to Africa where Jack Spang, head of the mob, is arriving to close down the last link in the diamond smuggling pipeline. After killing the diamond courier, he takes off in his helicopter but is shot down by Bond who fires a Bofors, 40mm artillery gun which destroys the helicopter and Jack Spang.

CAST

James Bond	007
M	Chief, M.I.6
Jacoby	Diamond Corporation
Sillitoe	DeBeers
Loelia Ponsonby	Bond's secretary
Rufus B. Saye (Jack Spang)	House of Diamonds
Moneypenny	M's secretary
Bill Tanner	Chief of Staff
Asst. Commisioner Vallance	Scotland Yard
Peter Franks	Diamond courier
Tiffany Case	Sprang employee
Sergeant Dankwaerts	Scotland Yard
Sergeant Lobiniere	Makeup artist
Seraffimo Spang	Spangled mob

Jack Spang .... Spangled mob
Michael (Shady) Tree .... Spang hood
Felix Leiter .... Pinkerton
'Lame Brain' Pissaro .... Spang hood
Tingaling Bell .... Jockey
Rosy Budd .... Horse trainer
Swinebroad .... Auctioneer
Wint .... Spang hood
Kidd .... Spang hood
Benie Cureo .... Cab driver
Frasso .... Spang hood
McGonigle .... Spang hood
Captain .... Freetown Garrison Force
Dentist.. Diamond smuggler
Corporal .... Freetown Garrison Force

FROM RUSSIA WITH LOVE

Smersh, the official murder organization of the Soviet government had devised a scheme: to lure James Bond into a trap using a beautiful Russian girl and the cipher machine spector as bait.

Chief Executioner Donovan "Red" Grant was assigned to kill them on the Orient Express and let it appear as a murder-suicide. English spy, a great scandal, professional killer, weakness for women etc. This would eliminate their most famous spy and discredit Britain's M.I.6. Tatiana Romanova, Corporal of State Security, was sent to Istanbul to front as a cipher clerk. Supposedly she had fallen in love with Bond from reading his file and seeing his picture. She would turn over the spector machine to the British if Bond would come and take her back to England where she would defect. What the Russian hadn't counted on though was that Tatiana fell in love with Bond.

After stealing the spector they board the Orient Express bound for Paris. Red Grant, pretending to be a British agent, nearly lures Bond to his death. In a vicious fight, Bond kills him. Bond and Tatiana go to Paris. Bond leaves Tatiana sleeping at the British Embassy and then goes to the Ritz Hotel to confront Rosa Klebb who had engineered the Bond plot. In a deadly fight she kicks Bond with the toe of her shoe which carries a poison tipped metal blade. Bond falls unconscious before he can leave the room.

Fortunately Rene Mathis is there to help Bond to the hospital. Rosa Klebb is sent to prison in England. In the film, Rosa Klebb is shot to death by Tatiana.

CAST

Krassno Granitay ("Red Grant")................... Chief Executioner, Smersh
Masseuse.. Smersh employee
Col. General Grubozaboyschikov .... Head of Smersh
Lt. General Slavin .... Head of G.R.V.
Lt. General Vozdvishensky .... R.V.M.I.D.
Col. Nikitin .... Head of Intelligence, M.G.B
Col. Klebb... Head of Otdyel II, Smersh, Operations/Executions
Kronsteen .... Head of Planning, Smersh

Makharov	Chess Champion
Tatiana Romanova	Corporal of State Security
Capt. Troop	Paymaster
Darko Kerim	Head of Station "T"
Loelia Ponsonby	Bond's secretary
Major Dansey	Former head of station "T"
Krilencu	Bulgarian refugee
Zora	Gypsy girl
Vida	Gypsy girl
Vavra	Head gypsy
Melchior Benz	M.G.B.
Kurt Goldfarb	M.G.B.
'Third man'	M.G.B.
Stefan Trempo	Kermin's son
Capt. Norman Nash	Red Grant, Smersh
Rene Mathis	Head of Deuxieme

DR. NO

Bond is sent to Jamaica to determine the whereabouts of Commander Strangeways, head of Station "C" and his assistant, Mary Trueblood. What begins as a routine investigation develops into a deadly game of murder and torture for Bond and his companion, Miss Honeychile Ryder.

After several attempts on his life, Bond and Quarrel land on Dr. No's Crab Key where they meet Honeychile. Bond and Honeychile are captured and Quarrel is killed by Dr. No's flame-throwing mobster. Taken to Dr. No's headquarters on the island, they are wined and dined by their host and then tortured. Bond survives to kill Dr. No and rescue Honey. They escape to Jamaica where Bond and Honey recuperate from their ordeal.

CAST

Commander Strangways	Head of Station "C"
Bill Templar	Brigadier General
Mary Trueblood	Asst. to Strangeways
Three Chigroes	Dr. No Hoods
M	Chief, M.I.6
Ex-Stocker Smith	M's chauffeur
Moneypenny	M's secretary
Sir James Molony	Neurologist[1]
Major Boothroyd	M.I.6 armourer
Dr. No	Nuclear engineer
Quarrel	Cayman Islander
Annabel Chung	Photographer
Pus–Feller	Restaurant owner
"P"	Acting Governor / Jamaica
Pleydell–Smith	Colonial secretary
Miss Taro	Secretary
Honeychile Rider	Shell collector

Sister Rose .... Receptionist
Sister Lily.. Receptionist
May .... Maid

[1] Author of *Some Psychosomatic Side-effects of Organic Inferiority.*

GOLDFINGER

Mr. Junius DuPont, who in 1951 had been one of the baccarat players with Bond at Royale-les-Eaux against Le Chiffre, recognized Bond in the Miami International Airport and approached him. He suspected a Mr. Goldfinger of cheating him at two-handed Canasta. Would Mr. Bond be a guest at his hotel, the Floridiana, and accept a $10,000 fee to possibly discover how Mr. Goldfinger did it? Bond accepted.

Entering Goldfinger's room, Bond discovers a girl giving Goldfinger the cards of his opponent with the aid of binoculars and earpiece. Over the microphone he tells Goldfinger to make out a check to Mr. DuPont for $50,000 or he will turn him over to the authorities. That night Bond and Jill Masterson take the Silver Meteor to New York. Back in London, 'M' assigns Bond to investigate Goldfinger's activities for gold smuggling. Bond learns that Goldfinger has a company, Thanet Alloys and residence at Reculver, England. Investigating the site, he discovers men to be fitting Goldfinger's Rolls-Royce with solid gold parts painted to simulate steel.

Goldfinger's operation consists of smuggling gold in this manner to his plant in Switzerland where it is then melted down and moulded into aircraft seats which are then installed in Mecca Airlines and flown to India where Mr. "G" sells the gold to bullion brokers at a hundred or two hundred percent profit!

Bond beats Goldfinger in the famous gold match at Royal[1] St. Marks at Sandwich, England, winning $10,000 and then pursues him across France to Goldfinger's plant in Switzerland[2]. Along the way he meets Tilly Masterson and learns that her sister has been murdered by Goldfinger. They are captured by Oddjob and Goldfinger prepares to torture Bond but at the last moment has a change of heart and hires him and Tilly as employees. The plot takes them to New York and then Kentucky where Goldfinger plans to contaminate the gold in Fort Knox. The plot is eventually foiled and in a jet, high above the Atlantic Ocean, Bond stabs Oddjob who is in turn sucked out of the plane window. Bond then chokes Goldfinger to death with his bare hands. This allows Bond to crash land the jet in the ocean, close to weathership Charlie, who takes Bond and Pussy Galore aboard.

[1] Goldfinger's golf game was filmed at the Royal St. Davids course in England.
[2] Pursuit of Goldfinger

The following is the route Goldfinger took across France with Bond in pursuit of the black and yellow Rolls-Royce. Sequence of events:

11:00AM
With the aid of custom officials, Bond plants Homer device in the boot of Goldfinger's Rolls-Royce.

12:00 Noon

Goldfinger and his Rolls-Royce take off on the Air Ferry at Lydd, England bound for Le Touquet, France. Tilly Masterson also leaves on the same flight with her dove-grey Triumph TR3 convertible.

2:00PM

Bond departs the same terminal bound for Le Touquet.

Upon arrival at Le Touquet, Bond's receiver picks up the Rolls-Royce on French highway N1 to Abbeville. It then turns onto N28 to Rouen[2], then south on N154 thru Dreux and Chartres. Following in the Aston Martin DBIII, Bond passes Tilly Masterson just outside of Chartres. Then just outside of Chateauneuf, Tilly passes Bond. Arriving in New Orleans, Goldfinger stays the night at the Arcades Hotel. Bond stays at the Hotel de la Gare.

[1] From the novel Goldfinger
[2] Where Joan of Arc was burned at the stake

Next day, 8:00AM

The Rolls-Royce takes N152 east to the N7 and south to Moulins. Goldfinger then heads east on the N73 and stops by a bridge on the N79 for lunch. Bond tucks his machine into an offset, out of sight. Continuing on to Macon and the suburb of St. Laurent, Bond spots Tilly's car as he parks in front of her for lunch. He purposely backs into her car and smashes the fan as a ploy to give her a ride.

Bond had to hurry to catch the Rolls-Royce, whose signal was fading. It had crossed the Saone River at Pont d'Ain, entered the foothills of the Jura Mountains, and wound its way thru the S-turns of N84 to the top of the pass. Then it continued down to the Swiss border and into Geneva. Bond followed two miles behind, dropping Tilly off at a hotel in Geneva. The Rolls-Royce continued up the left side of Lake Geneva with Bond following, to the tiny village of Coppet. There it turned into a walled compound whose sign read "ENTREPRISES, AURIC A.G."

Later that day, Bond and Tilly Masterson were taken prisoner by Oddjob.

CAST

James Bond	007
Junius Dupont	American millionaire
Jill Masterson	Goldfinger's companion
Auric Goldfinger	Industrialist
M	Chief, M.I.6
Colonel Smithers	Bank of England
Alfred Blacking	Golf pro
Hawker	Bond's caddie
Foulks	Goldfinger's caddie
Tilly Masterson	Jill's sister
Oddjob	Goldfinger's hood
Dr. Foch	Geneva M.D.
Jed Midnight	Shawdow syndicate
Billy Ring	Chicago "machine"
Helmut Springer	Detroit Purple Gang
Mr. Solo	Union Siciliano
Jack Strap	Spangled mob, Las Vegas

Miss Pussy Galore .... The Cement Mixers
Felix Leiter .... Pinkerton
Blackwall .... Import / Export merchant
Schwab .... Drug smuggler
'Big Mexican' .... Drug smuggler

THUNDERBALL

S.P.E.C.T.R.E., world criminal organization headed by Ernst Stavro Blofeld, has stolen a British bomber with two nuclear devices on board from a British air base. They demand of Great Britain and the U.S. 100,000,000 pounds in gold bullion or they will destroy two major cities. Bond is sent to the Bahamas where he meets Domino, mistress to Emilio Largo, and S.P.E.C.T.R.E.. Largo's headquarters is his yacht the "Disco Volante" by which he transports the nuclear devices. Bond is joined by Felix Leiter and together they discover the hidden bomber in shallow water. As Largo prepares to move the nuclear device, British and American forces thwart their attempt.

During the underwater fighting, Domino kills Largo with her spear gun and the nuclear bombs are recovered.

CAST

James Bond 007
M .... Chief, M.I.6
Moneypenny .... M's secretary
Joshua Wain .... Director Shrublands
Count Lippe .... S.P.E.C.T.R.E. villain
Patricia Fearing .... Shrublands therapist
Beresford .... Shrublands attendant
Sam .... Shrublands attendant
Ernst Stavro Blofeld .... Head of S.P.E.C.T.R.E.
Loelia Ponsonby .... Bond's secretary
Moneypenny .... M's secretary
May .... Bond's housekeeper
Giuseppe Petacchi .... Nato pilot
Vargas .... S.P.E.C.T.R.E. hood
Emilio Largo .... S.P.E.C.T.R.E. # One
Brandt .... S.P.E.C.T.R.E. hood
Kotze .... nuclear physicist
Maslov .... S.P.E.C.T.R.E. mechanic
Captain .... Disco Volante
Domino .... Largo's mistress
Roddick .... Bahamas Deputy Governor
Harling .... Nassau, Commisioner of Police
Mr. Pitman .... Chief, Immigration, Customs
Felix Leiter .... CIA
Constable Santos .... Nassau police
Commander P. Pederson USN .... Captain, USS Manta
Fonda, Johnson & Bracken .... USS Manta sailors
Dr. Stengel .... Nassau doctor

THE SPY WHO LOVED ME

Born and raised in Canada, Vivienne Michel is sent to finishing school in London at age sixteen. Losing her virginity to Derek after a brief affair, she goes to work for a local news agency where she meets Kurt and carries on a brief romance. Disillusioned with life, she returns to Canada and decides to travel to Florida. On the way she stops at the Dreamy Pines Motor Court in upstate New York where she is hired to close the place down for the winter. Appearing are two small–time gangsters hired by the owner to burn the place down for the insurance. They plan to kill her and make it all appear accidental. Before this can happen though, James Bond appears on the scene. In a final confrontation, after the two men have set the motel on fire, Bond kills both men in a shoot–out and makes love to Vivienne before he departs the scene. Eventually, Michel continues on her journey South to Florida.

CAST

James Bond	007
Vivienne Michel	Motel caretaker
Jed Phancey	Motel manager
Millicent Phancey	Wife
Derek Mallaby	Former boyfriend
Florence Toussant	Michel's aunt
Susan Duff	Michel's girlfriend
Manager	Royalty Kinema
Harling	Typesetter
Len Holbrook	Newspaper editor
Kurt Rainer	Former boyfriend
Trude	Kurt's girlfriend
Mr. Sanguinetti	Motel owner
Sol Horowitz	Small-time gangster
Sluggsy Morant	Small-time gangster
Lieutenant Morrow	Glen Falls police
O'Donnell	Glen Falls police
Captain Stoner	Glen Falls police

ON HER MAJESTY'S SECRET SERVICE

Playing Chemin de fer at Royale-les-Eaux, Bond meets La Comtesse Teresa di Vicenzo (Tracy) who has just lost two million francs. To save her honor, Bond steps in and pays the tab. In return, she invites Bond to her hotel room where they make love.

When he awakens she is gone, leaving him a note. The following day, on the beach, he prevents her from committing suicide. Her father, Marc-Ange Draco, head of the Union Course, has them picked up and brought to him. He offers Bond one million pounds to marry his daughter, hoping that will straighten her out. Bond turns him down but asks a favor in return: the whereabouts of Ernst Blofeld, who escaped prosecution for "Thunderball." Draco learns that Blofeld is somewhere in Switzerland. Bond discovers his location and assumes the pseudonym of Sir Hilary Bray, an expert in heraldy from the College of Arms as Blofeld desires to be accredited as the legitimate Count de Bleuville. Blofeld has devised[1] a plot to wage biological warfare against England by sending English girls he has hypnotized at his Piz Gloria clinic back to England with a deadly virus. It will destroy millions of acres of agriculture, livestock, and foul, ruining the English economy. However, the plot is foiled when the British apprehend each girl as she returns to England. Bond, with the aid of Draco, attacks Piz Gloria and destroys it, but Blofeld and Bunt manage to escape.

Later, in Munich, Bond marries Tracy. In leaving the city for their honeymoon, a car overtakes them and Tracy is killed by gunfire which was meant for Bond.[2] Bond catches a fleeting glimpse of Blofeld and Bunt as they disappear. Bond cradles Tracy in his arms.

[1] Count de Bleuville, supposedly the foremost authority of curing allergies at the Institute of Physiological Research, Piz Gloria Clinic.

[2] Tracy is killed on the Autobahn from Munich to Kufstein.

CAST

James Bond	007
Tracy	La Comtesse Teresa di Vicenzo
Phillope Bertrand	Sun bather
Madame Dufours	Sun bather
Yolande Lefeure	Sun bather
Monsieur Maurice	Hotel manager
Hood's #1 & 2	Union Course
Monsieur Pol	Chef de Jeu
Croupier	Casino
Marc-Ange Draco (Tracy's father)	Head of Union Course
Mary Goodnight	Bond's new secretary
Griffon Or	College of Arms
Sable Basilisk	College of Arms
Irma Bunt	Blofeld's mistress
Blofeld	Head of S.P.E.C.T.R.E.
Hier Muir	Head of Station "Z"
Lt. Commander Savage	Head of Station "M"
British Consul General	Munich
Consul General's wife	Munich
Georges	Helicopter pilot
Leathers	Scientific Research Section
Franklin	Ministry of Agriculture
Sir Ronald Vallance	C.I.D.
Marius	Marseilles taxi - driver
Toussant	Explosive expert
Che-Che	Union Course
Violet O'Neill, Pearl Tampion, Anne Charter, Elizabeth Mackinnon and Polly Tasker.	Piz Gloria girls
Shaun Campbell	#2, Station "Z"
Sir, George Dunbar	Piz Gloria guest
Lady Daphne Straight	Piz Gloria guest
Ursula Andress	Piz Gloria guest

Duke of Marlborough .... Piz Gloria guest
Mr. Whitney .... Piz Gloria guest
Policeman .... State police

YOU ONLY LIVE TWICE

Bond is sent on diplomatic assignment to Japan by 'M' who is concerned with Bond's physical and mental "well-being" after losing his wife Tracy on a previous assignment. Hopes are that this challenge will snap Bond out of his lethargy. His task: to establish a direct service liaison with the Japanese rather than to continue receiving their information second-hand through the CIA. M.I.6 does not have a Japanese station agent. Tiger Tanaka, head of the Japanese Secret Service is receptive to Bond, but in return has a request: to penetrate the castle of the mad Dr. Shatterhead and his wife. Dr. Shatterhead's garden of evil is filled with poisonous snakes, plants, trees, and lakes where people are encouraged to come and commit suicide.

Bond learns that the evil doctor and wife are in fact Ernst Blofeld and Irma Blunt. Under disguise as a Japanese coal miner and with the help of Tanaka and Kissy Suzuki, Bond breaches the castle, evading the garden of death and its guards. Bond is captured and is being prepared for torture when he breaks loose, killing Blunt and Blofeld.

Escaping the castle, Suzuki rescues him from the sea. Unfortunately, Bond suffers amnesia from a severe head wound and remembers nothing. After spending a year with Kissy on Kuro Island, the word "Vladivostok" strikes a note with Bond and he tells Kissy he must go there and try to discover his old identity.

In the end he leaves her and sets out on his journey.

CAST

James Bond 007
M .... Chief, M.I.6
Mary Goodnight .... Bond's secretary
Moneypenny .... M's secretary
Sir James Maloney .... Neurologist
Dikko Henderson .... Australian agent
Tiger Tanaka (1) .... Head, Japanese secret police
"Grey Pearl" .... Madame
"Trembling Leaf" .... Geisha girl
Porterfield .... Blades waiter
Col. Bill Tanner .... Chief of Staff
Melody .... Bartender
Dr. Guntram Shatterhead .... Ernst Stavro Blofeld
Mariko Ichiban .... Geisha girl
Mr. Mikimoto .... Founder, cultured pearl
Mrs. Shatterhead .... Irma Blunt
Kissy Suzuki .... Kuro island girl
Kono .... Blofeld guard
Kazama .... Blofeld guard
Shinto priest .... Kuro island

Doctor	Kuro island
Sex merchant	Fukuoka, Japan

THE MAN WITH THE GOLDEN GUN

Bond returns from Russia, having been hypnotized by the KGB in attempting to kill his M.I.6 Chief, 'M.' Bond attempts to gas 'M' with a cyanide gun but fails as 'M' drops a glass shield in front of his desk to protect himself. Bond is taken away and placed under the care of Sir James Maloney, the M.I.6 neurologist, who helps him to a complete recovery. 'M' supports Bond during this period and plans his next assignment which is to locate and kill Scaramanga, the paid assassin known as "The Man With the Golden Gun".

Arriving in Jamaica from Trinidad, Bond discovers Scaramanga to be living there and building the "Thunderbird Hotel" with syndicate money. Bond meets Scaramanga socially and is hired to be his bodyguard during a conference of underworld figures.

With the help of Felix Leiter and Mary Goodnight, Bond gathers incriminating evidence against Scarmanga and his illicit activities. Unfortunately, Scarmanga learns that Bond is a British agent and plots to kill him. The story builds to its climax aboard a private train taking the mob figures out for a day of fishing and a picnic. Gunfire erupts and Bond and Leiter are wounded but Bond manages to track Scaramanga through the jungle and kill him. The rest of the mob are killed as a bridge collapses under their train. 'M' recommends Bond for knighthood but he declines the honor. However, he and Leiter are awarded the Jamaican Police Medal for gallant and meritorius services.

CAST

James Bond	007
Captain Walker	Ministry of Defense
Col. Boris	KGB
Major Townsend	Ministry of Defense
Fred Robson	Ministry of Defense
Moneypenny	M's secretary
M	Chief, M.I.6
Col. Bill Tanner	Chief of Staff
Sir James Malony	Neurologist
Porterfield	Blades waiter
Lily	Blades waitress
Francisco Scaramanga	Assassin
Harold L. Peterson	Author
C.C.	Former history professor
Commander Ross	Head of Station "J"
Mary Goodnight	#2, Station "J"
Tiffy	Manager, Dreamland Café
Sarah & Lindy	Call girls
Mr. Henriks	Swiss financial representative
Sam Binion	Real estate
Leroy Gengerella	Gengerella Enterprises
Ruby Rotkopf	Las Vegas hotels

Hal Garfinkel	Teamster Union funds
Louie Paradise	Paradise slots
Mr. Travis	Assistant hotel manager
Felix Leiter	Pinkerton
Joe	Bartender
Nicholas Nicholson	CIA
King Tiger	Band leader
Mabel & Pearl	Dancers
Mr. C.	Castro
Flora	Tropical hurricane
Engineer	"The Belle"
Alec Hill	Head of Station "C"
Percival Sampson	Constable, Negril
Dr. Lister Smith	Savannah La Mar
Colonel Bannister	CIA
Commissioner of Police	Jamaica
Morris Cargill	Justice of the Supreme Court
Court Clerk	Jamaica
Nurse	Local hospital

A VIEW TO KILL

A Royal Signal Corporation dispatch rider is mysteriously shot to death while delivering secret documents to NATO headquarters in France. Bond happens to be in Paris enroute to London upon completion of another assignment. As he's enjoying a drink at Fouquets sidewalk café, he is approached by Mary Ann Russel, who informs him that 'M' needs him to investigate the incident.

Bond goes to NATO and interviews Col. Schreiber who is totally disinterested. Bond then sets up watch in the forest near where the killing took place. Eventually he discovers an underground hideout camaflouged by a rose bush. He observes men coming and going, one of which handles a BSA motor bike identical to the one the dispatch rider rode when he was killed. The man also wears an identical uniform.

The following morning Bond makes a dummy run up the same highway in an identical uniform. Four British SIS agents would serve as backup. Bond watches his driving mirror. Eventually he spots the killer approaching him from behind, and very fast. Bond brakes the bike and does a 45 degree turn, killing the engine as the other rider fires twice with his Luger, but misses. Bond squeezes off one shot killing the rider instantly.

Moving back to the underground hideout, Bond gives a whistle signal and the rose bush opens. Two men speaking Russian emerge. As they converge on Bond, one agent is shot by British backup agents as the other attacks Bond. As the muzzle of the Russian gun is about to go off in Bond's face, the Russian is shot to death by Mary Ann Russell.

FROM A VIEW TO A KILL

CAST
James Bond	007
M	M.I.6
Wing Commander Rattray	Head of Station F, Paris
Mary Ann Russell	Assistant, Station F
Bates	Dispatch rider
Col. G.A. Schreiber	Security Chief, NATO
Proctor	NATO security aide

FOR YOUR EYES ONLY (SHORT STORY)

The Havelock's, longtime friends of 'M', are brutally murdered on their plantation in Jamaica by Major Gonazales and his hoodlums on orders of Von Hammerstein who wants to buy their property, which they refused to sell. Now he and his group have taken up residence in a hideout retreat in Northern Vermont, just south of the Canadian border. At "M's" personal request, Bond flies to Montreal and with the assistance of Col. Johns, prepares for a trek through the wilderness to Hammerstein's retreat, to kill him. After a grueling eight hour march, he arrives only to run into Judy Havelock who is also intent on killing Hammerstein. They pair up and when the opportunity is right, she kills Hammerstein with her crossbow. In a wild shootout, Bond manages to kill Gonzales and his two hoods with his Savage 99f rifle with telescopic sight.

When it is all over, he and Judy prepare for the trip back through the forest to Canada, and then on to London.

CAST
James Bond	007
M	Chief, M.I.6
Mrs. Havelock	Wife
Col. Tim Havelock	Plantation owner
Jimmy Farquahasson	Jamaica resident
Ursula Farquahasson	Jamaica resident
Bill Aschenheim	Belais owner
Agatha	Housekeeper
Fay Prince	Second housekeeper
Major Gonazales	Cuban hood
Joshua	Gardner
Judy Havelock	Daughter
Von Hammerstein	Ex-Gestapo official
Col. Johns	Royal Canadian Mounted Police

QUANTUM OF SOLACE (SHORT STORY)

Bond has just finished an assignment in Nassau and was a dinner guest at the home of the British Bahamian Governor. In attendance were Mr. & Mrs. Harvey Miller.

Bond had found Mrs. Miller to be a crashing bore. When the Millers had left, he and the Governor sat talking over drinks. The Governor began a story about Foreign Service Officer Phillip Masters who years before had worked under him in Nassau.

Masters had met a lovely stewardess on a flight from Africa to England. They married and he was sent to Nassau as an under-secretary. Bored, his wife took up golf and met a handsome playboy at the club and took up with him. Carrying on her infidelity nearly destroyed Masters. He was sent on assignment to the "States" for five months.

In the meantime, Rhoda Masters' playboy had dumped her and she was once again prepared to become the dutiful wife. However, when Masters returned, he would have nothing to do with her and isolated her in the house to specific rooms. After a year he divorced her and left the Bahamas for another assignment. A broken woman, she eventually became a hotel receptionist in Jamaica where she met a wealthy Canadian who married her and took her back to Canada. Bond then learned she was none other than Mrs. Harvey Miller, the crashing bore he had sat next to during dinner.

CAST

James Bond	007
Harvey Miller	Canadian millionaire
Mrs. Miller	Wife
Governor	Bahamas
Phillip Masters	Colonial Service Officer
Rhoda Llewellyn Masters	Wife
Lady Burford	Governor's wife
Tattersall	Nassau playboy

RISICO (SHORT STORY)

'M' sends Bond to Italy to investigate a drug smuggling operation which is moving drugs into England. This, at the request of the Prime Minister. Bond's contact in Rome is Signor Kristados; this contact given to 'M' by the CIA. In a meeting in a Rome restaurant, Kristatos fingers Enrico Colombo as the drug kingpin who just happens at the time to be sitting at another table with Lisl Baum. In a "staged" fight with Colombo, Lisl Baum storms out of the café as Bond follows her. He explains he is a writer looking for drug information for a book he is about to write. She tells him to meet her in two days at a specified location just outside Venice. During this meeting, Bond is approached by three hoods who chase him up the beach and into the arms of Columbo and his men who are waiting for him. Bond is knocked unconscious by the butt of a pistol and awakens aboard Colombo's ship where he learns they are enroute to destroy a shipment of Kristatos drugs. Bond learns that Kristatos is the *real* drug smuggler, being supplied with raw opium by the Russians. Bond kills Kristatos as he tries to flee and Colombo's men destroy the opium shipment. Colombo gives Bond a hotel key where Lisl Baum is waiting for him.

CAST

James Bond	007
M	Chief, M.I.6
Signor Kristatos	Drug smuggler
Ronnie Valance	Special Branch
Enrico "The Dove" Colombo	Italian smuggler
Lisl Baum	Viennese whore

OCTOPUSSY (SHORT STORY)

At the end of WWII, Major Dexter Smythe, British Royal Marines, was second in command of "A" force of MOB (Miscellaneous Objective Bureau) near the Austrian Tirols of Europe. Examining captured the documents, he opened a wax-sealed envelope which contained a paper outlining the location of a secret cache of gold bars from the German Reichbank.

Recommended Austrian guide Hannes Oberhauser is arrested by Smythe and driven to the base of the mountain where the gold bars are hidden. Having climbed to its general location at the 10,000ft. level, Smythe murders Oberhauser and buries his body in a crevice; then locates the gold and moves it down the mountain. After the war he transports the gold to London, marries, and moves to the "North Shore" of Jamaica where he settles into a life of affluence. For fifteen years Smythe sells gold to the Foo brothers, as its needed, to maintain his comfortable lifestyle.

Bond, as a longtime friend of Oberhauser, is assigned to the case when Oberhauser's body is discovered at the base of a melting glacier. Bullets taken from the body match those of Smythe's Webley-Scott 45 cal. service automatic. Bond flies to Jamaica and confronts Smythe with the evidence, who in turn confesses. He is told that authorities will come for him in about a week. Smythe surmises that Bond is allowing him this time in which to commit suicide and save the government a lot of expense.

Later, with spear and mask intact, Smythe swims in the waters offshore in search of the deadly scorpion fish to feed his pet Octopussy. Smythe spears the deadly fish but not before its poisonous spines had punctured the flesh of Smythe's stomach.

Realizing that he had only about fifteen minutes to live, Smythe struggles to feed the Scorpion fish to his octopus. Unfortunately, Octopussy's tentacles encircle Smythe and pull him under the surface to drown.

In London, Bond wrote "found drowned" in Smythe's file and closed the case.

CAST

James Bond	007
Major Dexter Smythe	British Royal Marines, retired
Mary Parnell Smythe	Wife
Jimmy Greaner	Doctor
Professor Bengry	The "Institute"
Luna	Smythe's housekeeper
Colonel King	American CO
Hannes Oberhauser	Mountain guide
Foo Brothers	Import / Export merchants
Gieves	English tailor
Cahusac	Jamaican medical examiner

THE LIVING DAYLIGHTS (SHORT STORY)

'M' has ordered Bond to Berlin to prevent agent 272 from being assassinated as he crosses the East/West border. Bond's mission: kill the KGB agent before he can kill 272. From a flat overlooking the border, Bond and agent Sender keep a watchful vigil for 272. He is to cross within three nights. For the first two nights Bond watches a group of female musicians enter the same building the assassin will use, with their musical instruments. Bond is quite taken with one girl in particular.

She is a tall, beautiful, willowy blonde who carries a cello case. On the third night as agent 272 begins to cross the border, Bond's sniperscope sight is on the assassin's window when *she* appears; the same blonde musician, also known as "Trigger," the KGB agent. Bond hesitates for a split second, lets his sight drift just a hair, then squeezes off a shot which knocks her gun out the window and Bond presumes, wounded her in the left hand. Bond is glad he did not kill her. He and Sender then leave the flat.

CAST

James Bond 007
Corporal Menzies .... Q armory
Chief Range Officer .... Century Range / Bisley
M... Chief, M.I.6
272 .... British agent
Trigger .... Russian assassin
Col. Bill Tanner .... Chief of Staff
Capt. Paul Sender .... SIS resident agent

THE PROPERTY OF A LADY (SHORT STORY)

Miss Maria Freudenstein, British M.I.6 cipher clerk, is also known to the British as a KGB mole. For the past three years she has been supervisor of "Purple Cipher" dispatches. Unknown to her, M.I.6 has fed her a continuous stream of deceptive information which she passes on to the KGB and which they assume is authentic data.

In recognition of her service, and as payment, they have forwarded to her the Carl Faberge "Emerald Sphere," a priceless work of art. In turn, she has placed the sphere with Sotheby's for auction, where by all estimates, it should bring over 100,000 pounds.

M.I.6 assumes that the KGB are not aware of its true value and will have their resident agent at Sotheby's to act as an underbidder in order to push up the price. M.I.6 has never known the true identity of this individual. Bond's assignment is to attend the auction and try to determine his identity. Eventually, the "Emerald Sphere" goes to Mr. Snowman for 150,000 pounds and Bond discovers who the KGB agent really is at the conclusion of the bidding. M.I.6 continues to feed Miss Freudenstein false information for the KGB. With this knowledge the Foreign Office is able to declare Comrade Malinowski persona non grata and send him back to Russia.

CAST

James Bond 007
Mary Goodnight M.I.6
Moneypenny .... M's secretary
Dr. Fanshause.. Authority / antique jewelery
Maria Freudenstein .... KGB agent
A. Kenneth Snowman .... Faberge expert
Peter Wilson.. Head of Sotheby's
Piotr Malinowski .... KGB Resident Director / London

THE HILDEBRAND RARITY (SHORT STORY)

'M' sends Bond to the Seychelles Islands to check on security should the British fleet base need to relocate from the Maldives. Bond's friend, islander Fidele Barbey, has been hired by American millionaire Milton Krest to help him find a rare fish "The Hildebrand Rarity." He has agreed on condition he can bring along his diving expert, James Bond.

They board Krest's yacht and travel to Chagrin Island where it is reputed that the fish habitates. Mrs. Krest is lovely, charming, and fearful as Krest likes to beat her. Krest is an obnoxious bastard with a crude mouth, despised by many.

They discover and capture the rare fish in the shallow waters offshore and head back to the Seychelles. Enroute, Krest gets drunk and goes to sleep it off topside in a hammock.

Later, in the early morning hours, Bond awakens to discover that someone has murdered Krest by stuffing the rare "Hildebrand Rarity" into his mouth, on which he chokes to death. To prevent a complicated inquiry ashore, Bond replaces the fish in its container and dumps Krest overboard. The following morning Krest is discovered missing and presumed lost at sea. There will be statements taken by the authorities once they are ashore and then, all will be normal again.

Liz Krest invites Bond to travel on with her aboard the yacht to Mambasa. He agrees.

CAST

James Bond	007
Fidele Barbey	Seychelles resident
Milton Krest	Millionaire / Krest hotels
Liz Krest	Wife

COLONEL SUN

Admiral Sir Miles Messervey, head of M.I.6, is kidnapped by Red Chinese agents working for Colonel Sun Liang-tan. This is done to snare Bond so that both can be killed and involved in Col. Sun's grand scheme to bomb a Russian Summit Conference and implicate the British in the crime. Bond travels to Greece where he joins up with a beautiful Greek girl and Soviet agent, Ariadne Alexandrou and her friend Niko Litsas.

The three of them are eventually captured by Col. Sun who then tortures Bond. Fortunately he is saved by one of Sun's own Greek prostitutes. Bond in turn frees his two accomplices, together with 'M,' and disrupts Sun's evil plan.

In the finale, Col. Sun dies at the hands of James Bond.

Later, Bond was offered the Russian Order of the Red Banner for his services to peace, but declined the honor.

CAST

James Bond	007
M	Chief, M.I.6
Stuart Thomas	Head of Station G (Greece)

Col. Bill Tanner .... Chief of Staff
Ex-Chief Petty Officer Hammond .... M's houseman
Mrs. Hammond .... M's housekeeper
Dr. Allison .... Medical doctor
Sergeant Hassett .... Windsor policeman
Constable Wragg .... Windsor policeman
Inspector Crawford .... Windsor policeman
Sir Ronald Rideout .... Minister of Parliament
Asst. Commissioner Vallance .... Scotland Yard
Under-Secretary Bushnell .... Rideout's assistant
Mary Kyris .... Greek Embassy
Colonel Sun Liang-Tan .... People's Liberation Army
Doni Madan .... Prostitute
Luisa Tartini .... Prostitute
Evgeny Ryumin .... Sun's servant
Quantz .... Gunman
De Graaf .... Gunman
Dr. Lohmann .... Sun's doctor
Ariadne Alexandrou .... Soviet agent
Tzimas .... Soviet hood
Markos .... Soviet hood
Major Gordienko .... Russian state security
Kyrios Litsas .... Greek patriot
Yanni .... Greek sailor
Theoforou .... Gunman
Col. General Igor Arenski .... KGB
Gevrek .... Greek employee
Mily .... Greek employee
Boris .... Radioman
Mr. Aris .... Gunman
Ludwig von Richter .... Ex-Nazi
Willi .... Richter's assistant

LICENSE RENEWED

Anton Murik, famed nuclear physicist and the Laird of Murcaldy, codename "Warlock," has hired international terrorist Franco Oliveiro Quesacriado, codename "Foxtrot," to implement a plan of world nuclear blackmail against the US, Great Britain, France, Eastern and Western Germany.

Murik demands 50 billion in diamonds or his terrorist squads will shut down the cooling systems of six nuclear power plants, "Operation Meltdown", causing millions of deaths and worldwide contamination. Murik wants this wealth to build his own "safe" nuclear power facility and prove to the world that he is right and the world's leading nuclear genius.

Bond is assigned to infiltrate Murik's castle in Scotland, gain his confidence and learn Murik's plan. Bond learns he must stop Murik or the world will be thrown into catastrophic horror. The story builds to its climax high above the Mediterranean Sea in Murik's private aircraft. Bond fights

Murik and his henchmen to the death to prevent meltdown of world nuclear reactors. Men die but Murik escapes, only to be killed by Bond outside Murik's castle in Scotland when he attempts to flee with his vital papers.

After spending a week with Bond, Lavender Peacock returns to Scotland and her rightful inheritance as Lady Murik of Murcaldy.

CAST

James Bond	007
M	Chief, M.I.6
Col. Bill Tanner	Chief of Staff
Sir Richard Duggan	Director General M.I.5
David Ross	Head of Special Branch
Dr. Anton Murik	Nuclear physicist
Franco	International terrorist
May	Bond's housekeeper
Ann Reilly (Qute)	Assistant to 'Q'
Mary Jane Mashkin	Murik's mistress
Lavender Peacock	Murik's ward
Caber	Murik hood
Donal	Murik hood
Hamish	Murik hood
Malcolm	Murik hood

FOR SPECIAL SERVICES

James Bond was on British airways, flight 12, from Singapore to London when terrorists attempt to hijack the jumbo 747 for the two billion in gold, diamonds and currency which came aboard at Bahrain. Together with SAS Agents, Bond assists in killing all of them but not before one utters the word "S.P.E.C.T.R.E."

Bond is called to meeting with 'M' and introduced to Cedar Leiter, CIA agent and daughter of his old friend Felix Leiter. 'M' puts Bond on "special duty" to the US government at the request of the President. Together with Cedar they are to investigate Markus Bismaquer, wealthy American businessman, suspected of sinister operations and possible ties to S.P.E.C.T.R.E., who lives on Ranch Bismaquer outside Amarillo, Texas.

Previous agents sent had never returned. Since Bismaquer is a collector of rare prints, M.I.6 has supplied Bond a set of forgeries as bait. Bond and Leiter fly to New York where they are assaulted by hoods. Again in Washington, D.C. Finally, arriving by car in Amarillo, they are invited to Rancho Bismaquer. While there, Bond learns of the devious S.P.E.C.T.R.E. plot to steal the computer tapes of the US Space Wolves program from Norad headquarters in Cheyenne Mountain, Colorado and sell them to the Russians for billions. A battle develops but Bond is able to foil the plot. The climax is reached at S.P.E.C.T.R.E. house in the Louisiana Bayou where Bond discovers Nena Bismaquer to be none other than Blofeld's daughter! During a vicious fight with Bond she is accidentally killed by her giant python snakes. Bond and Cedar Leiter then take a month's holiday.

CAST

James Bond	007

M	Chief, M.I.6
Col. Bill Tanner	Chief of Staff
Moneypenny	M's secretary
Ann Reilly (Qute)	Assistant to 'Q'
Cedar Leiter	CIA Agent
Markus Bismaquer	American billionaire
Nena Bismaquer (Blofeld)	Chief of S.P.E.C.T.R.E.
Walter Luxor	S.P.E.C.T.R.E. hood
Fisher	S.P.E.C.T.R.E. hood
Mike Mazzard	Mazzard securities
Joe Bellini	Mazzard hood
Louis	Mazzard hood
Barquette brothers	French villains
Bjorn Junten	Swedish espionage agent
Kranko Stewart	New York gangster
Doner Richardson	New York gangster
Mr. de Luntz	S.P.E.C.T.R.E. agent
Askon Delville	Store owner
Criton	S.P.E.C.T.R.E. caretaker
Tic	S.P.E.C.T.R.E. cook
Freddie Nolan	S.P.E.C.T.R.E. employee
El Ahade	S.P.E.C.T.R.E. Executive Committee
Herr Treiben	S.P.E.C.T.R.E. Executive Committee
Michael Macro	S.P.E.C.T.R.E. Executive Committee
Frank Kenner	Air traffic controller
Felix Leiter	Former CIA agent
General James A. Banker	James Bond
Captain	Norad base
Colonel	Norad base

ICEBREAKER

The KGB requested British M.I.6 to assign Bond to "Operation Icebreaker," together with three other agents, US, Israeli, and Russian, to investigate the international terrorist organization called the National Socialist Action Army headed by Count Konrad Von Gloda.

Headquarters for the NSAA is the "Ice Palace," located in the far north on the Finnish-Russian border. From here Von Golda hopes to achieve world dominance with the "Fourth Reich." Von Golda is buying arms from the Russian depot at "Blue Hare" and stockpiling them, for further terrorist activities worldwide. Bond does not trust his fellow agents in "Operation Icebreaker" and senses he may be walking into a trap set by the KGB. As the story develops, Bond is attacked by foreign agents, severely wounded and betrayed by those around him. Eventually captured, he is brutally tortured by the NSAA. With the help of Paula Vacker, Bond manages to escape the "Ice Palace." In turn, it is destroyed by Russian aircraft, but Von Golda escapes.

Bond returns to Helsinki. The climax is reached when Bond kills Russian agent Mosolov and Count Konrad Von Golda with his powerful Ruger Super Redhawk 44 Magnum and is badly wounded himself. As we leave Bond, he is recuperating in hospital with the aid of Paula Vacker.

CAST

James Bond	007
M	Chief, M.I.6
Col. Bill Tanner	Chief of Staff
Moneypenny	M's secretary
Paula Vacker	Finnish intelligence agent
Rivke Ingber (Annie Tudeer)	Israeli agent
Nicolai Moslov	Russian agent
Brad Tirpitz (Hans Buchtman)	CIA agent
Annie Tudeer (Rivke Ingbeer)	NSAA agent
Count Konrad Von Gloda	Aarne Tudeer
Col. Aaarne Tudeer (NSAA Chief)	Nazi SS Officer
May	Bond's housekeeper
Erik Carlsson	Driving expert
Simo Lampien	Driving expert
Anatoli Pavlovich Grinen	KGB negotiator
Clifford Arthur Dudley	Stockholm resident agent
Col. Zwicka Zamir	Chief of Mossad
Simonsson	Finnish doctor
Trifon	Lapplander
Knut	Lapplander
Ingrid	Hospital nurse

ROLE OF HONOR

'M' orders Bond to publicly resign from the British Secret Service and set himself up as bait, as a disillusioned agent, making his services available to the highest bidder.

His real assignment is to determine if Jay Autem Holy, American computer genius, is really dead or has defected to the East. Bond discovers Holy to be operating under the guise of Professor St. John-Finnes in Nun's Cross, England. Heading a company called Gunfire Simulations, Ltd., Holy packages computer crime plans to anyone for a price. He and S.P.E.C.T.R.E. Chief Rahani have devised a plot to render both US and Russian nuclear missiles useless ("Operation Down Escalator").

As world leaders from the US, USSR, France, Germany and Great Britain hold a world summit in the Le Richemond Hotel in Geneva, Switzerland, Holy and Rahani plan to implement their scheme with false ciphers from the Goodyear Airship Europa overhead.

With them as a hostage is James Bond. But as events build, gunfire erupts and men die. Colonel Rahani, S.P.E.C.T.R.E. Chief, parachutes from the airship and escapes. However, S.P.E.C.T.R.E.'s plot is foiled and Bond takes a month's holiday with beautiful CIA agent Percy Proud.

CAST

James Bond	007
M	Chief, M.I.6
Bill Tanner	Chief of Staff
Q	Armorer, M.I.6

Anne Reilly (Qute)	Assistant to 'Q'
Jay Autem Holy	Pentagon computer genius
Percy Proud...	CIA agent
Colonel Tamil Rahani	S.P.E.C.T.R.E.
General Joe Zwingli....................................	Army
Lady Freddie Fortune	agent
Cindy Chalmer	agent
Moneypenny	M's secretary
Peter Amadeus	computer genius
Nick	Europa pilot
Simon...	S.P.E.C.T.R.E. hood
Arab boy	S.P.E.C.T.R.E. hood
Tigerbalm Balmer	hood
Happy Hopcroft	hood

NOBODY LIVES FOREVER

Bond goes on a driving holiday through Europe. What he doesn't know is that S.P.E.C.T.R.E. has placed a "price" on his head of ten million Swiss francs payable to whomever delivers him to S.P.E.C.T.R.E. alive. As Bond travels through Belgium, France, Switzerland, and Austria, strange occurrences beset him. He meets interesting women, dangerous assasins, and corrupt police officers, all out for the ransom money. Bond's housekeeper and Miss Moneypenny are kidnapped as leverage against Bond. Bond is taken prisoner by a Russian agent and flown to Key West, Florida where he is to be turned over to Col. Rahani of S.P.E.C.T.R.E.. However, he is rescued by Sukie Tempesta and Nannie Norrich.

Later, he leaves them and makes his way alone to Shark Island, Rahani's headquarters where he is again captured by Nannie Norrich who also wants the ransom money. May and Miss Moneypenny are also held prisoner on Shark Island. Bond is to be guillotined by none other than Norrich. Nevertheless, Bond manages to escape. He kills Col. Tamil Rahani with an explosive charge to the wheelchair, guillotines Norrich himself and rescues May and Moneypenny as Shark Island is destroyed and sinks into the ocean.

May and Miss Moneypenny return to England but Bond and Sukie Tempesta remain in Key West on holiday.

CAST

James Bond...	007
M..	Chief, M.I.6
Bill Tanner	Chief of Staff
Moneypenny	M's secretary
May	Bond's houskeeper
Tamil Rahani..	S.P.E.C.T.R.E. Chief
Sukie Tempesta	Wealthy widow
Nannie Norrich	Norrich Universal bodyguards
Steve Quinn	Rome agent, M.I.6
Inspector Heinrick Oster	Austrian policemen
Herr Doktor Kirchtum	Director, Klinik Mozart

Dr. McConnell .... Rahani's physician
Conrad Tempel .... Underworld assassin
Bernie Brazier .... Assassin
Paula Cordova (The Poison Dwarf) .... American assassin

NO DEALS MR. BOND

Bond's initial assignment is to rescue British double agents from Eastern Europe where their operation "Cream Cake" had been disclosed by one of them. But which one?

Bond brings them out via British Submarine. Five years later, although they have been under "deep cover" using pseudonyms, two of the agents are found murdered with their tongues cut out. Bond is called by 'M' to save the other agents and to stop the assassin.

The trail leads Bond from London to Ireland, Paris, and Hong Kong and a final confrontation with his old nemesis, General Kolya Chernov of Smersh, codename "Blackfriar." Bond is given his pistol with four bullets and told to defend himself from four well armed Russian "Robinsons." Hunted like an animal, Bond nevertheless manages to outwit and kill three of them. Richard Han, Swift's assistant, who unbeknownst to Bond, has followed him and killed the fourth assassin. Bond then kills the traitor who turns out to be Inspector Murray, captures General Chernov, and kills Heather Dare who proves to be the double agent.

CAST

James Bond 007
M .... Chief, M.I.6
Moneypenny .... M's secretary
Inspector Norman Murray .... Special Branch, Ireland
Rowena Mac Shine .... Watch Officer
Captain Dave Andrews .... Royal Marine
Lt. Joe Preedy .... Royal Marine
Lt. Commander Alec Stewart .... Submarine Captain
Ann Reilly (Qute) .... Q's assistant
Col. Maxim Smolin .... East German Intelligence
"Big" Mick Shean .... Irish underworld
"Black" Ingrid .... Assistant to General Chernov
General Kolya Chernov .... Head of Smersh
Richard Han .... Assistant to Swift
Swift .... Head of Operation Cream Cake
Ebbie Heritage .... Former SIS Agent
Heather Dare .... Former SIS Agent
Mischa .... Assistant to General Chernov
Susanne Dietrich .... East German Intelligence
Bridget Hammond .... Former SIS agent
Millicent Zampek .... Former SIS agent
Jungle Paisley .... Former SIS agent

SCORPIUS

A routine investigation into the death of a young girl leads to the discovery that she is a member of the cult, "The Meek One" headed by Father Valentine. Only later is it learned that Valentine and Vladimir Scorpius are one and the same man. Scorpius is a former arms supplier to all the world terrorist organizations.

Bond learns that Scorpius has developed a plot to threaten England and the world through assassination of political leaders. With the help of 'M', Harriet Horner, and "Pearly" Perlman, Bond battles Scorpius through ambushes, kidnappings, and torture. The climax is reached on the lawn of the White House in Washington, D.C. where Bond thwarts the assassination of the US President and the British Prime Minister and discovers the true identity of Scorpius' inside mole, none other than Detective Superintendent Baily of Special Branch, Metro Police, London.

CAST

James Bond	007
M	Chief, M.I.6
Moneypenny	M's secretary
Chief Superintendent Bailey	Special Branch
Miss Emma Dupre	Daughter of Peter Dupre
Lord Shrivnham	Banker
Trilby Shrivenham	Member of the "Meek Ones"
Sergeant Perlman	SAS Regiment
David Wolkovsky	CIA Agent
Scorpius	Father Valentine
Sir James Molony	Neurologist
Harriet Horner	IRS Agent
John Parkinson	M.I.6
Harper	Senior messenger
Ms. Boyd	Moneypenny's deputy
Mr. Hathaway	Scorpius hood
Danny DeFretas	Minder at safe house
Todd Sweeney	Minder at safe house
Lord Samuel Mills	Former Prime Minister
Mrs. Madeleine Findlay	Scatter's house minder
Ahmed el Kadar	Assassin

LICENSE TO KILL

Felix Leiter, Drug Enforcement Agent (DEA) and his best man, James Bond, are on the Seven Mile Bridge enroute to Key West where Leiter is scheduled to be married to Della Churchill. Moments later a giant Coast Guard helicopter sets down on the highway in front of them. Leiter is informed that Franz Sanchez, the Central American druglord has left Isthmus City headquarters enroute to Cray Cay in the Bahamas. Leiter and Bond board the helicopter, fly to Cray Cay, capture Sanchez and return to Key West where Leiter is married. Later however, Sanchez escapes. In turn, his hoods kill Della Churchill and throw Leiter to the sharks where he is badly mauled but still alive.

Bond investigates the Ocean Exotica Warehouse in Key West, owned by Milton Krest, a friend of Sanchez where Leiter was tortured and cocaine is stored for shipment. Later Bond is apprehended by British agents and taken to the Hemingway House where he is confronted by his boss 'M' who demands to know why he is not in Istanbul as ordered.

He is told to leave Sanchez to the American authorities but Bond insists on seeking revenge for the assault on Leiter. 'M' demands his resignation and his weapon but Bond bolts over the veranda railing and escapes. Later, Bond disrupts a drug exchange between Milton Krest's yacht the "Wavekrest" and a seaplane. He destroys the cocaine and boards the seaplane as it is taking off.

In a vicious fight, Bond kills the two pilots, takes control of the plane and flies to Ballast Key where he sinks the plane. With the cash in two suitcases and the aid of a friend, he returns to Key West and Leiter's house. In Leiter's computer file Bond discovers a meeting date for the following day at the Barrelhead Saloon on Bimini's West Island.

It is there that Bond meets Pam Bouvier, Leiter's contact. They are confronted by Sanchez's men but they escape. Bond hires Bouvier, a former army pilot for Air America, to fly them to Isthmus City where they check into the El Presidente Hotel and deposit the five million dollars in drug money in the Banco de Isthmus, a bank owned by Sanchez. That evening they attend Sanchez casino headquarters where Bond meets Sanchez face to face and develops a plot to kill him. 'M' sends 'Q' out to Isthmus City with a briefcase full of exotic equipment and weapons to give Bond support. However, Bond is captured and his plot foiled. Sanchez has developed a process whereby he can transport cocaine in gasoline tanker trucks, mixed in with the fuel undetected, and later retrieved intact. Sanchez has prepared a convoy of these trucks to deliver cocaine to the Chinese. Bond escapes with the aid of Pam Bouvier. They find the convoy and Bond is dropped onto one of the tankers. The story builds to a climax as Bond battles Sanchez's men and destroys the tankers.

During a final vicious fight, Sanchez's clothes have become drenched with gasoline. On the verge of being killed, Bond manages to extract his cigarette lighter and ignite Sanchez's clothes, turning him into a human torch.

Back at the El Presidente Hotel, Bond and Pam Bouvier lock in a passionate embrace.

CAST

James Bond	007
Felix Leiter	DEA Agent
Sharky	Driver
Della Churchill	Mrs. Leiter
Franz Sanchez	Druglord
Lupe Lamora	Sanchez girlfriend
Alvaraz	Drug smuggler
Hawkins	DEA agent
Mullins	DEA agent
Perez	Sanchez hood
Braun	Sanchez hood
Dario	Sanchez hood
Lizzie Owen	Artist
Pat	Wedding guest

Pam Bouvier	Pilot
Ed Killifer	DEA agent
Milton Krest	Drug smuggler
M	Chief, M.I.6
Clive	Wavekrest sailor
Seaplane pilots	Drug runners
Anna Rack	TV newscaster
President Hector Lopez	Isthmus
David Wolkowsky	Land developer
Steve	Wolkowsky employee
Moneypenny	"M's" secretary
William Truman-Lodge	Sanchez's accountant
Colonel Heller	Sanchez's security chief
Montolongo	Bank manager
Consuela	Bank assistant
Ms. Kennedy (Bouvier)	Bond's secretary
Kwang	Chinese drug smuggler
Miss Loti	Kwang's companion
Q	M.I.6 armourer
Nick Fallon	British agent
Captain Simon Rojas	Isthmus police
William	Sanchez's chief chemist
Professor Joe	TV evangelist

WIN, LOSE OR DIE

James Bond is promoted to Captain of the Royal Navy and 'M' has him transferred to active sea duty aboard the aircraft carrier HMS Invincible. British, Russian, and American naval forces are engaged in their annual four week exercise in North Sea, Landsea 89. During the exercise, a highly secretive "Steward's Meeting" is to take place aboard Invincible. In attendance are the leaders of the world's three most powerful countries. Prime Minister Margaret Thatcher, President Bush, and Mikhail Gorbachev. Placed in charge of British, Russian and American security forces aboard ship, Bond's orders are to protect the three world leaders from a possible terrorist attack. M.I.6 is aware that terrorist factions are planning some form of assault. But where and by whom?

Even before going to sea, several attempts are made on Bond's life. Aboard ship, a security man is murdered. Another attempt is made on Bond's life. Returning from a meeting at the US Naval Base at Rota, Bond is captured by terrorists who have infiltrated Invincible. He is locked in the brig but manages to escape and fly off Invincible in a British Sea Harrier V / STOL fighter.

The terrorists are demanding two hundred billion dollars for each of the world power leaders. Returning to Invincible with American and British forces from Rota, they quietly board ship. Gunfire erupts and terrorists die. All die except their leader, Bassam Baradj, head of B.A.S.T., the Brotherhood of Anarchy and Secret Terrorism, who has been directing the assault from his room in the Bear Hotel on Gibraltar.

Leaving his hotel, Baradj discovers he is being followed by Bond and agent Beatrice da Ricci. Together they pursue Baradj into the tunnel deep within Gibraltar where Bond finally comes face to face with the terrorist leader. Bond's pistol is shot out of his hand and as he awaits execution by Baradji. The terrorist himself is shot to death by Beatrice da Ricci.

In the final scene we find Bond and the beautiful Beatrice convalescing at the Villa Capricciani on the island of Ischia, just off the coast of Italy.

CAST

James Bond	007
Kiyoshi Akashi	Ship's Captain
Ogawa	Seaman
Zenzo Yamada	Hip's Officer
Ed Potts	Lt. Commander
M	Chief of M.I.6
Col. Bill Tanner	Chief of Staff
Sir Geoffrey Gould	Admiral of the Fleet
Moneypenny	"M's" secretary
Admiral Gudeon	US Navy
Admiral Sergei Pouker	Soviet Navy
Bassam Baradj (Robert Besavitsky)	Head of B.A.S.T.
Abou Hamarik	B.A.S.T. terrorist
Ali al Adwan	B.A.S.T. terrorist
Saphii Boudai	B.A.S.T. terrorist
Felipe Pantano	Spanish Navy pilot
Commander Bernie Brazier	Royal Navy
Clover Pennington (Saphii Boudai)	British Wren
Harry	Turbine engine representative
Bill	Fiber optics representative
Blackie Blackstone	Engineering petty officer
Beatrice da Ricci	Maid
Umberto & Franco	Gardeners
Julian Farsee (Ali al Adwan)	Second–in–command
Toby Lellenberg (Bassam Baradj)	Commanding Officer
Mac & Walter	American Naval Officers
Draycott	British Naval Officer
Read Admiral Sir John Walmsley	Captain / HMS Invincible
Nikola Ratnikov	Russian security
Ted Brinkley	British Special Branch
Martin Camm	British Special Branch
Surgeon Commander Grant	Ship's doctor
Sergeant Harvey	Royal Marines
Sarah Deeley	British Wren
Donald Speaker	Interrogation specialist
Lt. Commander Hallom	Royal Navy
Dan Woodward	US Naval Intelligence
Major	US Marine Corp.
Major	Royal Marines
Yevgeny Stura, Gennady Novikov, and Ivan Tivlashin	Russian security

Joe Israel, Stanley Hare, Bruce Trimble .... US Secret Service
Edgar Morgan .... British Intelligence
Margaret Thatcher .... British Prime Minister
George Bush .... U.S. President
Mikhail Gorbachev .... General Secretary, USSR

BROKENCLAW

On vacation in Victoria, B.C., Bond is ordered to San Francisco by 'M.' The same evening Bond arrives, he is witness to the murder of a FBI agent in Chinatown, apprehended by the FBI and eventually deposited aboard an aircraft carrier in San Francisco bay. There he meets 'M' together with U.S. and British Naval intelligence teams who are working on Operation Curve, designed to infiltrate Brokenclaw's operation.

Brokenclaw, a sinister Chinese / Indian international criminal, has kidnapped five British and U.S. electronic specialists who have perfected "Lords", an electronic device for detecting the location of allied nuclear submarines. This he will sell to the red Chinese government. Brokenclaw has also developed operation Jericho, a long-range plan for disrupting the New York Stock Exchange, creating an economic disaster which would bring about the collapse of the dollar and other world currencies. Posing as a red agent, Bond infiltrates Brokenclaw's domain but is eventually exposed. Gunfire erupts and men die. Bond escapes and confers with 'M'. Brokenclaw's headquarters is taken but he has managed to escape. Bond learns that Brokenclaw is hiding out in the Chelan mountains of Washington state. He pursues him. A final confrontation ensues with a fight to the death between the two. Bond kills Brokenclaw with an arrow to the throat.

CAST

James Bond 007
M .... Chief, M.I.6
Prof. Robt. Allardyce .... Founding Father of Lords
Lee Fu–Chu .... International criminal mind
Nolan & Wood .... FBI agents
Broderick .... FBI Bureau Chief, SF
Patrick Malloney .... FBI agent
Commander Ed Rushia .... US Naval Intelligence
Lt. Linsay Robertson .... US Naval Intelligence
Lt. Daniel Harvey .... US Naval Intelligence
Billy Heron .... Sr. Technician
Frankie McGregor .... US Petty Officer First Class
Lt. James Joseph Jepson III .... US Naval Officer
Lt. Commander Wanda .... US Naval Officer
Man Song Hing .... US Naval Officer
Billy Chinn .... US Navy pilot
Tony Man Song Hing .... Wanda's father
San Son-Ho .... Lee drug courier
Luk See .... Broken Dragon bouncer & doorman
Won Lo & Big Leu .... Lee employees
Bone Bender Ding &
   Frozen Stalk Pu & Fox .... Lee hoods

Sue Chi-Ho	CIA Operative
Bill Orr	SIS psychiatrist
Ann Reilly (Qute)	Assistant to 'Q'
Bill Tanner	M's Chief of Staff
Brian Cogger (The Scrivener)	SIS forger of documents
Franks (The Grand Inquisito)	SIS interrogator
Peter Argentbright	Agent, People's Republic of China
Jenny Mo	Agent, People's Republic of China
Grant	CIA Langley adviser
Mac	CIA agent
Marty Halman	Ice Age rock group
Mama Tai	Call House Madam
Chinese girl	Sales girl
General Hung Chow H'ong	Red Chinese army

THE MAN FROM BARBAROSSA

It began with the kidnapping of Joel Penderek in Hawthorne, New Jersey. A group called The Scales of Justice thought this man a Nazi war criminal by the name of Josif Varontson, a chief executioner of Jews in WWII. However, they had kidnapped the wrong man! 007's mission was to penetrate the inner circles of The Scales of Justice and discover their true intentions. Together with Bond are a Mossad agent and a Russian woman, Nina Bibikova.

Bond and his partners impersonate a British film crew hired by The Scales of Justice. Their job is to film a show trial thereby embarassing the Russian government over their treatment of Soviet Jews.

Simultaneously, General Yuskovich of the Red Army is planning his own personal coup, involving Iran, the forces of Desert Storm and nuclear weapons, to take over power in the Soviet Union. The ultimate climax to this macabre plan would be the total destruction of Washington, D.C.

Bond learns details of this plan and races to stop its implementation. The action reaches a deadly climax as General Yuskovich and his mistress are destroyed by a gigantic premature explosion.

In Moscow, Bond is awarded the Order of Lenin for thwarting the coup of General Yuskovich.

CAST

James Bond	007
Paul Blobel	SS Standartenfuhrer
Josif Vorontsov	Deputy SS Unterscharfuhrer
Franz Reichsleinter	SS Commandant
Joel Penderek	Jewish immigrant
Anna Penderek	Jewish immigrant
Debbie Monsell	Penderek neighbor
Ossie	Resturant proprietor
Moneypenny	M's secretary
M	Head of SIS
Colonel Abel	Russian spy
Gary Powers	American spy
Bill Tanner	Chief of Staff

Pete Natkowitz .... Israli Mossad
Federal Express delivery man
Mr. Leiberman (markus)
Mr / Mrs. Asher Lichtman
Mrs. Goldfarb
Brian Cogger .... The Scrivener (documents)
Nigsy Meadows .... British agent
Williamson .... British Embassy employee
General Brasilov .... Russian genereal
Major Henri Rampart .... GIGN
Major Stephanie Adore .... DGSE officer
Harriet Goode .... Red Army officer
General Yevgeny Yuskovich .... Red Army
Oleg Ivanovich (Krysim) .... 2nd Secretary, Soviet
Colonel General Viktor Mechaev .... 1st Chief Directorate Officer
Colonel Riuchev .... KGB
General Boris Stepakov .... Red army
Alex & Nicki .... Russian agents
Owen Gladwyn .... SIS
Gregory Findlay .... Head of Moscow Station, SIS
Nina Bibikova .... Russian agent
Vladamir Lyko .... Senior professor of English
Mikhail Bibikov (Michael Brooks) .... Nina's father
Emerald Lacy .... Nina's mother
Colonel Anatoli Lazin .... Air Force
Wilson Sharp .... British Cipher clerk
Dave Fletcher .... British SIS minder
Natasha .... The Scales of Justice agent
Clive .... The Scales of Justice agent
Gleb Yakovlevich Bzrzin .... Colonel, Red Army
Savall .... British cipher clerk
Nicola Chernysh .... Supervisor to the President's Secretariat.
Pansy Wright .... British SIS agent
Lopp .... Helper
Sergei Yakovlevich Batovrin .... Russian Officer

DEATH IS FOREVER

After the reunification of Germany, a joint British / American intelligence network, code name Cabal, in East Germany has disintegrated. Two of the case workers are murdered while trying to contact their undercover agents. James Bond and his counterpart Easy St. John of the CIA are sent to Berlin to investigate.

After contact with one agent the two are marked for death. Travelling across Europe by train and plane, they learn that Wolfgang Weisen, former head of East Germany's security service is attempting to eliminate all Cabal agents who may be a threat to his scheme to assasinate all of the European world leaders and destablize the European economy. Their pursuit of Weisen takes them to Paris, Venice, and Calais, France where the final confrontation between Bond and Weisen takes place.

With all the European heads of government aboard a train travelling through the channel tunnel, Weisen plants 500 pounds of Semtex plastique explosive to the underside of the train.

Racing to Calais from Venice, Bond alerts French and British forces of the sinister plot and orders them to cut electrical current to the rails. Upon arrival, he is taken into the tunnel where he has a final confrontation with Weisen as his men are planting the explosives. Through a small radio device Bond signals a series of clicks to restore power to the rails. Weisen and his men are electrocuted in a dance of death.

CAST

007	SIS agent
M	Head of M.I.6
Bill Tanner	Chief of Staff
Easy St. John	CIA
Oscar Vomberg (MAB)	Cabal agent
Crystal	Cabal agent
Ariel (Karl Kuckuck)	Cabal agent
Caliban	Cabal agent
Cobweb	Cabal agent
Orphan (August Wimper)	Cabal agent
Tester (Heini Spraker)	Cabal agent
Sulphur	Cabal agent
Puck	Cabal agent
Dodger	Cabal agent
Martin de Rosso	Controller at Langley
Markus Wolf	Spymaster General HVA
Wolfgang Weisen	Former East German Intelligence
Monica Haardt	HVA-Stasi
Heini Wachtel	Inferscope BV
Klaus Korgold	Foreign agent
Helmut	Taxi driver
Praxi Simeon (sulphur)	Cabal agent
Felix Wellerman	Weisen hood
Hexie Weiss	Weisen hood
Michelle Gris	French Foreign Intelligence
Antoine & Dulcie Amber	Hotel owners
Axel Ritter	Weisen agent
Carlos & Giorgio	Weisen guards
Franco & Antonio	Weisen boatment
Dimitri & Druvitch	Weisen golfers
Sprat	Weisen lackey
Dominic Jellineck	Political hood
Dorian Crane	Political hood
Libby Macintosh	Cabal agent
Elizabeth Cearns	CIA
Ford Puxley	SIS
Bogdan Stashinsky	KGB assasin

Lou Rebet .... Newspaper editor
Stepan Bandera .... Ukranian exiled leader
Simon Richards .... Attorney
Claude de Froid .... Agent
Harry Spraker (tester) .... Cabal agent

NEVER SEND FLOWERS

Four world figures had been systematically been assasinated. Then, when Laura March with M.I.5 was murdered in Switzerland, Bond was assigned by 'M' to the case. There he meets Fredericka von Grusse of Swiss Intelligence, also assigned to the case. Together they discovered that all of the killings were linked together and subsequent events then lead them to a German castle on the Rhine, home of the world-famous actor David Dragonpol, who they learn was Laura March's lover. When violence erupts, Bond and Flicka narrowly escape death.

Their pursuit of David Dragonpol now takes them to Milan and Athens but eventually reaches its climax at Euro Disney, just outside Paris. Here the killer intends to assassinate Princess Diana and her two sons.

Bond is given responsibility to stop the madman. Action builds to a violent climax in water surrounding the Mark Twain riverboat. In a gruelling death struggle, Bond accidently detonates the killer's explosive device which in turn incinerates his adversary.

CAST

James Bond 007
M .... Head of SIS
Father Paolo Di Sio .... Catholic Priest
His Holiness .... The Pope
General Claudio Carrousso .... Murder victim
Vatician Security Officer
Archie Shaw (MP) .... Murder victim
Angela Shaw .... Wife
Metropolitan Police Commander
Pavel Gruskochev .... Murder victim
Mark Fish (CIA) .... Murder victim
Laura March .... Murder victim
Moneypenny .... M's secretary
Gerald Grant MI5
Carmel Chantry MI5
Fredericka von Grusse .... Swiss Intelligence
Durzharna Sigurnost .... Former Bulgarian Intelligence
David March .... Murder victim
Christine Wright & Jessie Styles .... Murder victims
Bridget Bellamy & Betsy Sagar .... Murder victims
Janet Fellows & Anne Frick .... Murder victims
Superintendent Seymour &
Sergeant Bowles .... British police
Marietta Bruch .... Hotel clerk

Hotel Maid
Swiss Inspector Ponsin
Detective Bodo Lemphe .... Interlaken police
David Docking .... Assassin
Bill Tanner .... Chief of Staff
Gerda Bloom .... Swiss Intelligence
Man from MI5 Watcher Service
Street sweeper & London cab driver
David Dragonpol .... British actor
Maeve Horton .... Sister
Heather Barnabus .... Murder victim
Detective Sergeant Tibble
George Darby .... Detective Chief Superintendent
Policeman Meyer
Charles Colfer
Gianne-Franco Orsini .... Italian Intelligence
May .... Housekeeper
Robb .... Commander, Metropolitan Police
Ben .... Security Chief, Euro Disney
Colonel Fontaine.. GIGN (French Special Forces Unit)
Ann Reilly.. 'Q' Branch

SEAFIRE

Bond has been elevated to Director of the Double-O section of the SIS. 'M' has been placed in semi-retirement because of poor health. Fredericka von Grusse (Flicka) is once again on assignment with Bond in pursuit of billionaire Sir Maxwell Tarn, an illegal arms dealer who is obsessed with destroying the world of nations and resurrecting the Nazi party.

The story begins as Bond and Flicka are torpedoed on a cruise ship in the Caribbean. The trail of Tarn takes them from England to Spain, Israel, Germany and finally Puerto Rico. Through this maze Bond and Flicka are subjected to life threatening situations as they struggle to solve Operation SeaFire and prevent a catastrophic environmental disaster.

In the course of this pursuit, Flicka and Felix Leiter are captured by Tarn's men, tortured, and held prisoner on El Morro Castle. Trapped on board Tarn's submarine as he was planting explosives, Bond must escape the boat before the present time. The climax is reached high atop Morro Castle as Bond and Tarn face each other for the last time.

CAST

James Bond 007
M .... SIS
Bill Tanner .... SIS
Sir Maxwell Tarn .... Tarn International
Lady Trish Tarn .... Tarn's wife
Fredericka von Grusse .... SIS
Lt. Mark Neuman .... Ship's officer
Claude Wimsey... Police commissioner

Peter Dolmeck	Accountant
The Minister	Home office
Maurice Goodwin	Tarn staff mgr.
Anna & Cathy	Tarn hoods
Conrad Spicer	Tarn bodyguard
Susan Fawkes	Maid
George Drums	Valet
Hawkins	Driver
Beth	Tarn hood
Chastity Vain	Bond's secretary
Frobisher	M's nurse
Pete Natkowitz	Mossad
Pixie & Dixie	Tarn hoods
Thickness	Micro Globe One
Jane Smith	Micro Globe One
Judy Jameson	Security
Heidi	Tarn hood
Paulanerstuben	Waiter
Fritz Saal	Lawyer
Kurt Rollen	Tarn hood
Tony Hairman	Intelligence Service
Bill Burkeshaw	Intelligence Service
Lord Harvey	Joint Intelligence Committee
Ann Reilly	'Q' Branch
Felix Leiter	CIA
Vesta Motley	Biochemist
Afton Fritz	Biochemist
Rex Rexinus	Marine biologist
Jock Anerson	Submarine captain
Jim Dodd	Capt. 22nd SAS

COLD FALL

The date is March 1990. As Bradbury Airlines flight BD299 from London touches down at Dulles International Airport in Washington D.C., flames and explosions erupt from the aircraft. The 747 disintegrates down the runway in a ball of fire.

'M' assigns Bond to investigate and Bond learns that an old close companion of his was also possibly on board the ill-fated flight: the Principessa Sukie Tempesta, aka Susan Destry. She and Bond had shared danger and loving together in years past.

At Dulles, Bond unexpectedly runs into Sukie Tempesta who has been looking for him. Sukie had in fact not been on the Bradbury flight but had been instructed to come to D.C. immediately in a note supposedly from Bond. Years before, she had married Pasqual Tempesta. Together with his sons Luigi and Angelo, they were an organized crime family and connected with COLD, Children of the Last Days, an international terrorist organization. Sukie agrees to stay with Bond, but leaves to get her things at the Hilton. Upon his return from meetings, he receives a message from Sukie saying she is in danger and must "go to ground" for awhile.

Later police ask Bond to view the Lexus Sukie had been driving. A bomb had blown the roof off and a badly burned shape was viewable with what had once been a head, arms and hands curled into a fetal position.

Upon orders from 'M', Bond is sent to Quantico to see Eddie Rhabb, FBI supervisor. Here he meets Toni Nicolletti, FBI penetration agent and mistress of Luigi Tempesta. She agrees to help him get into the Tempesta Villa as an old friend.

Bond flies into Pisa, Italy, where he is met by Luigi Tempesta. Upon arrival at the Villa, Toni Nicolletti whispers to Bond that the brothers are going to kill them both and throw their bodies in the lake.

After lunch the brothers meet with Bond. He tells them he is looking for the killer of Sukie. They give him the name of retired General Brutus Clay. Sukie had turned down offers of marriage to him three times. Clay was a wealthy man who played war games in Idaho.

Fast forward: the brothers supposedly leave for a business meeting. Bond joins the women for dinner. Later, back in his room Giulliana appears and makes a play for Bond. Bond's door crashes open and Luigi, automatic in hand is prepared to kill both of them. At that moment Toni Nicolletti appears, shooting both Luigi and Giulliana with a high powered air pistol and tranquilizer darts.

From the boathouse, he and Nicolletti escape by jet skis to the port of Viareggio and an old farm house where they are met by 'M' and Eddie Rhabb, and debriefed. Bond is ordered to pursue General Clay. 'M' leaves for London but is kidnapped by Tempesta hoods and flown to Seattle. Bond flies to Coeur d' Alene. He phones General Clay who gives him map references and says he will allow him thirty minutes! After a drive of several hours Bond stops near a graveyard. Three dark shapes appear along with the sound of thunder. Bond heads for the nearby woods. Clay lands in his Cobra helicopter. Clay had orders from the Tempesta brothers to kill Bond. He orders Bond to come out of the woods. The Cobra only rested twenty feet from where Bond crouched. Inside, suspended on the straps of a safety harness, hangs 'M'.

Bond gains access to the Cobra without detection by Clay's men and lifted-off. Pursued by the two other helicopters, Bond fires his Tow missiles, destroying both aircraft. As he approaches Coeur d' Alene over the lake, the engine sputters and dies. Bond issues a mayday to the Spokane tower. Later, he regains consciousness in the hospital. 'M' had also survived the crash.

Having recovered with only superficial wounds, Bond and 'M' return to London. In the year that follows, information comes from Eddie Rhabb that General Clay had surfaced again, the Tempestas were up to more criminal dealings, and there had been a marked increase in the membership of COLD. Fast forward to 1994. Once again Bond hooks up with another M.I.6 agent, Beatrice da Ricci, with whom he had worked in the past.

It appears that COLD area commanders are meeting at the Villa Tempesta for a special briefing. COLD of course wants control of the USA to implement their isolationist policy. It would throw the entire world into the stone age!

Bond and Beatrice are briefed and equipped for operation anti-freeze: to secure and cut off the main leaders of COLD including the Tempesta brothers. After Beatrice had left for the Villa, Rhabb showed Bond a faxed color print of a girl who had arrived at the Villa. Bond was dumb-struck. He was looking at a beautiful picture of the Principessa Sukie Tempesta! Bond was sick and angry.

Bond parachutes onto the Villa Tempesta grounds where Beatrice will meet him. They will be followed by Italian Special Forces amd Royal Marine Commandos. Unfortunately they are discovered by Tempesta hoods and Sukie Tempesta. Sukie is glad to see Bond; she's getting married the following day and wants Bond to give her away. She tells him she is the one, using a remote, that detonated the explosives aboard the Bradbury flight. She also told him she had befriended a hotel chambermaid about her size, hired her as a personal maid, bought her expensive clothes and put her luggage in the trunk of the Lexus. Luigi Tempesta had sent someone in to do the car. Sukie sent her over to the hotel to meet Bond. Sukie activated the bomb as soon as she got out of the car. It was simple! Bond learns she is to marry Brutus Clay. Operation Blizzard would start on Christmas Day. Bombs are to explode around Times Square and The United Nations, and bombs are to explode across America, primarily in government buildings, accompanied by the seizing of TV and radio stations, National Guard armories, etc. It is time for Bond and Beatrice to twist the buckle of their belts which sends out a mayday signal. When the attack begins, General Clay forces Bond and Beatrice to accompany him through a maze of tunnels. Coming out in Clay's bedroom Bond views the body of Sukie Tempesta dead. She was murdered by Clay.

More tunnels take them to the boat dock and Clay's motor launch, the Clay Pigeon. As they depart the boat house, leaving a rooster tail of water behind, Italian Special Forces are arresting the Tempesta brothers and leaders of COLD. Beatrice retrieves a hidden pistol and fires, hitting Clay and knocking him overboard. Clay goes down several times, crying out that he could not swim, and then disappears.

Bond and Beatrice return to London and Bond's flat. An official envelop reveals that Bond is to report to M.I.6 immediately and the new 'M', a woman. Ying and Yang, a pair of M.I.6 minders, appear at the door to provide a personal escort.

CAST

James Bond	007
M	Chief, M.I.6
Moneypenny	'M's' secretary
Harley Bradbury	Bradbury Airlines
James Boldman	James Bond
Sukie Tempesta	The Principessa
Edward Mercer	Balpa Captain
Jack Hughes	Director/NTSB Team
Bill Alexander	Farnborough trio
Azeb	Hotel desk clerk
Peter Janson	Anti-terrorist department
John and Pam Smith	Anti-terrorist department
Eddie Rhabb and Barney Newhouse	FBI
Charles Grover	Bradbury attorney
Detective Pritchard	Washington D.C. police
Toni Nicolletii	FBI, Tempesta historian
Prime	FBI agent
Luigi and Angelo Tempesta	Italian hoods
Guilliana Tempesta	Luigi's wife
Maria Tempesta	Angelo's wife
Brutus Clay	Retired Air Force General
Pasqual Tempesta	Deceased husband of Sukie

Fillippo	Tempesta hood
Carlotta	Chambermaid
Felicio Heard Shifflet (Fliss)	FBI
David Brown	MD
Patti	Nurse
Jack "Pop" Hughes	NTSB
Daniel Paul	Bomb maker
Winston Mallard	Bomb maker
Wicked Witch of the Night	Black nurse
Ivor Bergman	Terrorist
Ruth Issacs & Nicola McBride	Provisional IRA
Frederika Von Gruisse (Flicka)	British SIS
Nick Carter	Anti-terrorist
Beatrice Maria da Ricci	British SIS
Dr. Samusi	Flicka's MD
Farmer and Allen	Tempesta hoods
General Bolletti	Italian army
Ying and Yang	SIS
Roberto, Tomaro, Edmunds, Allessandro, Giorgio, Enrico, Saul, Kauffburger	Tempesta hoods
The Davison's	Ms. housekeepers

GOLDENEYE

1986
'M' ordered James Bond, 007, and Alec Trevelyn, 006, to destroy the Archangel Chemical Weapons facility in the USSR. During the operation, 006 was killed by a Colonel Ourumov, but 007's explosives destroy the facility and Bond gets out alive.

1995
Driving the South coast of France, Bond is passed by a speeding yellow Ferrari. (In the movie the Ferrari is red.) In Monaco he discovers the Ferrari and the girl at the casino. Playing bacarat against her he wins 200,000 pounds. From M.I.6 he learns she is Xenia Onatopp with the Janus Crime Syndicate in the USSR. During the course of the following day she murders a US Admiral, two helicopter pilots and steals the latest French helicopter, the Tigre. Bond's efforts to stop her were not successful.

The scene is Severnaya radar station, USSR. Natalya Simonova, a computer technician manipulates a huge radio telescope dish locked onto a piece of Soviet space junk, in reality a fully operational satellite. She and co-worker Boris Grishenko are among a dozen men and women who work in a clean room far below the surface.

The Tigre lands at the station and out steps Xenia Onatopp and the now General Ourumov. They obtain the necessary codes, firing key and Goldeneye disc from the duty officer. They kill everyone in the station except Simonova who has hidden and Grishenko who disappeared. With the Goldeneye they proceed to arm the satellite, designating it to destroy the station, then leave.

Simonova survives the destruction, makes her way to St. Petersburg. Here she makes contact with Grishenko, who also survived and they agree to meet. Unfortunately, at their meeting, Grishenko is accompanied by Xenia Onatopp and is taken prisoner and drugged. Bonds meets with Jack Wade, CIA agent, who puts him in contact with an old nemesis of Bond's who can set him up to meet the head of the Janus Crime Sydicate. In the steam room of the Europa Hotel, Bond is attacked by Xenia Onatopp. He subdues her. Tied up, she agrees to take him to Janus in Statue Park. Out of the shadows steps Alec Trevelyn.

Bond is knocked unconscious and awakens to discover that he and Natalya Simonova are bound inside the Tigre helicopter. Its rockets have fired and are targeted to return. Bond hits the ejector switches with his nose and they are thrown clear, then taken prisoners by Russian Federal Intelligence. During interrogation by Viktor Mishkin, Minister of Defense, General Ourumov appears, and kills the Minister. Bond attacks Ourumov and escapes with Natalya. Natalya is again taken prisoner by General Ourumov, who flees in a black sedan. Bond commondeers a tank and pursues them.

The chase takes them to the Strategic (Rail) Weapons Depot where General Ourumov, Janus, and Xenia board the train. Taking a shortcut, Bond straddles his tank on the rails. As the train approached, Bond fired the 100 mm gun with an Armor piercing shell. After the explosion, Bond boarded the train. He kept his gun on Xenia and Trevelyan. General Ourumov appears with a gun pointed to Natalya's head. She breaks free and Bond kills Ourumov. Xenia and Trevelyn flee the car.

Through the computer, Natalya learns that Grishenko is in Cuba. Bond contacts Jack Wade of the CIA. He arranges plane tickets to the states, clothes, and the right visa for Natalya. Traveling under disguises, they go first to Paris, then to Miami and on to Puerto Rico where they are met by CIA agent, Jack Wade. He leaves a Piper Archer airplane for them at the nearest airport.

Wade also has brought Bond a briefcase with 'Q's' latest gagetry. The following morning as they are looking for the antenna and dish, a 140 mm rocket suddenly shears off half of their port wing and the plane crashes. Hovering above them is a helicopter with a rope ladder extended. Xenia grabs Bond with her legs in a scissor lock. Bond manages to grab her machine pistol and fire it up towards the pilot. The helicopter surges forward, pulling the ladder after it. Xenia is caught in the trees, killed, and the helicopter crashes in a ball of fire.

Far below the lake, Boris Grishenko is working the computer, transferring billions of dollars from the Bank of England into private accounts in other foreign countries. Then, they would activate the satellite to destroy London.

Bond and Natalya watch as three tall masts and a dish rise from the lake. They start to climb, then slip on the wet metal to the bottom of the dish. At the base they enter a maintenance blockhouse, and go down another rung ladder to a catwalk circling the control room. Guards begin firing at them and Bond pushes Natalya away. She heads for the mainframe computer room. Bond had planted mines around the fuel tanks and they are activated. Bond is captured and brought to Trevelan, who examined all his personal effects. Natalya had succeeded in deflecting the course of the satellite. Shots ring out. Explosions are heard. The liquid coolants suddenly explode. Boris Grishenko is suddenly enveloped in a freezing white mist. He becomes a frozen statue inside the doomed building. Pursued by Trevelyn, Bond drops through a trapdoor with his hands on the bottom rung of a ladder. Trevelyan slips and falls, with Bond grabbing him by one wrist. As he pleads for Bond to save him, Bond shouts, "Go to hell!" and lets him go.

As Bond dangles from the bottom rung of the ladder, Natalya has forced the pilot of a helicopter gunship to maneuver closer and closer to Bond. He brings the port landing skid just below Bond who manages to grab it just as everything around him seems to be collapsing. The gunship brings him down gently.

As he and Natalya begin to make love, Jack Wade and the Marines appear from out of the bushes.

CAST

James Bond	007
Alec Trevelyan	006
General Ourumov	Head of Security
Caroline	M.I.6
Xenia Onatopp	Janus Crime Syndicate
Chuck Farrel	U.S. Admiral
Natalya Simonova	Computer technician
Boris Grishenko	Computer scientist
Anna	Computer technician
Q	M.I.6
Viktor Mishkin	Defense Minister
Valantin Zukovsky	Ex-KGB/Criminal
Jake Wade	CIA
M	M.I.6 Chief
Irene	Mistress/singer
Dimitri	Thug
Janus	Alec Trevelyan
Mac	CIA

TOMORROW NEVER DIES

M.I.6 learns that Henry Gupta, a techno terrorist, has acquired an Atomic Clock Signal Encoding System (ACSES) of which there were supposedly only twenty-two in the world. This device, hooked up to a Global Positioning Satellite System (GPS) could, among other things, send a ship off course. What they didn't know was that Gupta was employed by Elliot Carver, a man who had inherited his father's wealth through blackmail and murder. He loved power and discovered that by manipulating the news he could increase his company's earnings and his personal wealth. In the 90's the Carver Media Group Network was second only to CNN. Its communication satellite was currently over Southeast Asia.

The HMS Devonshire is off the coast of China when it is ordered by Chinese MIGs to put into the nearest port or be fired upon. Commander Day replies that his ship is in international waters and will defend itself if attacked. What Day doesn't know is that Sea Dolphin II, a stealth ship, is following Devonshire. A device known as Sea-Vac, a jet engine drilling machine with rotary cutters for teeth and a video camera has been deployed. Fast forward as the Sea-Vac penetrates the hull of Devonshire, sinking it. Divers then enter the hull and remove one of its cruise missiles. Sea Dolphin II then destroys one of the Chinese MIGs. What has developed here is an international crisis between Great Britian and China. It is a crisis engineered totally by Elliot Carver whose media slogan is "tomorrow's news today!"

M.I.6 learns that one of the CMGN satellites over China, a news satellite that never got permission to broadcast, did in fact send a signal on the very same night. Somehow, war between Great Britain and China has to be averted.

In the next scene, Bond is sent to Hamburg where CMGN is having a grand opening of its world headquarters. At Avis Rental Car 'Q' instructs Bond in the latest techno weapons, the new BMW 750 and the Walther P99.

At the party Bond meets Carver's wife who turns out to be an old flame. Here too, he meets Wai Lin from Chinese intelligence. As the party progresses, Carter develops an instantaneous hatred for Bond and tries to have him killed by sending his henchmen to lure and attack him. Bond dispatches them, then again runs into Wai Lin. Bond sets off the automated fire alarm which creates total chaos and they escape the building with the fleeing crowd. Wai Lin disappears.

In Bond's hotel room, Paris Carver and Bond meet, reminisce and end up making love. Bond leaves to return to CMGN to investigate while Carver's men find Paris in the room and murder her.

In Henry Gupta's office Bond discovers the missing ACSES device. He flees the Carver building amid flying bullets. Back at the hotel Bond discovers Paris' body and tries to escape the parking garage in his exotic BMW but is forced to abandon it. However, by remote control, the BMW foils Carver's men. Bond directs the BMW to the rooftop and sends it flying into space, dropping six floors to the street below.

'M' orders Bond to Okinawa to meet with the CIA and find the Devonshire. To avoid Chinese radar Bond makes a high altitude, low opening (HALO) jump over the South China Sea where Devonshire went down. Finding the wreckage, he again discovers Wai Lin. Together they discover that none of the small missiles have been fired, which proves the Devonshire had not fired on the Chinese MIGs, and that one of the ship's cruise missiles had been taken. Upon reaching the surface, they are captured and taken to Carver's headquarters in Saigon. Needless to say, once again they make a dramatic escape and meet up at a bicycle repair shop, a front for Chinese Secret Service. Here they learn that Ha Long Bay is the logical location for the Carver stealth ship. Arriving at Ha Long Bay they discover Sea Dolphin II preparing to leave harbor to destroy the British ships.

The scene switches to Bond and Wai Lin boarding the ship from their inflatable raft. They plant limpet mines set for twenty minutes. Eventually they are discovered. Wai Lin is captured. Bond battles Stamper and his thugs, killing all of them. He rescues Wai Lin and they leave the ship in a raft just before the limpet mines and the HMS Bedford shells destroy Carver's ship.

CAST

James Bond	007
M	Chief, M.I.6
Bill Tanner	Chief of Staff
Bukharin	Russian General
Roebuck	British Admiral
Gustov Meinholtz	Former East German agent
Henry Gupta	Techno terrorist
Russian Co-Pilot	Russian pilot
Captain	HMS Chester
Commander Richard Day	Captain, HMS Devonshire
Lt. Commander Peter Hume	First Officer
Stamper	Carver thug
Elliot Carver	Head of CMGN
Wai Lin	People's External Security Force

Koh	Chinese general
Chang	Chinese general
Mr. Deng	Warehouse manager
Inga Bergstrom	Swedish language professor
Miss Moneypenny	'M's' secretary
Kelly	British Admiral
Paris McKenna	Carver's wife
Q	Major Boothroyd, armorer
Jack Trenton	Carver VP/PR
Tamara Kelly	News anchor
Dr. Kaufman	Carver hit man
Lord Roverman	Carver's father and MP
Hans Kriegler	Criminal
Mr. Schnitzler	Jewelry fence
Jack Wade	CIA
Dr. Dave Greenwalt	Lab Supervisor
Ramsey	Jamaican boy
James McMahon	British Captain
Satoshi Isagura	Chemical expert

ZERO MINUS TEN

On July 1, 1997 the British Crown Colony was to be transferred to the People's Republic of China. However, prior to that date, a series of terrorist acts occurred which threatened to disrupt the peaceful transfer of sovereignty between Great Britain and China.

June 17, 1997
The cargo ship Melbourne from Hong Kong is anchored off Portsmouth, England. Its cargo purportedly was tea and toys. Dockside, inspection reveals it to be heroin. A shoot-out follows killing two Hampshire Police officers and four Chinese women.

June 18, 1997
The following day in Hong Kong, a special event takes place aboard the floating restaurant Emerald Palace. John Desmond, CEO of EurAsia Enterprises, is retiring after thirty years. Guy Thackeray, whose great-great grandfather had founded the firm would be taking over. After his speech, Thackeray leaves the restaurant. Fifteen minutes later the Emerald Palace explodes into flames. Everyone is killed and the structure is completely submerged.

June 21, 1997
In Western Australia an aboriginal boy watches as two men bury something in the ground. After the men leave, the boy goes to inspect the burial mound. As he digs at the site, the mound explodes in his face. The nuclear explosion sends shock waves throughout the world. A special session of the United Nations is called. Australian officials are completely baffled.

Back in London, 'M' informs Bond that in the past week a solicitor from London, a Guy Donaldson, was killed in Hong Kong by a car bomb and two officials from Beijing were killed in a shopping mall by a man in military uniform. Bond also was told of the Emerald Palace explosion. There is growing tension between China and Great Britain. Both denied any involvement. Three of these explosions were connected to the EurAsia Enterprises, Ltd., a shipping and trading firm, operated by a long-established British firm.

'M' wants Bond to find out who is behind these terrorists acts and stop them. Also, to find a way to meet Guy Thackeray and size him up.

Bond stops at Q Branch for a briefing on 'Q's' latest array of weapons that Bond would take with him.

June 22, 1997
Bond arrives in Hong Kong and checks into the Mandarin/Oriental. He meets Station Head Woo and son Chen Chen. Woo briefs him on General Wong who is very militant, plus Thackeray, EurAsia Enterprises, and Li Xu Nan of the Dragon Wing Society triad.

Woo takes Bond to the Lisboa Hotel and Casino in Macau where he meets Guy Thackeray over a game of mahjong. After several hours of play, Bond's winnings amounted to approximately $ 41,200. He declares that he is out, reveals his hand and declares "Jade Dragon, maximum hand". Thackeray had been drinking heavily and Bond knew he had been cheating. Thackeray disappears into the men's room and Bond and Woo then leave the Casino.

June 23, 1997
The following day, Woo takes Bond to the Zipper Club, hopefully to meet Li Xu Nan, head of the Dragon Wing Society. Here he meets Sunni Pei, Zipper hostess, and persuades her to introduce him to Li Xu Nan. Bond interviews the triad leader, posing as a reporter for the Daily Gleaner of Jamaica. Li Xu Nan becomes enraged at Bond's questions and orders him to leave the club. Sunni slips him a note on his way out requesting he meet her behind the club in five minutes. The Triad thinks she betrayed them. She asks to stay with Bond until she knows what to do. Instead, they go to Sunni's apartment. They discover her mother has died of natural causes. As they prepare to leave, Triad hoods rush the apartment and Bond suffers a sever knife wound to his left arm. Gunfire erupts and Bond kills seven triad hoods in a wild shootout. Bond and Sunni flee and are picked up by Woo and Chen Chen and driven to their safe house where Bond and Sunni make love and spend the night.

June 24, 1997 3:55 PM
The following day Bond attends Guy Thackeray's press conference. Thackeray tells the news media he is selling his family's 59% in EurAsia Enterprises to the People's Republic of China. Thackeray leaves Statue Square and gets into the back seat of a black Mercedes. As it pulls away, a Chinese man dressed in black runs out into the intersection and throws something into the open window of the Mercedes.

The car explodes in flames and is totally destroyed. The CEO for EurAsia Enterprises has been assassinated while the whole city is watching. Bond sees the running man and takes after him. He goes up the escalator to the fifth floor, then on an elevator to the twelfth floor where Bond tackles him. He pushes Bond away and jumps a rail, falling 170 feet to his death. Bond reaches street level and walks away, then flags a cab. When he arrives at Woo's safe house, it has been burglarized. No one is inside the store. Woo and Sunni are missing. He returns to the Mandarin and contacts London. Tanner tells him that Woo and his son are safe, but knows nothing about the girl. Tanner tells him that 'M' still wants him on the job. If he can establish and prove the link between EurAsia and the Triad, he will have done his job.

Bond heads for the container port and Kwai Chung where EurAsia's warehouse is located. He breaches their security, lock-picks a rear door, enters and takes steps up to an office. Through a window he can see it is one of the Albino Chinese he had seen with Li Xu Nan at the Zipper Club. Down on the warehouse floor is a wooden sampan mounted on a wheeled platform.

It is brand new, painted brown with a red roof. The albino leaves the office, descends the steps and speaks to the workers who immediately wheel it out of the warehouse. Bond enters the office. He discovers a shipping itinerary on EurAsia letterhead; on it the name of a ship appears, "Taitai". It was now in the harbor. Its next stop is Singapore with a planned return of June 30. Inside a metal briefcase is thousands of dollars in Hong Kong currency. Bond studies a wall map with lines running from Hong Kong to a circled area in Yunan Province in China, the Golden Triangle, source of most of the world's heroin. Bond rifles the filing cabinet and discovers a folder marked Australia. There is a letterhead marked EurAsia Enterprises, Kalgoorlie, Australia, and a map of the Kalgoorlie mining facility. Bond takes the map and leaves the office.

He watches as the albino and another man open a crate on the forklift. Inside they find a burlap bag. After inspecting the contents, the two men leave. Bond checks the bag. It is refined heroin! Bond leaves the warehouse. A gray Rolls Royce is parked near the entrance. The man with the briefcase opens the back door and steps in, joining another man who is Li Xu Nan.

Bond has made the connection between EurAsia Enterprises and the Triad. As the Rolls pulls away, Bond flags a cab and follows the Rolls down an alley in Kowloon City. Li Xu Nan and the other man enter a shabby building. Bond manages to climb up to a second story window and slip inside. Looking down through the slats in the floor he could view everything below. For two hours he listens and watches. At the close of the ceremony they bring out Sunni Pei who was to be killed for betraying the Triad. When everyone has left, Bond drops to the floor and slips through the door where they had taken Sunni. He was immediately surrounded by Chinese thugs who took him to Li Xu Nan's private office. Here Bond learns that James Thackeray began supplying opium in 1836 to Li Wei Tam, Li's great-great-grandfather. In 1839 the Emporer ended the opium trade but James Thackeray managed to establish an illegal pipeline to continue his opium trade. In 1842 Hong Kong island was ceded to the British. James Thackeray needed more capital to start his own trading company. Thackeray would accept a loan from Li Wei Tan only on the condition that they made a provision by which Li could be repaid. Thus EurAsia Enterprises was born. The provision: should Hong Kong ever come under Chinese rule again, then Thackeray's assets in the company would be given to Li. It would become his company.

The agreement was handed down through the generations and kept intact. When the communists came to power, they seized all of Li Wei Tam's family property including the document between James Thackeray and Li Wei Tam. A General Wong was the silent partner who provided the heroin from the Golden Triangle. He was in possession of the original agreement that would automatically transfer ownership of EurAsia Enterprises at midnight on June 30, 1997. Guy Thackeray would be out and Wong would gain control of a multibillion corporation and increase his profit margin in the drug operation by one-third. If Bond would steal the original document from Wong, Li Xu Nan would spare his life and that of Sunni Pei.

June 26, 1997 8 AM

A James Pickard, representing EurAsia Enterprises, is arriving from London with an appointment to see General Wong. Li's men would make the switch at the airport and Bond would take his place. The following morning Bond is on the train to Guangzhou. Upon his arrival he is met and taken to

Wong's headquarters. Wong shows him the document and then declares him an imposter. Wong holds up a photo of the real James Pickard. Bond is forced to disrobe. Wong gives him ten lashes with a cane stick, then is called out of the room.

As two guards take him to a cell, he manages to kill both of them with his plastic dagger and take the AK-47 off the one guard. Bond finds Wong and a woman making love. He forces Wong to open the safe and give him the document, then kills him with his plastic dagger. Bond escapes the building and is picked up by Li's men. They board a hovercraft to Kowloon and Li's office where Bond gives him the document.

June 27, 1997, 12:01 AM

Bond tells Li about Australia. Li offers Bond and Sunni his private jet to Perth. Bond and Sunni pass through Immigration with their fake passports as John Hunter and Mary Ling. They rent a four-wheel Suzuki Vitara wagon. It is a seven hour drive to Kalgoorlie. They stop at the Star & Garter Motel. Having lunch in a local pub they meet Skip Stewart, a colorful bush guide. The following morning they drive to EurAsia's mining operations. Sitting on a flatbed truck is the dark brown sampan with the red roof Bond had seen at the EurAsia warehouse at Kwai Chung. Deep inside the mine they discover EurAsia Enterprises is mining uranium. Bond discovers an almost complete nuclear bomb. He returns to the room where he left Sunni and is confronted by three albino thugs. One is holding Sunni. The fourth man was Guy Thackeray, alive.

Thackeray intends to explode a nuclear bomb in Hong Kong harbor during the transition ceremonies creating total destruction, havoc, and contamination of the entire city. Bond is to be taken to a remote area by plane where he will be killed. Bond awakes aboard Thackeray's Cessna Grand Caravan. Harry the albino was sitting beside the pilot. Bond convinces him to remove Bond's duct tape. A fight develops and the pilot is accidently killed. Bond hits the emergency door lock and the albino falls to his death. He buckles himself into the pilot's seat and levels the plane out and brings it in for a crash landing.

June 29, 1997, 6:00 AM

Bond is uninjured. He walks all night and into the following afternoon. He comes upon an aborigine girl who shows him how to extract water from the roots of a plant. He tells her he is going to Uluru and she points in the direction he is traveling. He was correct!

It is 6 p.m. when Bond reaches Ayer's Rock and the park ranger station. Bond places a call to Skip Stewart in Kalgoorlie. Stewart agrees to fly into Ayer's Rock airport and pick Bond up. He then calls London and speaks to 'M'. She tells him to contact Captain Plante aboard the Peacock.

June 30, 1997 9:30 PM

Back in Hong Kong, Bond makes contact with Captain Plante. It dawns on Bond that Thackeray would put the bomb on the brown sampan with the red roof. Together with Li Xu Nan and his large yacht, they speed out into the harbor. Captain Plante calls the "Glory." This was actually the Taitai which had been repainted. They have about forty-five minutes to find the bomb and disarm it. Bond and Li's men board the Glory and a wild battle commences. Li Xu Nan is killed by Thackeray. Bond then kills Thackeray and boards the Sampan. He unties Sunni. While Bond disarms the bomb, Sunni applies her karate skills to Tom the albino and knocks him overboard. Bond finally extracts the battery to the timer with a pair of tweezers. The timer stops at 11:59.

Back on board the Peacock, 'M' puts Bond on leave for three months with pay and says that they will arrange a passport for Sunni.

July 1 1997 12:01 PM
A peaceful transition is made between great Britain and China. Hong Kong once again belongs to the People's Republic of China.

CAST

James Bond	007
Mr. Michaels	03
Stephanie Lane	05
Moneypenny	M's secretary
Major Boothroyd	Armourer ('Q')
Derek Plasket	Deceased Admiral/war hero
David March	Hampshire Constabulary
Charles Thorn & Gary Mitchell	Hampshire police officers
Guy Thackeray	CEO, EurAsia Enterprises
Chan Wo	Cook
Bobby Ling	Cook's assistant
John Desmond	Retired CEO, EurAsia Enterprises
Tom, Dick & Harry	Chinese albinos
Young	Aboriginal boy
Helena Marksbury	Bond's secretary
Bill Tanner	Chief of Staff
James Thackeray	Founder, EurAsia Enterprises
Gregory Donaldson	Lawyer
H. K. Woo	M.I.6 Station Head, Hong Kong
Woo Chen	Son
Ling Ling Chat	007 (in Cantonese)
Henry Ho	Manager of Man Wah Restaurant
Wong	Chinese General
Li Xu Nan	Leader/Dragon Wing Society
J. J. Woo	Boat captain
Simon Sinclair	Gen. Manager/EurAsia Enterprises
Sunni Pei	Club hostess
Scarface	Triad hood
Li Chen Tam	Father of Li Xu Nan
Li Wei Tam	Chinese warlord
San Yee On	Chinese Triad
Corinne Bates	EurAsia PR
Johnny Leung	Assistant to General Manager
Captain Charles Plante	Royal Navy
John Hunter	007
Mary Ling	Sunni Pei
Skip Stewart	Local bush pilot
Van Blaricum	Nuclear physicist

THE FACTS OF DEATH

In Los Angeles and Tokyo, dozens of people have died of mysterious symptoms. Halfway around the world in South Cyprus, Greek soldiers have died from an unknown chemical agent. Other soldiers have died from the nerve toxin sarin. Christopher Whitten, an M.I.6 agent in Athens, has died from what was believed to be ricin.

Bond is dispatched to Athens. Together with Niki Mirakos of the Greek National Intelligence Service, they attempt to learn what is behind the deaths. Eventually Bond returns to London and is briefed by 'M' who tells him that the chemical toxins had been smuggled into Athens in frozen sperm.

At a party at Sir Miles Messervy's home Bond meets Ambassador Alfred Hutchinson, escort of Barbara Mowdsley, the 'M' and head of M.I.6. Later that night he dies of repiratory failure from an unknown poison. His attorney Manville Duncan takes over his affairs.

Meanwhile, 'M' has learned that Hutchinson had a home in Austin, Texas and that his son supposedly lives there. Bond is dispatched to Austin to find him.

Bond's old friend Felix Leiter has retired to Austin and acts as an independent investigator. Together they learn that son Charles Hutchinson works as a courier for ReproCare, an infertility clinic owned by a European pharmaceutical firm called Biolinks. It is learned that he transports deadly toxic materials to Europe inside vials of sperm.

Meanwhile, back in Cyprus, a country divided between Turkey and Greece, four Turkish soldiers die at a checkpoint gate from the nerve agent sarin. In the Turkish city of Famagusta more soldiers are killed and foodstuffs in the cargohold of a ship were sprayed with an invisible and deadly germ. Back in London, Bond learns from Leiter that a home in Austin, being kept under surveillance, is owned by one Konstantine Romanos. On the Greek island of Chios, a group called the Decada met. Their leader called himself Pythagoras after the respected sixth-century B.C. scholar of mathematics and philosophy. What the world didn't know was that he was a terrorist. To his following he was known as the Monad, the One.

While in London, 'Q' checks Bond out with the new Walther P99 and the new company car from motor pool, the Jaguar XK8 coupe which has the ability to change colors and heal itself from bullet holes. Once again, Bond is dispatched back to Athens.

Bond enters Athens airport as John Bryce. He carries two Walthers; the PPK and the P99 in a special security briefcase to avoid detection. He is met by Niki Mirakos. She fills him in on Konstantine Romanos.

Romanos is a lecturer at Athens University, a noted author, brilliant mathematician and a refugee from North Cyprus. He is a Greek Cypriot who fled the Turkish invasion. No one knows how he acquired his wealth. He acquired a pharmaceutical firm in Athens called BioLinks. The President is a respected scientist named Milina Papas. Romanos was also head of the new Pythogoreans Society. Romanos usually plays baccarat on Friday nights at the Au Mont Parnes Casino in Athens.
Bond and Niki drive South to Cape Sounion in the Jaguar which 'Q' had shipped over from London. At the Temple of Poseidon police are standing by a body covered by a sheet. It is Charles Hutchinson, murdered by the Decada.

Bond goes to the casino which sits atop Mount Parnitha. He plays baccarat against Romanos, winning nearly five million drachmas from him. At the casino he meets Hera Volopoulos. Bond is "taken" with her. Going to her apartment, they make love, then eat Greek salads, one of which is drugged. Bond is then taken aboard Romano's ship, the Persephone, where he is tortured by Hera Volopoulos. She drags him topside so that authorities in a helicopter above will think everything is normal. Niki is piloting the helicopter. As Hera orders him below again, Bond hits her with a lifebelt which knocks the gun out of her hand. He dives off the stern of the ship. Bond swims to a cruise ship and hangs on to a propeller shaft as the ship proceeds into Santorini harbor.

Bond and Niki are together again at the Santorini police station. The Persephone was met by coast guard ships but Hera Volopoulos had escaped in a gyrocopter from the ship's deck.

All members of the Decada are vegetarians. Bond learns from 'M' that Hutchinson's attorney is a vegetarian. He tells 'M' that Manville Duncan is the one who will try to assassinate the President of the Turkish Republic of North Cyprus and possibly target Istanbul with a cruise missile.

To correspond with this attempt, Hera planned to fire sarin filled cartridges into the gathered crowd. Landing by helicopter, Bond is joined by Darko Kerim, Greek and Turkish soldiers. They rush to the palace where Duncan was prepared to jab the President with a ballpoint pen loaded with a ricin pellet. As the President stumbled out of the way, Bond shot Duncan with the P99.

Bond and Niki learn that the Pershing missile was hidden in a barn on the island of Chios. Fast forward to Anavatos, an ancient village built on a mountain. Bond thinks that Romano would want to place his missile somewhere high up.

Bond leaves Niki and the others behind and starts to climb up the path. He takes his P99 and night vision goggles. Reaching the building at the top of the summit, Bond enters through a ventilation grill. He enters a room and is discovered, disarmed, then taken to a large room which was the missile launching pad. Bond is secured to a table by cuffs on his ankles and wrists.

As Romano prepares to leave the site, Hera points her weapon at him and tells him his leadership has ended now. Melina Papas has a metal briefcase handcuffed to her wrist. She stands aside from the others. Inside the case she has what is called the Decada virus. Once infected with it, everyone that came in contact with it would become infected. Not only is the virus in there, but the only samples of the vaccine and its formula, as well. Hera had sent the virus to medical clinics all over the world, hidden in sperm samples. Hera shoots and kills Romanos.

Hera flips the switch which puts the timer in motion. Bond has four minutes in which to decide which wire to cut to abort the missile. It must be the red, blue or white wire. Suddenly his cuffs release him. Through logic and reasoning, Bond realizes that no decision is the right answer. He breaks the glass and flips the switch. The timer stops. The missile is lifeless. Reaching the surface, a sergeant informs Bond that they can catch them if they hurry.

Bond and the Greek Blackhawk helicopter catches up with the Huey that contains Hera, Melina, and the others. Hera's Huey had already destroyed one of the Greek's Apache helicopters. Now it launched another missile which blows the bottom struts off Bond's Blackhawk. As the Blackhawk is going down, Bond fires the hand-held stinger missile which hit the Huey head-on. It explodes in a fireball and falls 10,000 feet to crash into the sea.

Bond dives beneath the Blackhawk as it too, crashes. He finds Melina Papas' body intact with the briefcase. He hauls her out of the wreckage and brings her to the surface. Suddenly Hera breaks the surface next to him. Bond struggles with her, finally holding her head under water until she releases her grip on him. He then dives to retrieve Melina Papas once again.

Within twenty-four hours, hundreds of vials of the vaccine are on their way to the infected cities.

Two days later, Bond and Niki lay in the king-sized bed in his suite at the Grande Bretagne in Athens. "I guess I should call 'M'," he said.

CAST

James Bond/John Bryce 007
Carl Williams .... Hospital patient
Mrs. Williams .... Housewife
Hiroshi Nagawa .... Patient
Captain Sean Tully .... Naval officer
Ray Winninger .... London investigator
Ashcraft .... London investigator
Christopher Whitten .... M.I.6 Agent, Athens
Niki Mirakos .... Greek Nat'l Intelligence Service
May .... Scottish housekeeper
Sir James Malony .... Staff neurologist
Sir Miles Messervy .... Retired 'M'
Davison .... Former M's butler
Helena Marksbury .... Bond's personal assistant
Barbara Mowdsley 'M' .... Head of M.I.6
Moneypenny .... M's secretary
Major Boothroyd .... Q
Bill Tanner .... M's Chief of Staff
Hargreaves & Grey .... British Admirals
Haley McElwain .... Messervy's daughter
Alfred Hutchinson .... Ambassador
Manville Duncan .... Hutchinson's lawyer
Cynthia .... Duncan's wife
Inspector Howard .... Detective
Charles Hutchinson .... Courier
Manuela Montemayor .... FBI
Felix Leiter .... Retired CIA
Esmeralda .... Leiter's Dalmation
Dr. Ashely Anderson .... CEO/Repro Care
Jack Herman .... Redneck go-fer
Vassilis .... Thug
Tom Zielinski .... Doctor
Melina Papas .... President/Biolinks
James Goodner .... FBI Agent
Bill Johnson .... Rancher
Hera Volopoulos .... The Number Killer
Konstantine Romanos .... Terrorist
Panos Sambrakos .... Greek military police
Dimitris Georgiou .... Greek general
Christina .... Secretary
Nikos .... Romano's hood
Rauf Denktash .... President, Turkish Republic of North Cyprus
Stefan Tempo Kerim .... Station "T" Turkey
Lt. Colonel Gavras .... Greek Secret Service

BOOKS RELATING TO BOND & FLEMING

With the help of a friend, book dealer Percy Muir, Fleming collected "first editions" of books that he considered to be "milestones of human progress." His "first editions" had to be works published after 1800, and of medical, scientific, or social significance. The British government recognized the importance of his collection and during WWII it was stored by the Bodleian Library at Oxford, England. It has since been purchased by the Lilly Library, University of Indiana, Bloomington, where it may be viewed today.

When James Bond and his wife Mary Wickham Bond visited Ian Fleming at *Goldeneye* in Jamaica in 1964, Fleming inscribed his latest book *You Only Live Twice* to them as follows: "To the <u>real</u> James Bond from the thief of his identity, Ian Fleming, February 5, 1964 – A great day!"

This section comprises 164 major publications related to Bond and Fleming. Space does not permit inclusion of the hundreds of magazine articles, book and film reviews, picture books, gum cards, postcards, posters, sheet music and music books, audio cassettes, trivia books, jigsaw puzzles, Corgi toys, and plastic model kits. This material alone would warrant a separate publication.

However, major magazines from the past 32 years which have featured articles on Bond and Fleming would be *Life, Look, Playboy, American Film, Ladies Home Journal, GQ, Film Review, Peoples Weekly, Photoplay, Revue, Starlog,* and *TV Guide.*

You can consult the *Reader's Guide to Periodic Literature* in a library to help you find the appropriate issue dates.

Ian Fleming: The Man Behind James Bond by Andrew Lycett. Turner Published 1998.
Ian Fleming: A Catalogue of a Collection by Ian Campbell, Comersgate Ltd 1978
James Bond Bedside Companion by Raymond Benson. Dodd, Mead, 1984.
The Official James Bond Movie Book by Sally Hibben. Crown, 1987.
Ian Fleming: The Spy Who Came In With the Gold by Henry A. Zeiger, Duell, Sloan &Pearce, 1965.
Ian Fleming, 28th May, 1908 – 12 August, 1964 by William Plomer. Address given at the memorial service September 15, 1964. Privately printed, 1964. Westerham Press.
The Life of Ian Fleming by John Pearson. Jonathan Cape, Ltd. 1966.
Ian Fleming: Man With the Golden Pen by Eleanor and Dennis Pelrine, Swan Paperback, 1966.
FL*M*NG, I*N, Alligator A Harvard Lampoon parody, 1962.
You Only Live Once: Memories of Ian Fleming by Ivar Bryce, Weidenfeld & Nicolson, 1975. First American edition, 1984, University Publications of America, Inc. Frederick, Maryland.
The James Bond Dossier by Kingsley Amis. Jonathan Cape, Ltd. 1965. (US) New American Library.
The Bond Affair by Oreste Del Buono and Umberto Eco, Macdonald, 1966.
For Bond Lovers Only by Sheldon Lane. Dell, 1965.
James Bond: The Authorized Biography of 007 by John Pearson. Sidgwick & Jackson, 1973. (US) Signet.
007 James Bond: A Report by O.F. Snelling. Neville Spearman, Holland Press, 1964. (U.S.) Signet.
The Book of Bond, or Every Man His Own 007 by Lt. Col. William "Bill" Tanner (Pseudonym for Kingsley Amis) Jonathan Cape, Ltd. 1965. (U.S.)Viking Press.
How 007 Got His Name by Mary Wickham Bond. Collins, 1966. [1]
James Bond in the Cinema by John Brosnan. The Tantivy Press, 1972. (U.S.) A.S. Barnes. Revised Second Edition 1981.
The James Bond Films by Steven Jay Rubin. Arlington House, 1981. Crown Publishers, 1983.

Grimm Fairy Tales for Adults by Joel Wells. Macdonald, 1966. Contains an Ian Fleming Parody.

Ian Fleming's Incredible Creation by Paul Anthony and Jacquelyn Friedman, 1965.

For Bond Lovers Only Dell, U.S. Pictures, Girls, Guns. Words by Ian Fleming, Connery, Chandler, Deighton, 1965.

OMNIBUS EDITIONS

A James Bond Omnibus Cape, 1973. Contains *Live & Let Die, Diamonds are Forever*, and *Dr. No*.

FLEMING'S ONLY SIGNED LIMITED EDITION

On Her Majesty's Secret Service Cape, 1963. Edition of 250 numbered copies printed on special paper with frontispiece portrait of Fleming by his close friend Amherst Villiers and signed by Fleming.

BOOKS CONTAINING INTRODUCTIONS OR FORWARDS BY IAN FLEMING

Airline Detective by Donald Fish. Collins, 1962. Introduction by Ian Fleming.

All Night at Mr. Stanyhurst's by Hugh Edwards. Macmillan, 1963. Introduction by Ian Fleming.

The Seven Deadly Sins. Morrow, 1962. Foreward by Ian Fleming.

The Education of a Poker Player. London: Cape, 1959 by Herbert O. Yardley. Introduction by Ian Fleming.

Room 3603 by H.M. Hyde. Straus, 1963. Notes: Foreward by Ian Fleming.

Ian Fleming Introduces Jamaica (I) Andre Deutsch, 1965 & Hawthorn, 1965.

Pleasure Island: Book of Jamaica. Kingston, The Arawak Press, 1961. Edited by Ester Chapman, page 150 mentions Ian Flemings home in Jamaica.

BOOKS CONTAINING ARTICLES BY, SHORT STORIES OR EXCERPTS FROM NOVELS BY IAN FLEMING.

Kemsley Manual of Journalism. Cassell, 1950. "Foreign News" by Ian Fleming.

Holiday Magazine Book of the World's Fine Food. Simon & Schuster, 1960. "London's Best Dining" by Ian Fleming.

The Ivory Hammer: The Year at Sotheby's 219th Season 1962-1963 Holt Rhinehart & Winston, 1964. The James Bond story "The Property of a Lady" concerning an auction at Sotheby's was specially written for this book.

The Concise Encyclopedia of Crime and Criminals Edited by Sir Harold Scott. Andre Deutsch, 1961. Entry on Diamond Smuggling by Ian Fleming.

Encore Michael Joseph, 1962. Contains an excerpt from Thrilling Cities "My Monte Carlo System."

Encore: The Second Year Michael Joseph, 1963. Contains "A Golfing Nightmare" by Fleming and "The Terrible Dr. No" by Raymond Chandler.

The Twelfth Anniversary Playboy Reader Souvenir Press, 1965. Contains the James Bond short story "The Hildebrand Rarity."

House & Garden Weekend Book Conde Nast, 1969. Contains the piece "Jamaica" by Ian Fleming.

Best Gambling Stories edited by John Welcome. Faber, 1961. Contains "A Game of Bridge at Blades."

Best Motoring Stories edited by John Welcome. Faber, 1959. Contains "James Bond Drives."

To Catch a Spy edited by Eric Ambler. Atheneum, 1965. Contains "From A View To A Kill."

TWO UNIQUE BOOKS GIVEN BY IAN FLEMING TO MAUD RUSSELL, A FAMOUS SOCIETY HOSTESS OF THE 1930'S / 1940'S

On the Making of Gardens. An essay by Sir George Sitwell, introduced by Sir Osbert Sitwell with decorations by John Piper. A limited edition of 1000 copies, published by the Dropmore Press in 1949. No. 212 is inscribed "M" with love for Christmas 1949, "I."

Breviary of Love by Jean Aurelie Grivolin. Constable & Co., Ltd., London, 1938. Inscribed "Maud from I. 1938".

OTHER BOOKS RELATING TO BOND & FLEMING

Honor Blackman's Book of Self Defense by Honor Blackman. Andre Deutsch, 1965.

The Letters of Anne Fleming edited by Mark Amory. William Collins & Co., 1985.

Nobody Does it Better by Bob Simmons, with Kenneth Passingham. Javelin, 1987. James Bond movie stuntman.

The Complete Adventures of James Bond. Book One: *The Living Daylights & The Man With The Golden Gun.* Book Two: *Octopussy & The Hildebrand Rarity.* Titan Books, 1987. (Reprints of the Daily Express comic strips)

Keeping the British End Up by Roger Ryan & Martin Sterling. Coronet, 1987. (James Bond trivia)

Ian Fleming: The Fantastic 007 Man by Richard Gant. Lancer, 1966.

Chitty-Chitty-Bang-Bang by Ian Fleming. Jonathan Cape, Ltd. 1961. Random House, 1964. Illustrations by John Birningham.

The Noel Coward Diaries by Graham, Payne & Sheridon Morley, editors, Brown & Company, 1982. Note: Several references to Anne and Ian Fleming.

The Diamond Smugglers by Ian Fleming. Glidrose Productions, 1957. Macmillan, 1964.

Thrilling Cities by Ian Fleming. Cape, 1963.

State of Excitement: Impressions of Kuwait by Ian Fleming, 1960. Only one bound copy. Lilly Library, Indiana University.

James Bond: A Celebration by Peter Haining. W.H. Allen, 1987.

The Devil With James Bond! by Ann S. Boyd. John Knox Press, 1967.

James Bond Diary by Roger Moore. Fawcett, 1973.

Loxfinger by Sol Weinstein. Pocket Books, 1965. A thrilling adventure of Hebrew Agent OY-OY-7 (a parody).

Matzohball by Sol Weinstein, 1966. New York: Pocket.

On The Secret Service Of His Majesty, The Queen by Sol Weinstein, 1966. New York: Pocket.

You Only Live Until You Die by Sol Weinstein, 1968. New York: Trident.

Who's Who in Spy Fiction by Donald McCormick. Elm Tree Books, 1977. Ian Fleming is featured on pages 72 – 76.

Roger Moore by Paul Donovan. London, 1983.

Roger Moore: A Biography by Roy Moseley with Philip Martin. Masketer, London, 1985.

Roger Moore as James Bond 007. Pan, 1973.

Sean Connery by Michael Feeney Callan. Stein & Day, 1983.

The Liquidator by John Gardner. Viking, 1964. A Bond parody.

To James Bond With Love by Mary Wickham Bond. Sutter House, 1980.

The Second Oldest Profession by Phillip Knightley. Andre Deutsch Ltd. (UK) 1986., W.W. Norton & Co. (US) 1987, Viking Penquin Inc. (US) 1988. (Spies & Spying In The Twentieth Century).

The Book of Spies and Secret Agents by Janet Pate. Galley Press, 1978. Contains a chapter on James Bond.

My Name is Bond A pictorial survey of Sean Connery. Argus, 1983.

Best Secret Service Stories Edited by J. Welcome. Contains "Mister Big." London: Faber, 1960.

003 1/2: The Adventures of James Bond Jr. New York: Random House, 1968.

The James Bond Man: The Films of Sean Connery by Andrew Rissik. London: Elm Tree, 1983.

Heroes of the Movies: Sean Connery by Emma Andrews. Surrey: LSP, 1982.

Sean Connery A picture book in Japanese.

Sean Connery: A Biography by Kenneth Passingham. London: Sidgwick & Jackson, 1983.

The Company We Kept by Barbara Kaye (Mrs. Percy Muir) London: Sidgwick & Jackson, 1983.

"Ian Fleming: A Consideration of the Myth" in *The Rare Book Game* by George Sims. Philadelphia: Holmes, 1985.

Playboy Interviews Includes interview with Ian Fleming. Chicago: Playboy, 1967.

Jonathan Cape Publisher by Michael S. Howard. London: Cape, 1971.

The Manipulator by Diane Cilento. London: Hodder, 1967. Author is Sean Connery's first wife. Bondiana. Connery designed jacket and book is dedicated to him.

Birds of the West Indies by James Bond. NY: Houghton, 1985.

Die James Bond Filme by Erich Kocian. Wilhelm Heyne Verlag, Munich, 1991.

The Life of Raymond Chandler E.P. Dutton & Co., New York, 1976 by Frank McShane. Six page references to Ian Fleming.

True Britt Autobiography of Britt Ekland. Prentice Hall, 1980. By Britt Ekland. Bond girl of *The Man With The Golden Gun.*

Augustus John Autobiography. Cape, London, 1975. Augustus John printed a portrait of Mrs. Valentine Fleming when she was in her thirties. He made a drawing of her son, Ian, in 1942.

Blind in One Ear. Autobiography of Patrick Macnee. Toronto. Doubleday. Canada Ltd., Toronto, 1988. Co–star of *A View To A Kill.* Several page references to Roger Moore and the movie.

Majesty by Robert Lacey, Harcourt Brace Jovanonich, 1977. One page referrence to Ian Fleming.

Somerset Maugham Cape, London 1980. Many references to Ann and Ian Fleming.

The Sign of the Fish by Peter Quenell, Collins, London, 1960. Dedicated "To My Friend at Goldeneye."

The Sixth Column by Peter Fleming, London. Tondem Books, 1967. Dedicated "To my brother Ian."

Symbolizing America by Herve Varenne, editor. University of Nebraska Press, 1986. Contains "The Story of Bond" by Lee Drummond (pp. 65-89)

The Themes of 007: James Bond's Greatest Hits by David C. Olsen, editor. Columbia Pictures Publications, 1986.

Thrillers by Jerry Palmer. St. Martin's Press, 1979.

The Traveller's Tree by Patrick Leigh Fermor. Penguin Books, 1984. Note: Ian Fleming uses extracts from chapters 10 & 11 in Live & Let Die.

Triple'O'Seven by Ian R. Jamieson, Talonbooks, 1985. (Canada) Same title, same author, published by Mysterious Press, 1990. Completely different story.

United Artists: The Company that Changed the Film Industry by Tino Balio. University of Wisconsin Press, 1987. Note: "007: A License To Print Money" (chap 8).

Voices From the Sixties by Pierre Berton. Doubleday, 1967. Note: "Mrs. Ian Fleming: Widow to a Legend" interview (pp. 177-187).

What Became of Jane Austen? And Other Questions by Kingsley Amis. HBJ, 1970. Note: "A New James Bond" (pp. 65-77).

You Bet Your Life by Stuart Kaminsky. Charter, 1980.

The Primal Screen by Andrew Farris Simon & Schuster, 1973. Notes: "The 'Thriller' Thunderball" (pp. 180-182)

Private Lives of Private Eyes by Otto Penzler. Grosset & Dunlap, 1977. Note: Bond (pp. 17-23)

Reruns: 50 Memorable Films by Bosley Crowther. G.P. Putnam's sons, 1978. Note: "From Russia With Love" (pp. 175-178)

Roger Moore as James Bond 007 by Roger Moore. Pan, 1973.

Scarne on Cards by John Scarne. Crown, 1954. Note: "Bond's Bookshelf."

Sean Connery by Kenneth Passingham. St. Martin's Press, 1983.

Sean Connery: From 007 to Hollywood Icon by Andrew Yule. Donald I. Fine, 1992.

Secret Agents in Fiction by Lars Ole Sauerberg. St. Martins Press, 1984.

Selected Letters by Raymond Chandler by Frank McShane. Columbia University Press, 1981. Note: Contains two letters to Ian Fleming (pp. 396-398).

Snobbery With Violence by Calin Watson. St. Martins Press, 1971. Note: License To Kill (Ch. 18).

The Special Branch (The British Spy Novel, 1890-1980) by LeRoy L. Panek. Bowling Green University Popular Press, 1981. Note: Ian Fleming (pp. 201-219)

James Bond and Moonraker by Christopher Wood. Triad Panther, 1979.

The James Bond Girls by Graham Rye. Mallard Press, 1989.

The James Bond Story Book of the Movie A View to a Kill by Judy Alexander. Grosset & Dunlap, 1985.

The James Bond Trivia Quiz Book by Philip Gurin. Priam Books, 1984.

James Bond's World of Values by Lycurgus M. Starkey Jr. Abingdon Press, 1977.

The Letters of Evelyn Waugh by Mark Amory, editor. Ticknor & Fields, 1980.

The Life of Noel Coward by Cole Lesley. Penguin, 1988.

Literary Agents: The Novelist as Spy by Anthoney Masters. Basil Blackwell, 1987. Note: "Ian Fleming The Dashing Spy" (chapter 7) with other references to Fleming / Bond scattered.

The Making of Licence to Kill by Sally Hibbin. Harper & Row, 1989.

The Man Who Was 'M': The Life of Maxwell Knight by Anthony Masters. Basil Blackwell, 1987.

The Masks of Hate by David Holbrooks. Pergamon Press, 1972. Note: Includes a lengthy Freudian analysis of the novel *Goldfinger.*

Mass Culture Revisited by Bernard Rosenberg and David Manning White, editors. Von Nostrond Reinhold Co., 1971. Notes: "James Bond Unmasked" by Mordecai Richler (pp. 341-355).

Movies From the Mansion: A History of Pinewood Studios by George Perry. Elm Tree Books, 1982. Note: (pp. 7, 143, 147, 149, 175).

The Official 007 Fact File by Richard Holliss, Hamlyn, 1989.

The Official James Bond Movie Book by Sally Hibben. Hamlyn, 1987.

The Official James Bond Movie Poster Book by Sally Hibben. Hamlyn, 1987.

The Orient Express by Michael Barslay. Stein & Day, 1967. Note: References to Ian Fleming and From Russia With Love.

Peter Fleming: A Biography by Duff Hart-Davis. Jonathan Cape, 1974.

Playboy Interviews Playboy Press, 1967. Note: Playboy interviews Ian Fleming. (pp.14-29).

Previous Convictions by Cyril Connolly. Harper & Row, 1963. Note:"Bond Strikes Camp" (pp. 317-354).

The Evening Colonade by Cyril Connolly. HBJ, 1975. Note: Ian Fleming (pp 350-353).

Fifty Grand Movies of the 1960s and 1970s by David Zinman. Crown, 1986. Note: *Goldfinger* (pp 75-78)

Great Spy Stories by Allen Dulles, editor Castle, 1987. Note: Contains an excerpt from From Russia With Love (pp 364-369).

Hess by Roger Manvell and Heinrich Frenkel. Mac Gibbon and Kee, 1971. Note: mention of Ian Fleming and a plan to lure Hess to Britain by means of a fake horoscope (pp. 93-94).

A History of the British Secret Service by Richard Deacon. Taplinger Publishing Co., 1969.

Ian Fleming by Bruce A. Rosenberg and Ann Harleman Stewart. Twayne, 1989.

The Illustrated James Bond 007 by Richard Schenkman, editor James Bond 007 Fan Club, 1981.

The Incredible World of 007 by Lee Pfeiffer and Philip Lisa. Citadel Press.

James Bond 007 Tarot Book by Stuart R. Kaplan. U.S. Games Systems, 1973.

Anatomy of the Spy Thriller by Bruce Merry. McGill – Queen's University Press, 1977.

The Autobiography of William Plomer Jonathan Cape, 1975. Note: Mention in the postscript by Simon Nowell-Smith. (p. 437)

Bonded Fleming: A James Bond Omnibus by Ian Fleming. Viking Press, 1966. Note: An anthology containing *Thunderball, For Your Eyes Only* and *The Spy Who Loved Me.*

The Complete James Bond Movie Encyclopedia by Steven Jay Rubin. Contemporary Books, 1990.

Counterpoint by Roy Nequist, Simon & Schuster, 1964. Note: Interview with Ian Fleming (pp. 209-216).

Cunning Exiles: Studies of Modern Prose Writers by Don Anderson and Stephen Knight, editors Angus and Robertson, 1974. Note: Contains "James Bond: A Phenomenon of Some Importance," by Bernard Martin (pp. 218-230).

Deeper Into Movies by Pauline Kael. Little Brown & Co. 1973. Note: Film reviews of *On Her Majesty's Secret Service* (p. 85) and *Diamonds Are Forever.* (p. 388)

The Dynamics of Creation by Anthony Storr. Kingsport Press, 1972. Note: (pp. 17-21).

The Egoists by Oriana Fallaci. Henry Regnery Co., 1963. Note: "Sean Connery: The Superman" (pp. 19-36) which includes an interview with Sean Connery.

Entertainment Celebrity Register by Earl Blackwell. Visible Ink, 1991. Note: Short Biographies of Sean Connery, Roger Moore and Timothy Dalton.

Adrian Turner on Goldfinger Bloomsbury Movie Guide No.2 by Adrian Turner, Bloomsbury USA, 1999.

High Time to Kill by Raymond Benson, Hodder & Stoughton, 1999.

James Bond's Britain: A Guide to Locations by Gary Giblin, Daleon Enterprises, 1999.

Spy Toys: A History and Price Guide by Cramer Burks, Windmill Press, 1998.

The Bond Files: The Only Complete Guide to James Bond in Books, Films, TV and Comics by Andy Lane and Paul Simpson, 1998.

The Essential 007 by Lee Pfeiffer and Dave Worrall, Boxtree/Macmillan, 1998.

The Ultimate James Bond Trivia Book: A Citadel Quiz Book by Michael Lewis and Lee Pfeiffer, Citadel, 1984.

Bond and Beyond: The Political Career of a Popular Hero by Tony Bennetts, and Janet Wollacott, Houndmills (Basingstoke): Macmillan, and Methuen, 1987.

Diamonds Are Forever: A Files Magazine Update on the James Bond Files by John Peel, New Media Books.

From Russia With Love by Glenn A. Magee, New Media Books.

Goldfinger by Glenn A. Magee, New Media Books.

Live and Let Die, (The James Bond Files) by John Peel, New Media Books.

You Only Live Twice, (The James Bond Files) by John Peel, New Media Books.
Kiss Kiss, Bang Bang: The Unofficial James Bond Film Companion by Alan Barnes, Marcus Hearn, 1998.
The Making of Tomorrow Never Dies by Garth Pearce, 1997.
Goldeneye by Garth Pearce, 1995

BRITISH SECRET SERVICE (M.I.6)

HEADQUARTERS:
M.I.6 has moved its headquarters. It was a tall grey building overlooking Regent's Park. It is now located on the bank of the River Thames at Vauxhall.

BASEMENT:
Auto parking, electronic firing range, computer room.

LOBBY: (DIRECTORY)
1) Radio Tests, Ltd., 2) Transworld Consortium, 3) Delaney Bros. 1940 Ltd., 4) The Omnium Corp., 5) Enquires (Miss E. Twining, O.B.E.).

FOURTH FLOOR:
James Bond's office. Bond's personal secretaries: Loelia Ponsonby, Mary Goodnight, and new Secretary Chastity Vain (*Seafire*). Helena Marksbury, personal assistant (*The Facts of Death.*)

TOP FLOOR:
"M's" office, communications and a team of operators who are in constant touch with station heads throughout the world.

ROOF:
Three squat masts for one of the most powerful transmitters in England.

BROSNAN, PIERCE (BOND NUMBER FIVE)

Born May 16, 1951 in County Meath, Ireland. Moved with his family to London at age 11. Worked as a commercial illustrator and cab driver. Trained at the London Drama Center. Appeared professionally for the first time in 1976. Made his screen debut in 1980. Appeared in the TV series 'Remington Steele.' In 1986 Brosnan was announced as the next James Bond, but NBC would not let him out of his contract. His Australian born late wife Cassandra Harris appeared with Roger Moore in *For Your Eyes Only*.

TELEVISION
1980	Murphy's Stroke (British), The Professionals: Blood Sports, Hommer House of Heros; Carpathian Eagle.
1981	The Mannions of America
1982-1987	Remington Steele (91 episodes)
1982	Nancy Astor (BBC)
1984	Nancy Astor (PBS) Masterpiece Theatre
1988	Noble House

1989	Around the World in 80 Days, The Heist
1991	Murder 101, Victim of Love, Robin Hood (CBS)
1992	Great Golf Courses of the World (Ireland, Narrator) Live Wire, Running Wilde (NBC), Heartbreak Radio)
1993	Death Train, Entangled, The Broken Claw (TNT)
1994	Don't Talk To Strangers
1995	Night Watch (aka Detonator II: Nightwatch)

FILMOGRAPHY

1980	*The Long Good Friday, The Mirror Crack'd*
1986	*Nomads*
1987	*The Fourth Protocol*
1988	*Taffin, The Deceivers*
1990	*Mister Johnson*
1992	*Live Wire, The Lawnmower Man*
1993	*Entangled, Mrs. Doubtfire*
1994	*Love Affair*
1995	*Robinson Crusoe* (Originally filmed for TV)
1995	*Goldeneye* (as James Bond)
1997	*The Mirror Has Two Faces, Mars Attacks!, Dante's Peak, Tomorrow Never Dies*
1998	*The Nephew, The Thomas Crown Affair*
1999	*The World is Not Enough*

Pierce Brosnan purchased Ian Fleming's typewriter upon which he had written the original novels from Christie's at auction for 52,500 pounds sterling.

BROWN, ROBERT

Born 1918 in England. Since the death of Bernard Lee in 1981, Brown has portrayed Admiral Sir Miles Messervy, better known as 'M' in the James Bond films.

FILMOGRAPHY

1955	*Helen of Troy*
1956	*A Hill in Korea*
1957	*Campbell's Kingdom*
1959	*Ben Hur*
1960	*Sink the Bismarck*
1964	*The Mask of the Red Death*
1966	*One Million Years B.C.*
1971	*Private Road*
1977	*The Spy Who Loved Me* (Admiral Hargreaves)
1983	*Octopussy*
1985	*A View to a Kill*
1987	*The Living Daylights*
1989	*License to Kill*

James Bond (Sean Connery) and Domino Petachi (Kim Basinger) in a publicity photo from *Never Say Never Again*. (Rex USA Ltd.)

(Brown, Robert) continued

TELEVISION
Voyage of the Damned, The Forgotton Story (HTV), Ivanhoe (series), King John (BBC), The Move After Checkmate (Anglis), Cost of Living (Yorkshire), General Hospital (ATV), The Winds of War, Lion in the Desert, Mohammed, Messenger Of God.

THEATRE
Romeo & Juliet, Seasons Greetings, Last Summer in Chulminsk, Beethoven's Tenth with Peter Ustinov

CONNERY, SEAN (BOND NUMBER ONE)

Born Thomas Connery on August 25, 1930 in Edinburgh, Scotland.

At the age of nine he had his first job. Later he worked delivering milk. At sixteen, he joined the Royal Navy as a gunner and served three years before being discharged with an ulcer. In the years following he worked as a milkman, truck driver, cement mixer, bricklayer, steel bender, printer's devil, lifeguard, and coffin polisher.

His first break came as a dancer in the chorus line of South Pacific in 1950. He toured with South Pacific for eighteen months before joining a small repertory company. In 1956 he was given the leading role in a live television production, Requiem for a Heavyweight. This was followed by Anna Karenina opposite Claire Bloom and the BBC series Age of Kings. His first significant film role came in 1956 in No Road Back. In 1957 he signed a contract with Twentieth Century-Fox.

Connery is an experienced golfer, swimmer, and tennis player. He is happily married to his second wife, Micheline, whom he met during a golf tournament. They reside primarily in Marbella, Spain or the Bahamas, leading quiet, uncomplicated lives. Connery also has a residence in Scotland and an apartment in Hollywood.

FILMOGRAPHY
1954 .... *Lilacs in the Spring* (Bit)
1957 .... *No Road Back, Hell Drivers, Action Of The Tiger, Timelock*
1958 .... *Another Time, Another Place, A Night To Remember*
1959 .... *Darby O'Gill And The Little People, Tarzan's Greatest Adventure*
1961 .... *The Frightened City, Operation Snafu* (aka *On The Fiddle*)
1962 .... *The Longest Day, Dr. No*[1]
1963 .... *From Russia With Love*
1964 .... *Marnie, Women of Straw, Goldfinger*
1965 .... *The Hill, Thunderball*
1966 .... *A Fine Madness*
1967 .... *You Only Live Twice*
1968 .... *Shalako*
1970 .... *The Molly Maguires*
1971 .... *The Red Tent, The Anderson Tapes, Diamonds Are Forever*[2]
1973 .... *The Offence*
1974 .... *Zardoz, Murder on the Orient Express*
1975 .... *Ransom, The Wind and the Lion, The Man Who Would be King*

1976 .... *Robin and Marian, The Next Man*
1977 .... *A Bridge Too Far*
1979 .... *The Great Train Robbery, Meteor, Cuba*
1981 .... *Outland, Time Bandits*
1982 .... *Wrong is Right, Five Days One Summer*
1983 .... *Never Say Never Again*[3]
1984 .... *Sword of the Valiant*
1986 .... *Highlander, The Name Of The Rose*[4]
1987 .... *The Untouchables*[5]
1988 .... *The Presidio, Memories of Me*
1989 .... *Indiana Jones & The Last Crusade, Family Business*
1990 .... *The Hunt for Red October, The Russia House*
1991 .... *Highlander II, Robin Hood: Prince of Thieves*
1992 .... *Medicine Man*
1993 .... *Rising Sun*
1994 .... *A Good Man In Africa*
1995 .... *Just Cause, First Knight*
1996 .... *The Rock, Dragonheart*
1998 .... *The Avengers*
1999 .... *Entrapment, Playing by Heart*

[1] Salary for *Dr. No* was $16,500.
[2] Salary for *Diamonds Are Forever* was $1.25 million plus.
[3] Salary for *Never Say Never Again* purportedly $3 million.
[4] British Academy Award, Best Actor, *The Name of The Rose*.
[5] April 11, 1988. Academy Award, Best Supporting Actor. February 22, 1984, Man of the Year award from Harvard Hasty Pudding Theatrical Club.

Connery's favorite Bond film was *From Russia With Love*.

DAILY GLEANER NEWSPAPER, THE

Kingston, Jamaica. Established 1834. "The Gleaner" has been featured in four Bond novels, two short stories, and one film.

NOVELS

Casino Royale   *Dr. No*
The Man With the Golden Gun   *Zero Minus Ten*

SHORT STORIES

Octopussy   *For Your Eyes Only*

FILM

Dr. No

DALTON, TIMOTHY (BOND NUMBER FOUR)

Born in Colwyn Bay, Wales, March 21, 1944. A leading man of British stage and screen.

Dalton was educated in Manchester, Bellper and the Royal Academy of Dramatic Art. A former member of the Bellper Players Community Theatre and the National Youth Theatre. In 1964 he made his professional debut in Shakespear's Coriolanus at the Queen's Theatre.

His theatrical productions include: Little Malcolm and His Struggle Against the Eunichs, Richard II, As You Like It, Romeo & Juliet, Love's Labour's Lost, Black Comedy, The Lunatic, The Lover & The Poet, Henry IV, Anthony & Cleopatra, The Taming of the Shrew, Touch of the Poet.

Dalton's television credits include Mistral's Daughter, the Master of Ballantrae, Sins, Florence Nightingale, and the mini – series, Jane Eyre, Candida, Five Finger Exercise.

FILMOGRAPHY

1968 .... *The Lion in Winter*
1970 .... *Cromwell, Wuthering Heights*
1971 .... *Mary Queen of Scots*
1972 .... *Lady Caroline Lamb*
1975 .... *Permission to Kill*
1976 .... *El Hombre*
1978 .... *Sexette*
1979 .... *Agatha*
1980 .... *Flash Gordon, Centennial*
1981 .... *Chanel, Solitaire*
1985 .... *The Doctor and the Devils*
1987 .... *The Living Daylights*
1988 .... *Hawks*
1989 .... *Brenda Starr, License to Kill*
1990 .... *The King's Whore*
1991 .... *The Rocketeer*
1994 .... *Scarlett* (CBS mini-series) as Rhett Butler, *Naked in New York*

DENCH, DAME JUDI

Born December 9, 1934 in York, England. Educated at the The Mount School in York, and the Central School Speech Training and Dramatic Art. Leading lady and supporting player of British stage, screen, and television. She made her stage debut as Ophelia in a Old Vic Liverpool production of *Hamlet* and has since been highly regarded for her performances in Shakespeare and the classic repertoire. Her screen appearances have been few but memorable. She won British Film Academy Awards for *Four in the Morning* (1965) and *Handful of Dust* (1988).

Dench has portrayed Barbara Mowdsley, better known as 'M' in the James Bond films. She was awarded the Order of the British Empire (OBE) by Queen Elizabeth and is a Dame of the English Theatre. In 1999, she received the Best Supporting Actress Oscar for *Shakepeare in Love*.

FILMOGRAPHY

1964 .... *The Third Secret*
1965 .... *Four in the Morning, A Study in Terror*
1966 .... *He Who Rides a Tiger*
1968 .... *A Midsummer Night's Dream*

1973 .... *Luther*
1974 .... *Dead Cert*
1985 .... *Wetherby*
1986 .... *A Room With a View*
1987 .... *Charing Cross Road*
1988 .... *A Handful of Dust*
1989 .... *Henry V*
1995 .... *Jack and Sarah, Goldeneye*
1998 .... *Tomorrow Never Dies, Tea With Mussolini*

1981-1984 .... Television series: A Fine Romance

DESIGNERS: MAIN CREDITS

MAURICE BINDER:

Dr. No

You Only Live Twice

Diamonds Are Forever

The Man With the Golden Gun

Moonraker

Octopussy

The Living Daylights

Goldeneye

Thunderball

On Her Majesty's Secret Service

Live & Let Die

The Spy Who Loved Me

For Your Eyes Only

A View to a Kill

License to Kill

ROBERT BROWNJOHN:

From Russia With Love

Goldfinger

LESLIE DAILY

Never Say Never Again

DANIEL KLEINMAN

Tomorrow Never Dies

PRODUCTION DESIGNERS

KEN ADAM

Dr. No

Thunderball

Diamonds Are Forever

Moonraker

Goldfinger

You Only Live Twice

The Spy Who Loved Me

SYD CAIN

From Russia With Love

Live & Let Die

On Her Majesty's Secret Service

ALLAN CAMERON

Tomorrow Never Dies

PETER MURTON
The Man With the Golden Gun

STEPHEN GRIMES & PHILIP HARRISON
Never Say Never Again

PETER LAMONT
For Your Eyes Only	*Octopussy*
A View to a Kill	*The Living Daylights*
License to Kill	*Goldeneye*

DIRECTORS

TERRENCE YOUNG
Dr. No	*From Russia With Love*
Thunderball	

GUY HAMILTON
Goldfinger	*Diamonds Are Forever*
Live & Let Die	*The Man With the Golden Gun*

LEWIS GILBERT
You Only Live Twice	*The Spy Who Loved Me*
Moonraker	

JOHN GLEN
For Your Eyes Only	*Octopussy*
A View to a Kill	*The Living Daylights*
License to Kill	

PETER HUNT
On Her Majesty's Secret Service

IRVIN KERSHNER
Never Say Never Again

MARTIN CAMPBELL
Goldeneye

ROGER SPOTTISWOODE
Tomorrow Never Dies

DIRECTORS (SHORT BIOGRAPHIES)

JOHN GLEN
Born May 15, 1932, in Sunbury on Thames, England. Directed *For Your Eyes Only*, 1981, *Octopussy*, 1983, *A View To A Kill*, 1985, *The Living Daylights*, 1987, and *License To Kill*, 1989.

GUY HAMILTON

Born September, 1922 in Paris to English parents. Served with the British Navy in WWII. Worked as an assistant director in the noted post-war productions of *The African Queen* and *The Third Man*. Considered one of England's most proficient craftsmen. Directed four Bond films.

PETER HUNT

Born in 1928 in London. Educated in art and music. Entered the film industry in 1947 as a "clapper" boy. Became a film editor in the 50s and edited many of the James Bond films in the 60s. Directed *On Her Majesty's Secret Service*, 1969.

IRVIN KERSHNER

Born April 29, 1923 in Philadelphia, Pennsylvania. Educated in film at USC. During the 50s he made documentaries for the U.S. Information Service and later for TV. In 1958 he directed his first low-budget film and in the 60s established himself as a universally talented director. Directed *Star Wars*, 1979, *The Empire Strikes Back*, 1980, and *Never Say Never Again*, 1983.

TERRENCE YOUNG

Born June 20, 1915 in Shanghai, China to British parents. Educated at Cambridge. Began his film career in 1936 as a screenwriter and after WWII service he began directing in 1948. He came to world prominence with his talents on the Bond films, directing three of them.

EQUIPMENT USED BY BOND (BOOK & FILM)

DR. NO
Silencer, Geiger counter.

FROM RUSSIA WITH LOVE
From the novel: Converted Swaine & Adeney Attache Case. Contained 1) 50 rounds of .25 cal. ammunition, 2) two flat throwing knives from Wilkinson, 3) hidden compartment in handle for a cyanide pill, 4) silencer packed inside a tube of Palmolive shaving cream, 5) 50 gold sovereigns.

From the film. Contained 1) AR-7 Survival rifle, 2) 40 spare rounds of ammunition, 3) infrared telescopic sight, 4) 50 gold sovereigns, 5) throwing daggers, 6) tear gas cannister in a talcum powder container.

Chamois holster: This is the holster in which Bond carried his .25 cal. Beretta for years. However, on this assignment his Beretta caught in the holster and nearly cost him his life. Bond also used a flare pistol.

GOLDFINGER
Echo Tracer: Transmits a short signal, frequently, when it receives a radio beam with a specific frequency. This tracer was placed in the boot of Goldfinger's Rolls – Royce and tracked by Bond on a viewing screen installed in the Aston Martin. Identigraph machine: Illustrate's a person's facial features as they are described. Other equipment: Gun that fires a grappling hook, plastic explosive, detonator and timing device. Homing device in heel of shoe. M3 Leica camera, MC exposure meter, K2 filter & flash holder.

THUNDERBALL

Rocket Jet Pack: Bond made a miraculous escape with this one-man jet pack that propelled him over the wall and rooftops to his waiting Aston Martin DB5. Built by Bell for the US army. Other equipment: Steel scuba tanks. Waterproof Rolex watch with built-in Geiger counter. Underwater camera with infrared film. Radio-active homing device pill. Flare pistol. Miniaturized breathing apparatus. Dye container.

YOU ONLY LIVE TWICE

Pencil flashlight. Small steel file. X-Ray Safecracker. Gyro-copter "Little Nellie". Helmet with camera.

ON HER MAJESTY'S SECRET SERVICE:

Syncraphone: A light, plastic radio receiver the size of a pocket watch. Can be beeped on receiver in 10 mile range. Automatic Safecracker: Unlike the X-Ray Safecracker which is the size of a pocket calculator, this equipment is rather odd in appearance and very bulky. Bond had to move this unit with a crane and a bucket. Other equipment: Radioactive lint. Aston-Martin DB6. Computerized safe-opener and copying machine.

DIAMONDS ARE FOREVER

A giant, silver plastic ball. Schermuly Pains-Wessex Speedline, a rocket powered line-throwing device which contains 891' of rope. Simulated fingerprints developed by 'Q' which can be applied and removed like a Band-aid. Finger trap. Fire extinguisher.

OCTOPUSSY

Acid pen: Dispenses a stream of acid capable of cutting through iron bars and sheet metal. 'Q' included a microphone and receiver in this pen so Bond could pick up transmissions and conversations from the Faberge egg. Avram tracer: When planted in the Faberge egg, Bond was able to follow its whereabouts during this mission. Bond also used a wristwatch with a miniature TV screen.

NEVER SAY NEVER AGAIN

Rocket pen. Bond used this deadly device to kill Fatima Blush. Other equipment: Wristwatch with laser beam apparatus. Motorcycle.

A VIEW TO A KILL

Flare gun: Bond destroyed a Russian helicopter with this device. Other equipment: Magnetized device to unlock windows. Bug detector under head of electric razor. Sunglasses which can see through darkened windows. Miniature camera set in ring. Shotgun.

THE LIVING DAYLIGHTS

Special keys developed by 'Q' and used by Bond which open 90% of the world's locks. Phillips key ring; responds to "Rule Britannia" by emitting stun gas. A wolf whistle creates an explosion. Infrared night viewer goggles.

DIAMONDS ARE FOREVER

Voice synthesizer: A portable piece of equipment which electronically will match callers voice you wish to store and use at another time. Blofeld used this device to simulate the voice of Willard Whyte and control his giant corporation. Bond also used this device on the same assignment.

LIVE & LET DIE

Delta Wing hang glider, Champion harpoon gun, Wilkinson commando dagger and underwater torches. Compressed air shark pistol, cigarette case & lighter which become a projector. Magnetized, rotary saw watch. Sword. Magnetic Rolex watch. Gastron power boat.

THE MAN WITH THE GOLDEN GUN

Homing device and detector. American Motors Hornet Hatchback-SanPan.

THE SPY WHO LOVED ME

Cigarette case & lighter that form a microfilm reader. Printer/receiver watch with a short wave receiver, paper punch for short message. Lotus Car. Wet Bike. Parachute for pre-title sequence.

MOONRAKER

Detonator watch. Holly Goodhead and Bond are imprisoned below the space shuttle rocket by Drax. With only seconds to spare before blast–off, Bond manages to open an obstructed air vent grille using this device. X-Ray Safecracker: The size of a pocket calculator. Employs a battery and viewing screen. Bond used this device to open the Drax safe. 007 miniature camera and poison pen. High speed gondola, hovercraft, speedboat. Sword.

FOR YOUR EYES ONLY

Grappling hook. Underwater diving equipment, underwater Lotus car, skis. Identicast machine; this unit can illustrate a person's facial features as they are described to the machine.

LICENSE RENEWED

Covert Operations Accessory Pack. Contains 1) flare device 2) explosives 3) killing knife 4) garroting wire 5) pen which fires steel needles by compressed air. Other equipment: Receiver/ recorder with miniature tape cassette and headset. Dunhill lighter, filled with anesthetic Halothane gas used by Bond in fight with Caber. Money belt, an ingenious accessory developed by 'Q' branch for 00 agents; access via the belt buckle and a hidden razor-sharp knife; each two-inch section of the belt carries a foreign currency in paper notes, French francs, German marks, Dutch guilders. VL22H Countersurveillance Receiver, the size of a walkie-talkie, comes with head phones, handheld probe, pen alarm with instant signal communication to M.I.6 headquarters. Also contains micro-homing device so headquarters can follow Bond in the field; small enough to carry in the breast pocket. Bausch & Lomb binoculars with Zeiss lenses. Infrared night viewer goggles; approximate range 500'; permits visual amplification at night.

FOR SPECIAL SERVICES

Infrared night viewer goggles, pocket pager and Polaroid glasses. Swaine & Adeney bag; contains 1) throwing knifes 2) chloroform pad 3) steel picklocks 4) 3" jimmy bar and other miniature tools 5) padded leather gloves 6) six detonators 7) lump of plastic explosive 8) length of fuse 9) 35' nylon rope, ½" diameter 10) miniture grappling hooks 11) Smith & Wesson revolver.

ICEBREAKER

Spade, field rations, flares, maps and Schermuly Pains – Wessex Speedline, small infrared camera, military compass, telephone scrambler, and small electronic box adapted to a regular telephone allowing Bond to illegally bypass a nation's phone service when calling another country. VL34 Counter-Surveillance Personal Privacy Protector; finds electronic bugs in seconds; verifies and evesdropping device, ultra-miniaturized.

ROLE OF HONOR
Super 1000 long range telephone.

NOBODY LIVES FOREVER
Belt tool kit fitted with 1) small explosive charges 2) electronic connectors 3) four small packets of plastique explosive 4) four short lengths of fuse 5) extra-thin electric wire 6) six tiny detonators 7) miniature penlight torch 8) set of miniature tools, screwdrivers, picklocks. CC500 telephone scrambler. Super 1000 long range telephone.

NO DEALS MR. BOND
Super 1000 long range telephone, CC500 telephone scrambler. Harmonica bug, a miniature surveillance and sound stealing device.

SCORPIUS
Pen activated homing device.

COLONEL SUN
Two wafer thin Tungsten hacksaw blades sewn into the lapels of Bond's suit. Miniature pick lock fitted into the right heel of his shoe and homing device hidden in left heel of shoe.

THE MAN WITH THE GOLDEN GUN
Walkie talkie

LICENSE TO KILL
Briefcase which contained the following: 1) travelling alarm clock, size of a cigarette package, stuffed with explosives 2) passport; James Boldman, which activates mace 3) two king size tubes of toothpaste with C-4 plastique explosive 4) fountain pen which contains selection of detonators; pen converts to a remote with a couple of triple-A batteries 5) steel tube which connects to a portable grappling iron with four curved heads & spring – loaded nylon rope 6) a long, slim dull black metal tube which converted into a simple rifle. Bond also used pinlight torch, lockpicking device known as a "rake," a soft mallet, chisel, and W-9 pickups (bugs) used in conjunction with a receiver. A small rubber seriel dinghy. A solid gold DuPont cigarette lighter. A British passport which would explode if opened improperly. A Poloroid camera which fired a laser beam and took X-ray pictures, and a signature gun with optical palm reader.

WIN, LOSE OR DIE
Dictating machine, communications telephone, intelligence computer.

BROKEN CLAW
No special equipment used.

THE MAN FROM BARBAROSSA
Minature shortwave transmitter, tape recorder, computer, homing device, small penlight, hypos (syringes), RDX – based C-4 explosives, detonators, fuse wire, long killing knife, H.E. magnetic grenades.

DEATH IS FOREVER
Buckmaster survival knife with anchor pins for grappling hooks, Haley & Waller Dartcord rapid opening systems, explosive charges in strip form with primers and detonators, stun grenades, steel

leatherman which converts to heavy duty pliers, knife screwdriver, file, etc., pen gun, three passports & 2,000 pounds sterling.

NEVER SEND FLOWERS
State of the art telephone, Electronic Countermeasure Telephone (ECMT), Squeal phone, anti–bug scanner, waterproof hand flares, radio.

SEAFIRE
Applegate Fairboirn knife, parachutes, plastic explosives, fuse and electronic timing advice, compact tool kit, radio, fieldglasses, flashlight, miniature camera, gloves, lock picks, maps and documents.

COLDFALL
Parachute, implanted homer device, communication pack, mayday signal, emergency pack into belt, jumpsuit, canvas shoes.

GOLDENEYE
BMW Z3 Convertible Roadster with a self-destruct system and Stinger missiles. A leather belt with buckle that fires seventy-five feet of a high tensile wire, Parker exploding pen. X-ray document scanner. A detonator 'Omega" Seamaster watch with built-in laxer and magnetic charges. Electronic mayday flasher. Insulated ski mask. Electronic door opener. Binoculars with computer disk. Wet suit, parka, parachute, timer and charges, four grenades. T-55 tank with 100mm gun. Dunhill lighter with explosives.

TOMORROW NEVER DIES
BMW 750 IL with voice assisted navigation system, GPS tracking, bullet-proof body, self-inflating tires, jets emitting tear gas, rack of rockets concealed in sun-roof, metal spikes behind rear bumper, metal cutter hidden under BMW badge. The body work produces electric shock to unauthroized personnel. Other equipment: DUI CF200 drysuit of durable crushed neoprene designed for extremely cold tempuratures. Hard-sole boots and neoprene gloves, integrated weight system. SeaQuest black diamond buoyancy compensator, two aluminum Dacor cylinders each with 100 cubic feet of air compressed to 3200 psi, DacorExtreme Plus regulator, Mares ESA mask, Mares Plana Avanti fins, SeaQuest Sumto EON LUX air-integrated dive computer, Rolex submarine watch/wrist altimeter, shock parachute, inflatable Zodiac boat, magnetic limpet mines, Daewoo .380 automatic pistols, wet suits, regulators, fins and masks. BMW R1200 C motorcycle. Cellular telephone equipped with explosives.

ZERO MINUS TEN
X-ray proof wire cutter and file, plastic dagger, microfilm maps, inflammable shoe laces, flint and steel. Medicines including antiseptics, tweezers, acetaminophen tablets, generic amoxicyllin, bandages, sun block, petroleum jelly.

THE FACTS OF DEATH
Device to check telephone for bugs, Wilson gas mask, utility belt, portable flippers with elastic bonds, Bentley Turbo R, PPK 7.65 mm, P99, Jaguar XK8 Coupe, belt buckle with lockpick, night vision goggles, Ericsson cellphone, remote control device which fits in heel of shoe, alarm sensor deactivates any alarm within a twenty-five yard radius.

Note: No matter what other equipment is used, Bond always carries a service weapon on each assignment.

FILM

DR. NO

Bond is sent to Jamaica by M to investigate the strange disappearance of Commander Strangways, head of Station C, and his secretary. Arriving in Kingston, Bond's investigation leads him to a Professor Dent, a geologist, who does an analysis of rock samples Strangways had picked up on Crab Key. After discovering they are radioactive, Bond realizes that Dent had lied to him. Another suspect is Miss Taro, an employee of Government House who lures him up to her place in the Blue Mountains. On the way, a car tries to run him off a cliff. Bond has her arrested and waits at her place until Dent arrives to kill him. After Dent unloads his gun on a dummy Bond has placed in the bed, Bond kills him. Bond meets Felix Leiter from the CIA who is investigating Dr. No who they suspect of interferring with the course of their rockets which have been landing in South American jungles rather than the South Atlantic. Quarrel takes Bond to Crab Key where they meet Honey Rider, a collector of shells. Pursued by Dr. No's headquarters, they are imprisoned, later to be tortured. Bond manages to remove a grill in his cell and crawl down a shaft which leads to Dr. No's reactor room. A fight develops and Bond kills Dr. No by forcing him into the liquid core of the reactor. Bond manipulates the reactor dials forcing it to overheat. He frees Honey and they flee Crab Key in a small boat as Dr. No's island fortress explodes.

THE CAST

James Bond	Sean Connery
Honey Rider	Ursula Andress (re-voiced)
Dr. No	Joseph Wiseman
Felix Leiter:	Jack Lord
M	Bernard Lee
Professor Dent	Anthony Dawson
Quarrel	John Kitzmiller
Miss Taro	Zena Marshall
Sylvia	Eunice Gayson
Miss Moneypenny	Lois Maxwell
Puss-Feller	Lester Prendergast
Strangways	Tim Moxon
Girl Photographer	Margaret LeWars
Jones	Reggie Carter
Major Boothroyd ('Q')	Peter Burton
Duff	William Foster-Davis
Playdell-Smith	Louis Blaazer
Sister Rose	Michele Mok
Sister Lily	Yvonne Shima
Mary	Dolores Keater
The Byron Lee Band	Themselves
General Potter	Colonel Burton
Stewardess	Margaret Ellery

THE PRODUCTION STAFF

Produced by	Harry Saltzman and Albert R. Broccoli
Directed by	Terrence Young

Screenplay	Richard Maibaum, Johanna Harwood, Berkley Mather
Music Composed by	John Barry Orchestra, conducted by Eric Rogers
Orcherstrated by	Burt Rhodes
James Bond Theme	Monty Norman
Director of Photography	Ted Moore, B.S.C.
Production Designer	Ken Adam
Production Manager	L.C. Rudkin
Editor	Peter Hunt
Main Titles Designed by	Maurice Binder[1]
Animation	Trevor Bond and Robert Ellis
Art Director	Syd Cain
Make–up	John O'Gorman
Special Effects	Frank George
Continuity	Helen Whitson
Assistant Director	Clive Reed
Cameraman	John Winbolt
Sound Recording	Wally Milner & John Dennis
Hair Stylist	Eileen Warwick
Assistant Editor	Ben Reyner
Dubbing Editors	Archie Ludski and Norman Wanstall
Costumes	Tessa Wellborn
Set Dressing	Freda Pearson
Stuntman	Bob Simmons (Double for Connery)
Stuntman	George Leech (Double for Wiseman)

[1] The gun barrel logo was designed by Maurice Binder using a .38 calibre revolver. Bob Simmons, stuntman, was shown in Dr. No as Bond for this sequence.

Derived from a plot series called "Commander Jamaica" which Ian Fleming originated for NBC, and which was never telecast.

FROM RUSSIA WITH LOVE

A young Russian Army clerk informs the British Secret Service she wishes to defect with a Russian "Lector" decoding machine on condition that Bond meet her in Istanbul. 'M' knows this is a trap but sends Bond as they have wanted a Lector for years. However, they do not realize this is a trap to lure Bond to Turkey, to kill him and discredit the British M.I.6. Tatiana Romanova thinks she is working for the Russians but she has been deceived by Rosa Klebb, who now works for S.P.E.C.T.R.E. Bond meets Tatiana and ultimately, with her help, steals the Lector from the Russian Embassy. They flee and catch the Simplon-Orient Express to Paris. On board with them are Kerim Bey, British Head of Station T, Turkey and several enemy agents. In due course, Bey is killed and S.P.E.C.T.R.E. agent Red Grant comes aboard posing as a British Agent. A dramatic fight ensues and Bond kills Grant. He and Tatiana then leave the train and flee. A Russian helicopter tries to kill them but Bond destroys it with his AR-7 survival rifle. Stealing a patrol boat, they are confronted by more Russians but manages to elude capture and go to the Ritz Hotel in Paris where Grant was supposed to meet Klebb and get his payoff. She tries to kill Bond but is shot to death by Tatiana.

THE CAST

James Bond	Sean Connery
Tatiana Romanova	Daniela Bianchi
Kerim Bey	Pedro Armendariz
Rosa Klebb	Lotta Lenya
Red Grant	Robert Shaw
M	Bernard Lee
Sylvia	Eunice Gayson
Morzeny	Walter Gotell
Vavra	Francis de Wolff
Train Conductor	George Pastell
Kerim's Girl	Nadja Regin
Miss Moneypenny	Lois Maxwell
Vida	Aliza Gur
Belly dancer	Leila
Zora	Martine Beswick
Kronsteen	Vladek Sheybal
Foreign Agent	Hasan Ceylan
Krilencu	Fred Haggerty
Rolls-Royce Chauffeur	Neville Jason
Benz	Peter Bayliss
Mehmet	Nushet Ataer
Rhoda	Peter Brayham
Boothroyd ('Q')	Desmond Llewelyn
Masseuse	Jan Williams
McAdams	Peter Madden
Turkish Guide	Muhammat Kohen
Blofeld	Anthony Dawson
Voice of No. 1	Eric Pohlman
British Agent Nash	Bill Hill

THE PRODUCTION STAFF

Produced by	Harry Saltzman and Albert R. Broccoli
Directed by	Terence Young
Screenplay	Richard Maibaum
Adapted by	Johanna Harwood
Director of Photography	Ted Moore, B.S.C.
Editor	Peter Hunt
Production Manager	Bill Hill
Art Director	Syd Cain
Title Song written by	Lionel Bart
"From Russia With Love" sung by	Matt Monro
"James Bond Theme" written by	Monty Norman
Orchestral Music Composed And Conducted by	John Barry
Assistant Director	David Anderson
Second Unit Cameraman	Robert Kindred

The Orient Express dining car where Red Grant places a knock-out drug in Tatiana's drink. (Venice Simplon-Orient Express New York)

Camera Operator	John Winbolt
Continuity	Kay Mander
Make-up	Basil Newall and Paul Rabiger
Hairdresser	Eileen Warwick
Location Manager	Frank Ernst
Istanbul Production Assistant	Ilham Filmer
Special Effects by	John Stears assisted by Frank George
Production Liaison	Charles Russhon
Stuntman	Jack Sholomir
Pilot of S.P.E.C.T.R.E. helicopter	Capt. John Crewdson
Stunt Work arranged by	Peter Perkins
Sound Recordists	John W. Mitchell and C. Le Messurier
Dubbing Editor	Norman Wanstall and Harry Miller
Assembly Editor	Ben Reyner
Costume Designer	Jocelyn Rickards
Wardrobe Mistress	Eileen Sullivan
Wardrobe Master	Ernie Farrer
Assistant Art Director	Michael White
Set Dresser	Freda Pearson
Titles Designed by	Robert Brownjohn, assisted by Trevor Bond

Stuntman .... Bob Simmons (Connery's double)
Stuntman .... Jack Cooper (Shaw's double)

Music Recorded at C.T.S. Studios, London.

GOLDFINGER

Through Felix Leiter, 'M' has ordered Bond to investigate Goldfinger and coincidentally, Goldfinger is staying at the Fountainbleau Hotel in Miami where Bond is also staying. Goldfinger is cheating another guest at cards. Bond discovers Jill Masterson in Goldfinger's room calling out the cards to him thru binoculars and a radio transmitter. Bond thwarts this plan, forces Goldfinger to lose to his opponent and then beds lovely Jill. Knocked unconcious by Oddjob, Bond awakens to discover Masterson painted head to toe with gold paint and quite dead.

Back in England, Bond meets Goldfinger on the golf course and beats him in a $10,000 match[1] Planting a homing device in the boot of Goldfinger's Rolls-Royce, he tails him across France to his plant in Switzerland.

Along the way he meets Tilly Masterson, Jill's sister. After a high speed chase in the Aston Martin DB5, Tilly is killed and Bond is captured. After being knocked out with a tranquilizer gun, Bond awakens aboard Goldfinger's private jet piloted by Pussy Galore.

Arriving in Kentucky, Bond learns of Goldfinger's plan, "Operation Grand Slam," to detonate a nuclear device inside Ft. Knox and contaminate all the gold which will drive the price of Goldfinger's gold up. Bond, aided by Pussy, Felix Leiter, the US Army, foil Goldfinger's plan. While doing so, Bond kills Oddjob by electrocution.

On his way to meet the President aboard an executive jet piloted by Pussy, he is confronted by Goldfinger. In a vicious fight, Goldfinger is sucked out of the plane and Bond and Pussy parachute to safety.

[1]In the golf match with Goldfinger, Bond used a Penfold Hearts golf ball, Goldfinger a No. One.

CAST

James Bond .... Sean Connery
Pussy Galore .... Honor Blackman
Auric Goldfinger .... Gert Frobe (1)
Jill Masterson .... Shirley Eaton
Tilly Masterson .... Tania Mallet
Oddjob .... Harold Sakata
M .... Bernard Lee
Felix Leiter .... Cec Linder
Miss Moneypenny .... Lois Maxwell
Q .... Desmond Llewelyn
Solo .... Martin Benson
Simmons .... Austin Willis
Midnight .... Bill Nagy
Capungo .... Alf Joint

Bonita the Flamenco Dancer .... Nadja Regin
Sierra .... Raymond Young
Colonel Smithers .... Richard Vernon
Brunskill .... Denis Cowles
Kisch .... Michael Mellinger
Johnny .... Peter Cramwell
Stewardess .... Mai Ling
Pussy Galore's co-pilot .... Tricia Muller
Gatekeeper .... Varley Thomas
Mr. Ling .... Bert Kwouk
Strap .... Hal Galili
Henchman .... Lenny Robin
Dink .... Margaret Nolan
Brigadier .... John McLaren
Atomic Specialist .... Robert Macleod
Blacking .... Victor Brooks
Hawker .... Gerry Dugan
Nude, gold girl who danced in the credits .... Vicki Kennedy
Maid .... Janette Rowsell

[1]Speaking role re-dubbed by the late actor Michael Collins

THE PRODUCTION STAFF

Producers .... Albert R. Broccoli and Harry Saltzman
Director .... Guy Hamilton
Assistant Director .... Frank Ernst
Scriptwriters .... Richard Maibaum & Paul Dehn
Director of Photography .... Ted Moore, B.S.C.
Production Designer .... Ken Adam
Special Effects .... John Stears, assisted by Frank George
Action Sequences .... Bob Simmons
Art Director .... Peter Murton
Sound Effects .... Norman Wanstall (Academy Award)
Editor .... Peter Hunt
Main Title Designer .... Robert Brownjohn
Music .... Composed and conducted by John Barry
Title Song.. Lyrics by Leslie Bricusse and Anthony Newley
                                                                               Sung by Shirley Bassey
Production Manager .... I.C. Rudkin
Dubbing Editors .... Norman Wanstall and Harry Miller
Sound Recordists .... Dudley Messengart and Gordan McCullum
Hairdresser .... Eileen Warwick
Wardrobe Supervisor .... Elsa Fennell
Wardrobe Mistress .... Eileen Sullivan
Choreographer .... Selina Wylie
Publicity .... Tom Carlisle
Production Liaison .... Charles Russhon

Assembly Editor	Ben Rayner
Set Dresser	Freda Pearson
Wardrobe Master	John Hilling
Assistant Art Directors	Michael White and Maurice Pelling
Camera Operator	John Winbolt
Continuity	Constance Willis
Make-up	Paul Rabiger & Basil Newall
Stuntman	Bob Simmons (Doubled for Michael Mellinger who is thrown off the top of Fort Knox by Oddjob; Doubled for Connery)
Stuntman	George Leech (One of England's finest stuntmen; drove the Aston Martin DB5 into the wall at Auric Enterprises)
Stuntgirl	Phyllis Cornell (Doubled for Tilly Masterson).

The James Bond theme by Monty Norman.

THUNDERBALL

The international crime syndicate S.P.E.C.T.R.E. have stolen two nuclear bombs and are attempting to hold Great Britain and the U.S. hostage unless their demands are met. Bond is sent to the Bahamas where he meets Domino, sister to the pilot who stole the Vulcan bomber and who in turn is killed by Largo's men. Domino is Largo's mistress.

When Bond tells her that Largo is responsible for her brother's death, she tells him where she thinks Largo has hidden the bombs. Bond discovers them but is captured and sealed in the underground tomb. Bond takes a radioactive pill which allows Leiter to discover his location and he rescues Bond with helicopter and winch. They notify the proper authorities who send out aqua paratroopers.

Bond and the U.S. force battle with Largo's men and defeat them but Largo escapes to his yacht with Bond in pursuit. On board, Bond battles Largo and his men. Just as Largo is about to kill Bond, he is himself killed by Domino with her speargun. Bond and Domino jump just in time before Largo's yacht hits a reef and explodes. They are rescued by the Air Force.

THE CAST

James Bond	Sean Connery
Domino	Claudine Auger
Largo	Adolfo Celi
Fiona Volpe	Luciana Paluzzi
Felix Leiter	Rik Van Nutter
M	Bernard Lee
Paula Caplan	Martine Beswick
Count Lippe	Guy Doleman
Miss Moneypenny	Lois Maxwell
Q	Desmond Llewelyn
Patricia Fearing	Molly Peters
Home Secretary	Roland Culver
Pinder	Earl Cameron
Derval	Paul Stassino

Madame Boivard .... Rose Alba
Vargas .... Philip Locke
Kutee .... George Pravda
Janni .... Michael Brennan
Group Captain .... Leonard Sachs
Air Vice Marshall .... Edward Underdown
Kenniston .... Reginald Beckwith
U.S. Air Force Officer .... Charles Russhon
Quirt .... Bill Cummings
Domino Double .... Evelyn Boren
Bond Double .... Frank Cousins
Mademoiselle La Porte .... Mitsouko
Hydrofoil Captain .... Harold Sanderson[1]
Jack Boivard .... Bob Simmons

[1]Also Connery's stand-in.

The voice of Blofeld was Joseph Wiseman.

THE PRODUCTION STAFF

Producer .... Kevin McClory for Eon Productions
Executive Producers .... Harry Saltzman & Albert R. Broccoli
Director .... Terence Young
Assistant Director .... Gus Agosti
Scriptwriters .... Richard Maibaum, John Hopkins. Based on an original screenplay by Kevin McClory, Jack Whittingham, and Ian Fleming.
Director of Photography .... Ted Moore, B.S.C.
Production Supervisor .... David Middlemas
Assembly Editor .... Ben Rayner
Art Director .... Peter Murton
Camera Operator .... John Winbolt
Assistant Art Director .... Michael White
Blofeld's voice .... Joseph Wiseman
Set Dresser .... Freda Pearson
Dubbing Editors .... Norman Wanstall & Harry Miller
Hairdresser .... Eileen Warwick
Wardrobe Mistress .... Eileen Sullivan
Wardrobe Master .... John Brady
Continuity .... Joan Davis
Make-up .... Paul Rabiger & Basil Newall
Sound Recordists .... Bert Ross & Maurice Askey
James Bond Theme .... Monty Norman
Costumes Designer .... Anthony Medelson
Production Liasion .... Charles Russhon
Underwater Sequences .... Ivan Tors Underwater Studios Ltd.
Underwater Director .... Ricou Browning
Underwater Cameraman .... Lamar Boren[1]

Underwater Engineer .... Jordan Klein
Underwater Scenes .... Evelyn Boren doubled for Claudine Auger
Underwater Scenes .... Frank Cousins doubled for Connery
Fight scene in pre-title sequence.................. Bob Simmons & Harold Anderson

[1]Lama Boren of La Jolla, California, one of the world's most experienced underwater cameramen, helped pioneer underwater photography. He assembled over sixty divers and $85,000 worth of diving equipment for this film.

Story derived from a manuscript by Ian Fleming and Kevin McClory titled "James Bond of the Secret Service." Title later changed to "Longitude 78 West." Later changed to "Thunderball."

ACKNOWLEDGEMENTS

Royal Air Force   Royal Navy
United States Air Force   United States Coast Guard

YOU ONLY LIVE TWICE

Sent to Japan to investigate the loss of U.S. space ships, Bond discovers Osaka Chemicals is a front for Blofeld's S.P.E.C.T.R.E. organization. They in turn make several attempts on his life. Working with Tiger Tanaka, head of the Japanese Secret Service and his agent Aki, Bond discovers S.P.E.C.T.R.E.'s space operation at the bottom of an extinct volcano. During the course of this investigation, Aki is murdered and Bond fights an aerial duel in the skies over Japan with the Wallis autogyro "Little Nellie," shooting down all four S.P.E.C.T.R.E. aircraft. He penetrates the space operation and sends Kissy Suzuki back for help. Bond is captured but manages to destroy the Spectre spacecraft which intends to destroy the Russian spacecraft and create a confrontation with the U.S. government. American paratroopers arrive and gain control of Blofeld's headquarters. However, on the verge of blowing up, everyone flees and Bond and Kissy escape in a small boat.

THE CAST

James Bond... Sean Connery
Aki .... Akiko Wakabayashi
Tiger Tanaka .... Tetsuro Tamba
Kissy Suzuki .... Mie Hama
Osato .... Teru Shimada
Helga Brandt .... Karin Dor
Ernst Stavro Blofeld .... Donald Pleasence
M.. Bernard Lee
Miss Moneypenny .... Lois Maxwell
Q .... Desmond Llewelyn
Henderson .... Charles Gray
Chinese Girl .... Tsai Chin
American Leader .... Alexander Knox
Leader's Aide... Robert Hutton
British Police Officer .... Patrick Jordan
British Police Officer .... Anthony Ainley
S.P.E.C.T.R.E. 4 .... Michael Chow
S.P.E.C.T.R.E. 3 .... Burt Kwouk
Car Driver .... Peter Fanere Maivia

Hans .... Ronald Rich
Bedroom Assassin .... David Toguri
Bond's Masseuse .... Jeanne Roland
Submarine Captain .... John Stone
Japanese Sumo Wrestler .... Sadoyanama
1ST American Astronauts .... Norman Jones and Paul Carson
2nd American Astronauts .... Bill Mitchell and George Rouricek
Russian Cosmonauts .... Laurence Herder and Richard Graydon
Hawaii Radar Operative .... Ed Bishop
Hawaii Control .... Shane Rimmer
Stuntgirl .... Jenny Le Free (Doubled for Karin Dor)

Tetsuro Tamba, Akiko Wakabayashi, Mie Hama, were under contract to Toho Studio in Japan. Wakabayashi and Hama also appeared in the Bond spoof "What's Up, Tiger Lilly?"

THE PRODUCTION STAFF

Producers .... Harry Saltzman and Albert R. Broccoli
Director .... Lewis Gilbert
Scriptwriter .... Roald Dahl
Director of Photography .... Freddie Young
Production Designer .... Ken Adam
Special Effects .... John Stears
Film Editor .... Thelma Connell
Action Sequences .... Bob Simmons and George Leech
Second Unit Director &
supervising editor .... Peter Hunt
Main Title Designer .... Maurice Binder
Music .... Composed, conducted and arranged by John Barry
Title Song .... Lyrics by Leslie Bricusse, sung by Nancy Sinatra
Cameramen: 2nd Unit, Aerial, underwater .... Bob Huke, John Jordan, Lamar Boren
Additional story material .... Harold Jack Bloom
Art Director .... Henry Pottle
Production Supervisor .... David Middlemas
Assistant Director .... William P. Cartlidge
Location Manager .... Herbert Watts
Camera Operator .... Ernie Day
Continuity .... Angela Martelli
Make–up .... Paul Rabiger and Basil Newall
Production Liasion .... Charles Russhon
Aviation consultant .... Group Captain Hamish Mahaddie, RAF
"Little Nellie" Pilot .... Wing Commander Kenneth H. Wallis, RAF, Retired
Dubbing Editors .... Norman Wanstall and Harry Miller
Assembly Editor .... Robert Richardson
Sound Recordists .... John Mitchell and Gordon McCallum
James Bond Theme .... Monty Norman
Wardrobe Mistress .... Eileen Sullivan
Hairdresser .... Eileen Warwick

Set Decorator .... David Folkes
Technical Advisor .... Kikumaru Okuda

The British destroyer HMS Tenby dropped Bond's body into the bay, in this film. Scene was filmed in Gibraltar harbour. The rescue of Bond's body from the bottom of Hong Kong Harbour was filmed in the Bahamas.

The hollow volcano set cost Eon Productions 400,000 pounds sterling. To construct Blofeld's secret rocket base, Ken Adam used, among other materials, two hundred miles of tubular steel, seven hundred tons of structural steel, two hundred tons of plasterwork, 8,000 railroad ties for the monorail and 25,000 square yards of protective canvas. In the final scene, 120 stuntmen were employed.

HELICOPTERS USED IN THE FILM

By S.P.E.C.T.R.E. agents .... Hiller
On rocket launch pad .... Brantley
To film sequences .... French Alouette
Bond flew .... Wallis WA-116 (XR-943) Auto Gyro
                                                     ("Little Nellie")

The James Bond theme by Monty Norman

CASINO ROYALE (1967)

THE CAST (PRINCIPALS ONLY)

M .... John Huston
Le Chiffre .... Orson Welles
Sir James Bond .... David Niven
Vesper Lynd .... Ursula Andress
Miss Goodthighs .... Jacqueline Bissett
Evelyn Tremble .... Peter Sellers
Cooper .... Terence Cooper
Detainer .... Daliah Lavi
Mata Bond .... Joanne Pettet
Dr. Noah .... Woody Allen
Miss Moneypenny .... Barbara Bouchet
Cameo roles by: .... Debora Kerr, William Holden, Charles Boyer,
                                                     George Raft, Jean-Paul Belmondo, Tracy Reed,
                                                     Kurt Kasznar, Gabriella Licudi

Ian Fleming sold the film rights to Casino Royale for $6,000 to director Gregory Ratoff in 1955. His widow sold the film rights to Charles K. Feldman in 1960. Unfortunately, he turned the film in to a parody on Bond and it became simply an abortion, with an $8 million budget and no plot!

THE PRODUCTION STAFF (PRINCIPALS ONLY)

Producers .... Charles K. Feldman and Jerry Bresler
Directors .... John Huston, Ken Hughes, Val Guest, Robert Paris,
                                                       Joseph McGrath

Director / Photography .... Jack Hildyard B.S.C.
Location / Photographers .... Nicolas Roeg B.S.C. and John Wilcox B.S.C.
Screenplay .... Wolf Mankowitz, John Law, Michael Sayers
Music .... Burt Bacharach
Title Song .... Herb Alpert and The Tijuana Brass
Other Song .... "The Look of Love"
Sung by .... Dusty Springfield
Lyrics by .... Hal David
Production Designer .... Michael Stringer
Costume Designer .... Julie Harris
Film Editor .... Bill Lenny
Special Effects .... Richard Williams
Associate Producer .... John Dark
Assistant Directors .... John Stoneman, Douglas Pierce, Barrie Melrose, John Merriman, John Howell, Lionel Couch, Dick Talmadge, Anthony Swire

Columbia Pictures, Technicolor, Panavision. Filmed in Englan, Monte Carlo and Shepperton and Pinewood Studios, England.

ON HER MAJESTY'S SECRET SERVICE

In his search for Blofeld, Bond meets Tracy di Vincenzo, prevents her from committing suicide by drowning, then saves her from disgrace when she loses at the casino by paying her losses, and finally makes love to her in her room that night. Not a bad day's work!

The following day he meets her father, Draco, who wants Bond to marry her and take care of her and in turn he will give Bond a million dollars. Bond refuses but asks a favor in return. Can he learn the whereabouts of Blofeld with his connections as head of the Union Corse, the French Mafia. He can and does.

Bond returns to England and is given the green light by M to pursue the matter. Bond travels to Piz Gloria, Blofeld's headquarter's in the Swiss Alps, posing as Sir Hilary Bray, a specialist in heraldry, because Blofeld wants to be declared the legitimate Count Balthazar de Bleuville. Blofeld has brainwashed his patients at Piz Gloria and intends to send them back to England with a deadly virus to destroy England's economy with biological warfare. Bond learns all this, then escapes and returns to England to sound the alarm. He returns to Piz Gloria with Draco and his men and destroys it but Blofeld has escaped. Later, Tracy and Bond are married in Munich with their friends in attendance. On their way to their honeymoon, a car speeds by them and shots ring out. Bullets meant for Bond hit and kill Tracy and Blofeld escapes again.

THE CAST

James Bond .... George Lazenby
Tracy .... Diana Rigg
Blofeld .... Telly Savalas
Irma Bunt .... IIse Steppat
Draco .... Gabriele Ferzetti
Grunther: .... Yuri Borienko
Campbell .... Bernard Horsfall

James Bond's (Pierce Brosnan) assignment is to retrieve the stolen access codes for Goldeneye, the awesome space weapon that can fire a devastating electromagnetic pulse toward Earth. This action sequence was filmed in the Cuban jungle headquarters of former agent 006. (Rex USA Ltd.)

James Bond (Pierce Brosnan) is pitted against Xenia Onatopp (Famke Janssen) in a serious game of baccarat at a Monte Carlo casino in Goldeneye (Rex USA Ltd.)

James Bond (Roger Moore) and Francisco Scaramanga (Christopher Lee) are set to count off ten paces in *The Man With the Golden Gun*. Bond with his Walther 7.65mm PPK and Scaramanga with his "golden gun." (Rex USA Ltd.)

James Bond (Pierce Brosnan) and Wai Lin (Michelle Yeoh) in a scene from *Tomorrow Never Dies*. (Rex USA Ltd.)

Alec Trevelyan (006) (Sean Benn) and James Bond (007) (Pierce Brosnan) are deep inside a Russian dam which houses a top secret Soviet nerve gas facility. Their assignment: destroy it! (Rex USA Ltd.)

Roger Moore and the women of *A View to A Kill,* including, left to right, Jenny Flax (Alison Doody), Pola Ivanova (Fiona Fullerton) and Stacey Sutton (Tanya Roberts) (Rex USA Ltd.)

In *License to Kill,* Pam Bouvier, CIA pilot (Carey Lowell) and James Bond, 007 (Timothy Dalton) make a handsome, but deadly couple. (Rex USA Ltd.)

As US soldiers prepare to rush Fort Knox, Goldfinger, wearing a US uniform, prepares to shoot his own men in order to escape. (Rex USA Ltd.)

Jane Seymour in a publicity shot for *Live & Let Die*. She never fired a gun in the film. (Rex USA Ltd.)

James Bond (Roger Moore) and Octopussy (Maud Adams) in their first embrace after Octopussy's invitation to Bond to be a house guest. (Rex USA Ltd.)

Things become a little tense as James Bond (Pierce Brosnan) physically makes his point to CIA agent Jack Wade (Joe Don Baker) in *Goldeneye*. (Rex USA Ltd.)

On board a train bound for Sardinia in *The Spy Who Loved Me,* James Bond (Roger Moore) is attacked by Jaws (Richard Kiel). Fortunately, Bond is able to smash a lamp and place the live wire to the teeth of Jaws. Reeling from the shock, Jaws is pushed through the compartment window and off the train by Bond. (Rex USA Ltd.)

Tracy (Diana Rigg) and Bond (George Lazenby) in *On Her Majesty's Secret Service* prepare to leave on their honeymoon. However, within the hour Tracy would be dead as Blofeld opens fire with a machine gun from a passing car, killing her instantly. (Rex USA Ltd.)

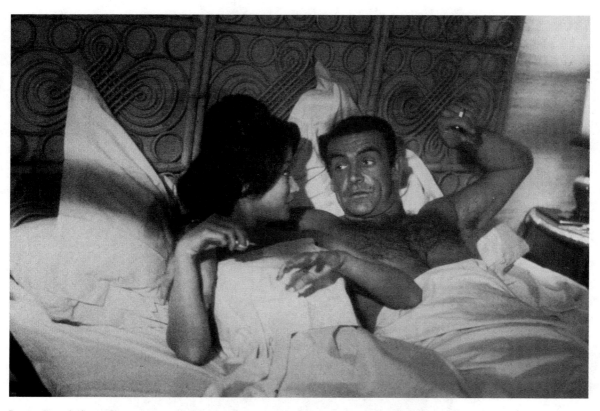

James Bond (Sean Connery) and Miss Taro (Zeno Marshall) in *Dr. No*. Miss Taro was actually a spy for Dr. No (Joseph Wiseman) and was ordered to lure Bond into her cottage in the Blue Mountains to be killed. Fortunately, she failed! (Rex USA Ltd.)

Tatiana Romanova (Daniela Bianchi) seduces James Bond (Sean Connery) in this scene of *From Russia With Love*. Tatiana thinks she is working for the KGB but in reality, unknown to her, it is Smersh. (Rex USA Ltd.)

At Goldfinger's Kentucky horse farm, Pussy Galore (Honor Blackman) prepares to teach James Bond (Sean Connery) some manners through the art of ju-jitsu. (Rex USA Ltd.)

In the pre-title sequence of *The Living Daylights,* James Bond (Timothy Dalton) has just parachuted from a flaming truck on to a luxurious yacht where the "lady on the boat" (Kell Tyler) is looking for a real man. Bond borrows her phone to call MI6. She invites him to stay awhile. (Rex USA Ltd.)

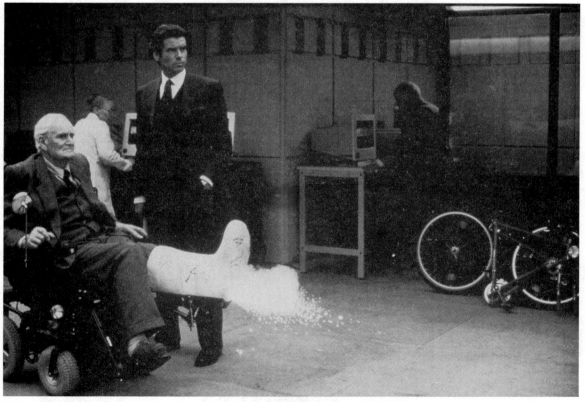

Major Boothroyd (aka "Q") demonstrates a new weapon to James Bond (Pierce Brosnan) at MI6 headquarters in London. (Rex USA Ltd.)

In a scene from *A View to A Kill,* Max Zorin (Christopher Walken) tells May Day (Grace Jones) to watch Bond and keep him away from Stacey Sutton (Tanya Roberts) as he doesn't trust him. (Rex USA Ltd.)

Elliot Carver (Jonathan Pryce), head of the global conglomerate Carver Communications, is prepared to make an announcement from his headquarters in Hamburg, Germany. (Rex USA Ltd.)

Sir Hilary Bray .... George Baker
M.. Bernard Lee
Miss Moneypenny .... Lois Maxwell
Q .... Desmond Llewelyn
Ruby.. Angela Scoular
Nancy .... Catherine von Schell
   Piz Gloria Girls:
American Girl .... Dani Sheridan
Scandinavian Girl .... Julie Ege
English Girl.. Joanna Lumley
Chinese Girl .... Mona Chong
Australian Girl .... Anoushka Hempel
German Girl .... Ingrid Back
Italian Girl... Jenny Hanley
Indian Girl... Zara
Jamaican Girl .... Sylvana Henriques
Israeli Girl .... Helena Ronee
   Draco's Men:
Toussaint .... Geoffrey Cheshire
Che Che .... Irvin Allen
Raphael .... Terry Mountain
Klett .... Bill Morgan
Driver... Richard Graydon
   Blofeld's Men:
Felsen .... Les Crawford
Braun .... George Cooper
Driver... Reg Harding
Gumbold .... James Bree
Olympe .... Virginia North
Manuel .... Brian Worth
   At The Casino:
Amercian Guest .... Bessie Love
Greek Tycoon... Steve Plytas
Chef de Jeu .... Robert Rietty
American Guest .... Elliott Sullivan
Chef de Jeu Huissier .... Martin Leyder
Janitor .... Norman McGlen
Hall Porter... Dudley Jones
Draco Helicopter Pilot .... John Crewdson
Piz Gloria receptionist .... Josef Vasa

THE PRODUCTION STAFF

Producers .... Harry Saltzman and Albert R. Broccoli
Associate Producer .... Stanley Sopel
Director .... Peter Hunt
Scriptwriter .... Richard Maibaum
Director / Photography .... Michael Reed

Production Designer	Syd Cain
Special Effects	John Stears
Stunt arranger; Stock Car sequence	George Leech and Anthony Squire.
Editor and Second Unit Director	John Glen
Main Title Designer	Maurice Binder
Music	Composed, conducted and arranged by John Barry.
Song	"We Have All The Time In The World." Lyrics by Hal David. Sung by Louis Armstrong.
Cameraman	Ken Higgins
Production Supervisor	David Middlemas
1st Asst. Director	Frank Ernst
Continuity	Joan Davis
Cameraman	Alec Mills
Camera Focus	Ron Drinkwater
Sound Mixer	John Mitchell and Gordon McCallum
Art Director	Bob Laing
Set Dresser	Peter Lamont
James Bond Theme	Monty Norman
Construction Manager	Ron Udell
Costume Designer	Marjorie Cornelius
Wardrobe Supervisor	Jackie Cummins
Wardrobe Master	John Brady
Make–up	Basil Newall and Paul Rabiger
Hairdresser	Eileen Warwick
Dialogue Coach	Job Stewart
Assembly Editor	Robert Richardson
Stunt Arranger	George Leech
Stuntman	Chris Webb
Dubbing Editors	Nicholas Stevenson and Harry Miller
Additional Dialogue	Simon Raven
Stuntmen	Leu Heinz and Robert Zimmerman doubled for Blofeld and Bond.
Austrian Professional Rally Driver, Stock Car Sequence	Erich Glavitza
Stuntmen	Chris Webb and Richard Graydon doubled George Lazenby
Cameramen 2nd Unit	Egil Woxholt, Roy Ford, Willy Bogner, Jr., Alex Barbey, and John Jordan[1].

[1]John Jordan lost a foot while filming a helicopter sequence in *You Only Live Twice*. Later, they had to amputate his entire leg. But he came back and was able to film action sequences during this film. Unfortunately, after this, he was killed while filming *Catch 22* in Mexico.

ACKNOWLEDGEMENTS

Her Majesty's College of Arms and Heralds
Music Recorded at CTS Studios

Ford Motor Company

DIAMONDS ARE FOREVER

To stop illegal trafficking in stolen diamonds, Bond takes the place of a diamond courier, intending to follow the pipeline to the top. In the course of the events he meets Tiffany Case, flies to New York and on to Los Angeles, and then by car to Las Vegas, pretending to transport his dead brother for burial. In actuality, the casket carries the diamonds inside the remains. In Las Vegas several attempts are made on his life. Blofeld has, through manipulation, taken control of Willard Whyte's industrial empire, holding Whyte hostage. Bond learns of Whyte's whereabouts and frees him with the aid of Felix Leiter and FBI agents. Blofeld has kidnapped Tiffany and fled to his headquarters on an oil rig. A battle ensues, Blofeld is killed, Bond and Tiffany escape as the rig is about to blow up. The scene now shifts to the Queen Elizabeth liner in New York. Bond and Tiffany board for England. Also aboard are two assassins of Blofeld. Posing as waiters, they make an attempt on Bond's life but both end up overboard. Bond and Tiffany are now alone!

THE CAST

James Bond	Sean Connery
Tiffany Case	Jill St. John
Ernst Stavro Blofeld	Charles Gray
Plenty O'Toole	Lana Wood
Williard Whyte	Jimmy Dean
Burt Saxby	Bruce Cabot
M	Bernard Lee
Miss Moneypenny	Lois Maxwell
Mr. Kidd	Putter Smith
Q	Desmond Llewelyn
Felix Leiter	Norman Burton
Dr. Metz	Joseph Furst
Gangster #1	Marc Lawrence
Tom	Shane Rimmer
Klaus Hergescheimer	Ed Bishop
Mr. Slumber	David Bauer
Shady Tree	Leonard Barr
Thumper	Trina Parks
Bambi	Donna Garratt
Mrs. Whistler	Margaret Lacey
Peter Franks	Joe Robinson
Doctor	David de Keyser
Sir Donald Muner	Lawrence Naismith
Girl on the Beach: "Marie"	Denise Perrier
Gangster #2	Sid Haig
Gangster #3 and #4	Michael Valeute
Dentist	Henry Rowland
Maxwell	Burt Metcalf
Barker	Larry Blake
Doorman: (Tropicana)	Nicky Blair
Aides to Professor Metz	Constantin de Goquel, Jonos Kurucz
Immigration Officer	Clifford Earl
Agent	Karl Held
Airline Representative	John Abineri

Blofeld's double	Max Latimer
Controller (Moon Crater)	Bill Hutchinson
Guard	Frank Mann
Sir Donald's Male Secretary	Mark Elwes
Man in Fez	Frank Olegario
Vondenburg Launch Director	David Healy
Vandenburg Aide	Gordon Ruttan
Houseboy	Brinsley Farde
Maxie	Ed Call
Helicopter Pilot	Raymond Baker
Boy	Gary Dubin
Welfare Worker	Catherine Dreney

THE PRODUCTION STAFF

Producers	Albert R. Broccoli and Harry Saltzman
Associate Producer	Stanley Sopel
Director	Guy Hamilton
Screenplay	Richard Maibaum and Tom Mankiewicz
Assistant Directors	Jerome M. Siegel and Derek Cracknell
Continuity	Del Rose and Elaine Schreyeck
Camera Operators	Bill Johnson and Bob Kindred
Art Directors	Bill Kenney and Jack Maxsted
Set Decorators	John Austin and Peter Lamont
Special Effects	Whitney McMahon and Leslie Hillman
Production Buyer	Ronnie Quelch
Jill St. John's Costumes	Don Feld
2nd Unit Cameraman	Harold Wellman
Visual Effects	Albert Whitlock and Wally Veevers
Stunt Arrangers	Paul Baxley and Bob Simmons and George Leech
Location Managers	Eddie Saeta and Bernard Hanson
Dubbing Editors	Teddy Mason, Jimmy Shields, Christopher Landcaster
Dubbing Mixer	Gordon McCallum
Sound Recordists	Al Overton and John Mitchell
Wardrobe Supervisors	Ted Tetrick and Elsa Fennell
Main Title Designer	Maurice Binder
Car Stunt 2-wheels	Buzz Bundy
Stuntman	Jack Sholomir
Production Managers	Milton Feldman and Claude Hudson.
Editors	John W. Holmes, ACE and Bert Bates
Production Designer	Ken Adam
Director / Photography	Ted Moore, B.S.C.
Music	Composed, conducted and arranged by John Barry
Lyrics	Don Black
James Bond Theme	Monty Norman
Title Song Sung by	Shirley Bassey

The auto chase scenes in Las Vegas involved the use of 53 cars, of which 24 were totally destroyed.

Connery donated his salary for this film to the Scottish Education Trust, the charity he himself established to aid deprived Scottish children.

The plastic water bed featured in Diamonds Are Forever was filled with some 3,000 tropical fish. The bed, 7x6 feet in diameter, was in the Bridal Suite of the Riviera Hotel in Las Vegas.

The P & O luxury liner, the Canberra, came out of a Southhampton dry dock after a clean–up to feature in the fade–out sequence of the film.

ACKNOWLEDGEMENTS

Ford Motor Company   Aston Martin LaGonda Ltd.
Honda Motor Company   The Dover Harbour Board
P & O Lines   David Morris Jewelers
The Rivera Hotel   The Sands Hotel
The Dunes Hotel   The Landmark Hotel
The International Hotel   The Tropicana Hotel
The Mint hotel   Circus Circus Hotel

All of the above hotels are in Las Vegas, Nevada.
Music recorded at C.T.S. Studio, London.

LIVE & LET DIE

Three British agents have been killed in the past 24 hours. One in San Monique, one in New Orleans, and one in New York. The agent in New York was investigating Dr. Kanga, minister from San Monique; also known as Mr. Big, drug smuggler and owner of numerous restaurants and houses of prostitution Harlem. Bond flies to New York and an attempt is immediately made on his life as he rides in a taxi to Manhattan. Felix Leiter, CIA agent, provides Bond with the address where he suspects the car is registered. Bond goes to the Occult Vodoo Shop, watches as Dr. Kanaga and his hoods leave and tails them in a taxi which takes them up town to Harlem and the Filet of Soul restaurant. Seated in a booth, it revolves Bond into a back room where he meets Solitaire who is playing cards and Kanaga's hoods who are told to take him out and waste him. Solitaire is Mr. Big's ward and soothsayer. As he is about to be killed, he knocks out the two hoods and is picked up by a CIA agent who has been following him. Leiter tells him that Kanaga is leaving for San Monique. Bond follows. In San Monique he meets Rosie Carver, a British agent who is actually in the employ of Mr. Big. On their way to Mr. Big's she is killed by his men. Bond enters Big's house, makes love to Solitaire and they leave together. They discover Mr. Big's drug fields and are attacked by a helicopter. Making their way to the village of San Monique, they steal a double decker bus and outrun the police to a dock where they catch a boat and leave the island. Arriving in New Orleans, they are captured by Mr. Big. Bond escapes and meets Felix Leiter in New Orleans. They go to the Filet of Soul restaurant where once again Bond is captured by Mr. Big's men and taken to an alligator farm where he is left to be eaten alive. But Bond escapes by way of the Louisiana bayous in a Glastron powerboat.

Arriving back in San Monique, he rescues Solitaire and has a final confrontation with Mr. Big himself. Captured, he and Solitaire are placed on a platform and are being lowered into a pool of waiting sharks. But Bond utilizes his magnetized watch to free his bonds and fights Mr. Big. Bond shoves a compressed air pellet into Big's mouth and he blows up like a balloon and explodes. On the train to New York, they are attacked by Mr. Big's hood Tee Hee. Bond manages to cut the cable to Tee Hee's claw hand and it locks into the window sill. Bond then tosses him through the window.

Note: Roger Moore's first words as Bond were, "Hello Felix, what are you doing here?"

THE CAST

James Bond .... Roger Moore
Dr. Kananga/Mr. Big .... Yaphet Kotto
Solitaire .... Jane Seymour
Sheriff Pepper .... Clifton James
Tee Hee .... Julius Harris
Baron Samedi .... Geoffrey Holder
Felix Leiter .... David Hedison
Rosie Carver .... Gloria Hendry
M... Bernard Lee
Miss Moneypenny .... Lois Maxwell
Quarrel Junior .... Roy Stewart
Whisper.. Earl Jolly Brown
Adam .... Tommy Lane
Sister Love (Band Singer) .... Brenda Arnau
Strutter .... Lon Satton
Cab Driver .... Arnold Williams
Mrs. Bell .... Ruth Kempf
Charlie .... Joe Chitwood
Miss Caruso .... Madeline Smith
Dambala (High Priest) .... Michael Ebbin

Above, and next three pages: Four chase scenes from Roger Moore's first Bond film *Live & Let Die,* filmed in Louisiana. (Glastron Boats)

Salesgirl	Kubi Chaza
Hamilton	Bob Dix
Jazz Assassin	"Kid" Thomas Valentine
Crabman	Don Topping
Baines (CIA Agent)	Dennis Edwards

THE PRODUCTION STAFF

Producers	Albert R. Broccoli & Harry Saltzman
Director	Guy Hamilton
Screenplay	Tom Mankiewicz
Continuity	Elaine Schreyeck
Camera Operator	Bob Andred
Cameraman, 2nd Unit	John Harris
Production Supervisor:	Laurel Staffell
Makeup	Paul Rabiger
Hairdresser	Colin Jamieson
Construction Manager	Leon Davis
Props	Patrick Weymouth
Production Managers	Stephen F. Kesten & Steven P. Skloot
Assistant Director	Alan Hopkins
Unit Manager	Michael Rauch
Location Coordinator	Jack Weis
Art Director	Stephen Hendrickson

Camera Operators .... George Boullett & Warren Rothenberger
Stunt Scenes .... William Grefe
Moore stand-in .... John Woods
Bus stunt scene .... Maurice Patchett
Supervising Art Director .... Syd Cain
Art Directors .... Bob Laing & Peter Lamont
Special Effects .... Derek Meddings
Optical Effects .... Charles Staffel
Speedboat Stunt Driver .... Murray Cleveland
Car Stunt Driver... Jim Heck
Car Driver .... Al Gross
Boat Organizer .... John Kerner
Director, 2nd Assistant .... Joel Rosen
Cook .... Tom Hardy
Camera Operator .... Bob Kindred
Location Caterer .... George Crawford
Production Secretary .... Jane Ascroft
Still Photographer .... Terry O'Neill
American Publicist .... Vic Hentschy
Still Photographer .... John Bryson
Clapper / Loader .... Colin Davidson
Publicity Director... Derek Coyte
Asst. Director .... Richard Jenkins
Editors... Bert Bates, Raymond Poullen, John Shirley
Dubbing Editors .... Teddy Mason, Jimmy Shields, Chris Lancaster
Sound Recordists .... John Mitchell and Ken Barker

Stunts Coordinated by	Bob Simmons, Ross Kananga, Eddie Smith, Joe Chitwood, Jerry Conneaux, Bill Bennett
Choreography	Geoffrey Holder
Costume Design	Julie Harris
Stuntman for Roger Moore	Martin Grace
Production Liaison	Charles Russhon
Casting Director	Weston Drury, Jr.
Main Title Design	Maurice Binder
Production Supervisor	Claude Hudson
Assistant Director	Derek Cracknell
Location Manager	Bernard Hanson
Director / Photography	Ted Moore, B.S.C.
Title Song Composed by	Paul and Linda McCartney
Performed by	Paul McCartney and Wings
Music Score	George Martin
James Bond Theme	Monty Norman

"Oh For A Closer Walk With Thee" performed by the Olympia Brass Band.
"Live & Let Die" and "Filet of Soul" sequence by B.J.Arnau.

ACKNOWLEDGEMENTS

Chevrolet Motor Division, General Motors Corporation
Glastron Boat Company
Evinrude Motors
Harley Davidson Motors Company, Inc.
Budget Rent-a-Car

A.M.F. Inc.
Exotic cars by Durham Coach of New Jersey
Pan American World Airways
Rolex, Inc.
Visi-Tel Corporation
Pulsar, the Time Computer
The Black Stuntmen's Association, Hollywood, California
Tarot Cards by Fergus-Hall, Courtesy of Portal Gallery, London

In New Orleans:
Police Department
International Airport
Levee Board
Lakefront Airport and Tenants Association

In New York:
Mayor's Office of Film Coordination
Police Department
Department of Commerce and Industrial Development

In Jamaica:
Jamaica Defense forces
Jamaica Tourist Board
Jamaica Swany Safari Ltd.

THE MAN WITH THE GOLDEN GUN

'M' is sent a golden bullet with Bond's 007 number on it. Since Bill Fairbanks, agent 002 was killed by Scaramanga, the man with the golden gun, in Beirut in 1969, Bond goes there first to pick up the trail and retrieves the bullet from a belly dancer who used it as a navel ornament. Back in London, 'Q' determines from the bullet that it came from a custom gun builder in Macao. Bond learns from the builder that he is sending an order of golden bullets to Scaramanga. Following the bullets takes Bond to a gambling casino where they are picked up by Andrea, Scaramanga's girlfriend. He follows her to Hong Kong. She tells him that she is the one that sent the bullet and hopes he will kill Scaramanga so she can be free of him. Scaramanga has developed a solar energy device which could revolutionize industrial and military development. She is to meet Bond with it. However, Scaramanga suspects and kills her. Bond meets Mary Goodnight, British agent who is sent as his backup. They learn that Hi-Fat has hired Scaramanga to kill Bond for one million dollars. The trail leads to Hi-Fat's residence in Bangkok where Scaramanga kills Hi-Fat to take over his business interests. Scaramanga kidnaps Goodnight and Bond follows her to Scaramanga headquarters on an island off South East Asia. He kills Scaramanga, rescues Goodnight, retrieves the solar device and they escape as the island is about to blow up.

On board the Chinese junk taking them to Hong Kong is the dwarf, Nick Nack, Scaramanga's assistant. He tries to kill Bond but Bond manages to trap him in a suitcase and hoists it to the top of the junk's mast. Bond and Goodnight sail off into the sunset.

THE CAST

James Bond	Roger Moore
Scaramanga	Christopher Lee
Mary Goodnight	Britt Ekland
Andrea	Maud Adams
Nick Nack	Herve Villechaize
Sheriff J.W. Pepper	Clifton James
M	Bernard Lee
Hip	Soon-Taik Oh
Miss Moneypenny	Lois Maxwell
Q	Desmond Llewelyn
Hi-Fat	Richard Loo
Rodney	Marc Lawrence
Lazar	Marne Maitland
Calharpe	James Cossins
Chula	Chan-Yiu-Lam
Salda	Carmen Sautoy
Navy Lieutenant	Michael Osborne
Doubles for Moore	Mike Lovatt, Colonel Claire
Frazier	Gerald James

THE PRODUCTION STAFF

Producers	Harry Saltzman and Albert R. Broccoli
Director	Guy Hamilton
Scriptwriters	Richard Maibaum and Tom Mankiewicz
Director / Photography	Ted Moore and Oswald Morris
Production Designer	Peter Murton
Special Effects	John Stears
Editors	John Shirley and Raymond Poulton
Main Title Designer	Maurice Binder
Music	Composed, conducted, arranged by John Barry
Title Song	Lyrics by Don Black
Title Song performed by	Lulu
James Bond Theme	Monty Norman
Astro spiral car jump	W. Jay Milligan
Performed by	Bumps Willard
Art Director	Peter Lamont
Construction Manager	Leon Davis
Assistant Director	Derek Cracknell
Wardrobe Supervisor	Elsa Fennell
Production Supervisor	Claude Hudson
Location Managers	Frank Ernst and Eric Rattray
Associate Producer	Charles Orme
Camera Operator	Bob Kindred

Special Effects	Derek Meddings
Casting Director	Weston Drury, Jr. and Maurice Spector
Props	Patrick Weymouth
Production Coordinator	Reginald Barkshire
Dubbing Editors	June Shells, Christopher Lancaster, Charles Crawford
Editors	John Shirley and Raymond Poulion
Continuity	Elaine Schreyeck
Cameraman, 2nd Unit	John Harris
Sound	Gordon Everett
Make–up	Paul Engelen
Production Accountant	Brian Bailey

ACKNOWLEDGEMENTS

Stuntmen furnished by American Thrill Show, J.M. Productions, Inc.
AMC Astro spiral jump—mathematical and computer technology furnished by Calspan Corporation, Buffalo, New York
American Motors Corporation
Colibri Lighters, London, England
Music recorded at CTS Studios, Wembley, England

THE SPY WHO LOVED ME

Karl Stromberg has developed a system for tracking and locating nuclear submarines as they travel beneath the sea. Each country has lost one. They decide to team up and each assign an agent to investigate. Bond's travels take him to Egypt where several attempts are made on his life and where he and Major Anya Amasova, the Russian agent are teamed together by their superiors. Given a new lead, they travel together to Sardinia where Stromberg's "Atlantis" headquarters is located submerged off the island.

After meeting with Stromberg as a marine biologist, Bond's cover is revealed by Jaws, who has confronted them in the past and Stromberg orders them killed. Several attempts are made on their lives. The nuclear submarine U.S.S. Wayne, with Bond and Amasova aboard is swallowed up by Stromberg's super tanker "Liparus" and they are taken prisoner. Bond manages to escape and free the submarine crew. In the meantime, Stromberg has programmed his computer to have the Russian and American submarines destroy each other with their respective missiles. Bond switches the trajectory to have the missiles destroy each other in mid-flight. He and the submarine crew escape as the tanker is sinking but Amasova has already been taken to "Atlantis" by Stromberg where he holds her prisoner. Skipper of the Wayne has been ordered to destroy "Atlantis" but Bond convinces him to wait until he rescues Amasova. On board "Atlantis" he kills Stromberg, rescues Amasova, and they escape as "Atlantis" sinks.

THE CAST

James Bond	Roger Moore
Major Anya Amasova	Barbara Bach
Karl Stromberg	Curt Jurgens
Jaws	Richard Kiel
Naomi	Caroline Munro
M	Bernard Lee
Minister of Defense	Geoffrey Keen

General Gogol .... Walter Gotell
Captain Benson .... George Baker
Miss Moneypenny .... Lois Maxwell
Q .... Desmond Llewelyn
Captain Carter .... Shane Rimmer
Commander Talbot .... Bryan Marshall
Sergei .... Michael Billington
Felicca .... Olga Bisera
Shiek Hossein .... Edward de Souza
Max Kalba .... Vernon Dobycheff
Hotel Receptionist .... Valerie Leon
Liparus Captain .... Sidney Tafler
Fekkesh .... Nakim Sawalha
The Cabin Girl .... Sue Vanner
Rubelvitch.. Eva Reuber-Staier
Admiral Hargreaves .... Robert Brown
Stormberg's Assistant .... Marilyn Galsworthy
Sandor .... Milton Reid
Bechmann .... Cyril Shaps
Markovitz .... Milo Sperber
Barman... Albert Moses
Cairo Club Waiter .... Rafiq Anwar
Arab Beauty .... Felicity York
Arab Beauty .... Dawn Rodriques
Arab Beauty .... Anika Pavel
Arab Beauty .... Jill Goodall and the Egyptian Folklore Group
Anthony Forrest .... John Sarbutt
Garrick Hagon .... David Auker
Ray Evans .... Dennis Blanche
Vincent Marzello .... Keith Buckley
Nicholas Campbell .... Keith Morris
Ray Jewers .... Jonathan Bury
George Malloby .... Nick Ellsworth
Christopher Muncke .... Tom Gerrard
Anthony Pullen .... John Salthouse
Dean Warwick .... Kazik Michalski

The Stronberg Crew
George Roubicek
Lenny Rabin
Irvin Allen
Yasher Adem
Peter Ensor
Eric Stine
Robert Sheedy
Don Stanton
Stephen Temperley

U.S.S. Wayne Crew
Capt. Shane Rimmer
Bob Sherman
Doyle Richmond
Murray Salem
John Truscott
Peter Whitman
Ray Hassett

HMS Ranger Crew
Capt. Brian Marshall
Michael Howarth
Kim Fortune
Barry Andrews
Kevin McNalley
Jeremy Bulloch
Sean Bury

THE PRODUCTION STAFF

Producer	Albert R. Broccoli
Director	Lewis Gilbert
Scriptwriters	Christopher Wood & Richard Maibaum
Director / Photography	Claude Renoir[1]
Production Designer	Ken Adam (Academy Award nomination)
Cameraman; ski, & underwater	Willy Bogner, Lamar Boren
Special Effects	Derek Meddings & Alan Maley
Directors, 2nd Unit	Ernest Day & John Glen
Action Arranger	Bob Simmons
Ski Jump	Rick Sylvester
Editor	John Glen
Main Title Designer	Maurice Binder
Music	Marvin Hamlisch (Academy Award nomination)
Song	'Nobody Does It Better' sung by Carly Simon Lyrics by Carole Bayer Sager (Academy Award Nomination)
Photographer & pilot, Lotus submersible	Don Griffin
Pilot to the Shark Hunter II	Keith Anderson
Expert climber	Bob Richardson
Parachute Expert	Jim Buckley
Production Coordinator, Canada	Rene DuPont
Principal Cameraman	Alan Hume
Assistant Director	William P. Cartlidge
Special Effects (studio)	John Evans
Construction Manager	Michael Redding
Script Editor	Vernon Harris
Wardrobe Mistress	Rosemary Burrows
Production Manager	David Middemas
Assistant Director	Ariel Levy
Assistant Director, 2nd Unit	Chris Kenny
Location Manager (Egypt)	Frank Ernst
Location Manager (Canada)	Golda Offenheim
Production Coordinator (Canada)	Rene Dupont
Art Director	Peter Lamont
Production Asst	Brian Bailey
Special Asst. to Director	Michael G. Wilson
Script Advisor	Richard Kennan
Asst. Art Director	Ernie Archer
Sound Recorder	George Everett
James Bond Theme	Monty Norman
Costumes	June Randall
Production Assistant	Marguerite Green
Assistant Editor	John Grover
Hairdresser	Maud Spector, Weston Drury, Jr. & Barbara Ritchie
Make–up	Paul Engelen
Production Coordinator	Reginald Barkshire

Designer .... Gordon K. McCallum & Allen Soles
Assistant Editor .... Allan Stichon

[1]His grandfather was the famous French impressionist painter, Pierre Auguste Renoir and whose uncle Jean Renoir was a famous film-maker.

ACKNOWLEDGEMENTS

Royal Navy	Hotel Cala di Volpe
Shell Oil	Ford Motor Company
Sony Corporation	Commonwealth of the Bahamas
Kawasaki Motorcycles	Egyptian Film Theatre and Music Organization
Lotus Cars[1]	Perry Corporation
Ski Suits by Willy Bogner	Seiko Watches
Parks Canada	

[1]Six Lotus Esprits were used in the production of this film.

MOONRAKER

A 747 carrying a space shuttle craft designated for the British is destroyed in flight but no sign of the space craft exists. Bond is sent to Southern California to investigate Hugo Drax of Drax Industries who builds the shuttle. He meets Holly Goodhead who works for Drax as a space scientist and is later revealed to be a CIA agent. An attempt is made on his life.

Bond makes love to Drax's beautiful helicopter pilot and she assists him in cracking the Drax safe which contains secret documents. Drax discovers this and has her murdered.

Bond returns to London where Drax papers are examined. This affords a clue which takes Bond to Venice, Italy and Drax laboratories where a deadly gas is being manufactured. Here, he again meets Goodhead and another attempt is made on his life.

The trail leads to South America where Goodhead is captured by Drax and eventually, so is Bond. Drax places them below a rocket so the exhaust blast will incinerate them but Bond manages to free them and escape. Drax has boarded a shuttle bound for his station in space. Bond and Goodhead follow. At Drax space colony they battle Drax and Bond pushes Drax through an air lock, out into space. The space station is destroyed by forces from Earth as Bond and Goodhead chase the satellites that contain the deadly gas designed to kill the world's population. They destroy each one and Earth is saved.

THE CAST

James Bond	Roger Moore
Holly Goodhead	Lois Chiles
Drax	Michael Lonsdale
Jaws	Richard Kiel
Corrine Dufour	Corinne Clery
M	Bernard Lee
Manuela	Emily Bolton
Chang	Toshiro Suga
Blonde beauty	Irka Bochenko
Minister of Defense	Geoffrey Keen

Miss Moneypenny .... Lois Maxwell
Q .... Desmond Llewelyn
General Gogol .... Walter Gotell
Dolly .... Blanche Ravalec
Colonel Scott .... Michael Marshall
Hostess on Private Jet .... Leila Shenna
Museum guide .... Anne Lonnberg
Pilot / private jet .... Jean Pierre Castaldi
Mission Control Director .... Douglas Lambert
Consumptive Italian .... Alfie Bass
Shuttle Pilot .... Brian Keith
Captain of 707 .... George Birt
RAF Officer .... Kim Fortune
Russian Girl .... Lizzie Warville
Ambulanceman .... Guy Di Rigo
Drax Technicians .... Chris Dillinger & Georges Beller
Man in The Coffin .... Claude Carliez
Boeing 707 Officer .... Denis Seurat
Drax's Girls .... Christina Hui, Beatrice Libert, Catherine Serre, Nicaise Jean Louis, Francoise Gayat, Chichinou Kaeppler
Stunt Team .... Claude Carliez, Martin Grace, Richard Graydon, Dorothy Ford, Michel Berreur, Guy Di Rigo, Paul Weston, Daniel Breton
Drax's Boy .... Nicholas Orbez
Funambulist .... Johnny Traber

The boat Bond used in South America when being pursued by Drax thugs. (Glastron Boats)

THE PRODUCTION STAFF

Producer .... Albert R. Broccoli
Executive Producer .... Michael G. Wilson
Director .... Lewis Gilbert
Scriptwriter .... Christopher Wood
Director / Photography .... Jean Tournier
Production Designer .... Ken Adam
Action Unit Directors .... Ernest Day & John Glen
Visual Special Effects .... Derek Meddings (Academy Award nomination)
Stunt arranger .... Bob Simmons
Editor .... John Glen
Main Title Designer .... Maurice Binder
Music .... John Barry
Title Song .... Lyrics by Hal David, sung by Shirley Bassey
Script Editor .... Vernon Harris
Assembly Editor .... John Grover
Visual Effects Art Director .... Peter Lamont
Associate Producer .... William P. Cartlidge
Optical Effects .... Robin Browne
Production Coordinator .... Reginald Barkshire
Art Directors .... Max Douy & Charles Bishop
Production Accountant .... Brian Bailey
Cameraman, 2nd Unit .... Jacques Renoir
Action Sequences .... Bob Simmons
Visual Effects Cameraman .... Paul Wilson
Assistant Director .... Michel Cheyko
Set Director .... Peter Howitt
Location Manager (Brazil) .... Frank Ernst
Unit Manager (France) .... Rober Saussier
Unit Manager (UK) .... Chris Kenny
Location Manager (Italy) .... Philippe Modave
Location Manager (USA) .... John Comfort
Production Managers .... Jean-Pierre Spiri-Mercanton, Terence Churcher
Dolby Consultant .... John Isles
Dubbing Editors .... Allan Sones, Dino de Campo, Collin Miller
Re-recording Mixers .... Gordon McCullum, Nicholas Le Messurier, Graham V. Hartstone, Jacques Touilland
Process Consultant .... Bill Hanbard
Process Effects (France) .... Louis Lapeyre
Optical Effects (France) .... Michel Francois Films
Camera Operators .... Alec Mills, Michel Deloire, Guy Delatre, James Davis, John Morgan
Art Directors, 2nd Unit .... Peter Bennett, Meyer Barreby
Assistant Director, 2nd Unit .... Chris Carreras
Special Effects .... John Evans, John Richardson, Rene Albouze, Serge Ponvianne, Charles Abbola
Hairdresser .... Pierre Vade, Mike Jones

Roger Moore's Hair .... Mike Jones
Production Secretary .... Simone Ebcoffier
Production Assistant .... Marguerite Green
Production Secretary .... Dominique Back
Construction Manager .... Michael Redding
Continuity .... Josie Fulford, Gladys Goldsmith, Elaine Schreyeck
Sound Mixer .... Daniel Brisseau
Assistant Sound Mixer .... Gerard De Lagarde, Jean Labourel
Space Consultant .... Eric Burgess
Space Art Director .... Harry Lange
Props .... Pierre Roudeix, Raymond Le Moigne
Costume Designer .... Jacques Fonteray
Sound Effects .... Jean Pierre LeLong
Models .... Gareth Tandy
Assistant Art Directors .... Marc Frederix, Jacques Douy, Serge Douy, Ernie Archer, John Fenner
Set Dressers .... Pierre Charron, Andre Labussiere
Buyers .... John Lanzer, Alan Guyard, Jean Nassereau
Production Accountant (France) .... Paul Beuori
Make-up .... Monique Archambault, Paul Engelen
Visual Effects (France) .... Jean Berard
Stunt Arranger (France) .... Claude Carliez
Location Manager (Brazil) .... Andy Armstrong
Casting .... Budge Drury, Margot Capelier
Wardrobe Mistress .... Colette Baudot
Wardrobe Master .... Jean Zay
Dialog Editor .... Catherine Kelber
Assistant Unit Manager (France) .... Robert Boulic
Assistant Editors .... Michael Round, Peter Davies, Luce Gruenwald
Key Grip .... Rene Strasser
Camera Grip .... Chunky Huse
Unit Publicist .... Steve Swan & Gilles Durieux
James Bond Theme .... Monty Norman

ACKNOWLEDGEMENTS

Rockwell International Space Division   United States Air Force
United States Marine Corp.   Dept. Of National Parks, Brazil
Government Of Argentina   Florida State Film Commission
Paris Airport   Glastron Boat Company
Seiko Watches   Seven - Up
Bollinger Champagne   Air France
Marlboro   Christian Dior
Cannon Cameras   British Airways
Varig Airways   NASA

FOR YOUR EYES ONLY

British spy ship and fishing trawler, the "St. George", struck a mine and sank. Everyone drowned before they could destroy the British secret ATAC (Automatic Targeting Attack Communicator). The Russians would like to recover it. So would Kristatos, Greek drug smuggler, who would then sell it to the Russians. Bond's assignment: recover it!

Meanwhile, Timothy Havelock, working with the British, has discovered the location of the "St. George" but before he can reveal its location, he and his wife are murdered by Major Gonzales. Their daughter, Melina Havelock vows revenge. On the trail of Gonzales, Bond is captured and taken to their headquarters but before he can be interrogated, Gonzales is killed with a crossbow fired by Melina Havelock. Bond and Melina escape to her father's yacht, the "Triana." Bond makes her promise she will not interfere any further until he can unravel who is behind the plot. He meets with Kristatos and is told that another Greek smuggler, Columbo, is the man he will have to contend with in a showdown. Bond then meets and makes love to Countess Lisl, friend of Columbo, but she is murdered the following morning by Kristatos men. As they prepare to take Bond prisoner, he is rescued by Columbo's men and taken aboard Columbo's ship where he learns that Kristatos is the real enemy. Columbo and Bond sail to Kristatos ship, overpower its crew and destroy Kristatos drug shipment.

Back on board the "Triana", Bond and Melina search her father's papers and ultimately learn the location of the "St. George." They dive to it and recover the ATAC but after coming back aboard their yacht, are captured by Kristatos men who tie them up and drag them through the water, in hopes they will to be eaten by the sharks or drowned.

Bond manages to free them and they escape. Kristatos, taking the ATAC with him, has left for his retreat high atop a mountain in northern Greece where he is waiting for General Gogol to arrive and take the ATAC. Bond, with Melina and Kristatos follow.

Bond scales the mountain top, kills several guards, and the rest follow. They overpower Kristatos and his men and Melina kills Kristatos with her crossbow. General Gogol arrives by helicopter but Bond throws the ATAC off the mountain top to be destroyed.

Bond and Melina then return to her father's yacht for a swim.

THE CAST

James Bond	Roger Moore
Melina Havelock	Carole Bouquet
Columbo	Topol
Bibi	Lynn-Holly Johnson
Kristatos	Julian Glover
Countess Lisl	Cassandra Harris
Jacoba Brink	Jill Bennett
Emile Locque	Michael Gothard
Sir Timothy Havelock	Jack Hedley
Iona Havelock	Toby Robins
General Gogol	Walter Gotell
Miss Moneypenny	Lois Maxwell
Q	Desmond Llewelyn
Kriegler	John Wyman

Minister of Defense .... Geoffrey Keen
Gonzales .... Stefan Kalipha
Luigi Ferrara .... John Moreno
Margaret Thatcher .... Janet Brown
Dennis Thatcher... John Wells
Bill Tanner, Chief of Staff .... James Villiers
Aide to 'Q' .... Jeremy Bullock
Claus .... Charles Dance
Apostis .... Jack Klaff
Mantis Man... Graham Hawkes
Karageorge .... Paul Angelis
Santos .... Alkis Kritikos
McGregor.. William Hoyland
Bunky .... Paul Brooke
Vicar .... Fred Bryant
Nikos .... Stag Theodore
First Sea Lord .... Graham Crowden
Vice Admiral... Noel Johnson
Rublevich .... Eva Rueber-Staier
Parrot's voice (Max) .... Percy Edwards, animal mimic
Girl in Flower Shop .... Robbin Young
Girl at Casino.. Max Vesterhalt
Girls at the Pool .... Lalla Dean, Evelyn Drogue, Laoura Hadzivageli, Koko, Chai Lee, Kim Mills, Tula, Vanya, Viva, Lizzie Warville, Alison Worth

THE PRODUCTION STAFF

Producer.. Albert R. Broccoli
Executive Producer .... Michael G. Wilson
Director .... John Glen
Scriptwriters.. Richard Maibaum & Michael G. Wilson
Director / Photography .... Alan Hume
Production Designer .... Peter Lamont
Action Unit Director .... Arthur Wooster
Special Effects .... Derek Meddings
Cameramen; underwater, Aerial, ski .... Al Giddings, James Devis, Willy Bogner
Action Sequence Arrangers .... Bob Simmons, Remy Julienne
Editor .... John Grover
Main Title Designer .... Maurice Binder
Music .... Bill Conti
Title Song.. Lyrics by Michael Leeson, sung by Sheena Easton (Academy Award nomination)
Climbing Stunts .... Rick Sylvester
Associate Producer .... Tom Pevsner
Assistant Director, 2nd Unit .... Gerry Gavigan
Continuity, 2nd Unit .... Phyllis Townsend
Assistant Directors 2nd Unit .... Terry Madden, Gareth Tandy, Michael Zimbrich, Tony Broccoli

London Contact .... Van Jones
Production Assistants .... Iris Rose & Sally Ball
Greek Wedding Scene: Bouas-Danilia Village,
Corfu
Sound Effects .... Jean Pierre LeLong
Additional Editor .... Eric Boyd-Perkins
Assembly Editors .... Peter Davies, Derek Trigg
Additional Art Directors .... Michael Lamont, Mike Karapiperis, Franco
Fumagalli
Dubbing Editors .... Colin Miller, Bill Trent, Vernon Messenger
Music Mixer .... John Richards
Re-recording Mixer .... Gordon McCallum, Ken Barker
Camera Operator .... Alec Mills
Production Coordinator .... Reginald A. Barkshire
2nd Unit Director & Photographer .... Arthur Wooster
Production Managers .... Mario Blasetti, Philip Kohler, Aspa Lambrou
Assistant Director .... Anthony Waye
Sound Mixer .... Derek Ball
Art Director .... John Fenner
Director / Publicity .... Charles Juroe
Production Accountant .... Douglas Noakes
Continuity .... Elaine Schreyeck
Visual Effects Photography .... Paul Wilson
Set Director .... Vernon Dixon
Production Supervisor .... Bob Simmonds
Secretary to the Executive Producer .... Joanna Brown
Casting .... Maude Spector & Deborah McWilliams
Costume Designer .... Elizabeth Waller
Wardrobe Master .... Tiny Nicholls
Wardrobe for Miss Bouquet & Miss Harris .. Raemonde Rahvis, London
Assistant Art Director .... Ernie Archer
Illustrator .... Dennis Rich
Scenic Artist .... Ernest Smith
Camera Operators, 2nd Unit .... Jack Lowin, John Morgan, Dewi Humphreys,
Robert Kindred.
Boom Operator .... Ken Nightingall
Make–up .... George Frost, Eric Allwright
Hairdresser .... Stephanie Kaye, Marsha Lewis
Special Effects .... John Evans
Stills .... Keith Hamshere
James Bond Theme .... Monty Norman
Construction Manager .... Michael Redding
Electrical Supervisor .... John Tythe
Camera Grip .... Chunky Huse
Property Master .... Brian Humphrey
Marine Advisors .... David Halsey & Barry Goldsmith
Skating scenes staged by .... Brian Foley

Optical Effects .... Michel Francois Films
Unit & Location Managers .... Vincent Winter, Peter Bennett, Michalis Lambrinos,
Redmond Morris, Umberto Sambuco

Note: Screenplay for this movie is based loosely on the Ian Fleming short stories "For Your Eyes Only" and "Risico."

THE STUNT TEAM

Martin Grace, Pat Banta, Cyd Child, Jo Cote, John Eaves, Hans Hechenbichler, Michel Julienne, Woldgang Junginger, George Leech, Wendy Leech, Gavin McKinney, Gareth Milne, Bernard Pascual, Frances Young.

THE AERIAL TEAM

Marc Wolff, Albert Werry, John Crewdson, Robin Browne, Andrew Von Preussen, Nigel Brendish, Czeslav Dyzma.

THE SKI TEAM

Gerhard Fromm, Peter Rohe, George Ostler, Gerhard Huber, Christian Troschke, Wolfgang Kleinwaechter, Michael Ratajczak, Sabine Boueke, Victor Tourjanski, Verena Baldeo, Giovanni Dibona.

THE UNDERWATER TEAM

Ken Court, Walter Clayton, Charles Nicklin, Steve Bowerman, Arlette Greenfield, Doug Laughlin, Randolph Johnson, Terry Kerby, Jack Monestier, Richard Mula, Pete Romano, Moby Griffin, John Bremer.

THE CLIMBING TEAM

Rick Sylvester, Herbert Raditschnig, Chester Brown, Bill Fox
Unit & Location Managers: .... Vincent Winter, Peter Bennett, Michalis Lambrino,
Redmond Morris, Umberto Sambuco

ACKNOWLEDGEMENTS

The town of Cortina D'Ampezzo	The Ministry of Tourism and the Government of the Bahamas
Ski Suits by Bogner	The Greek National Tourist and Ministry of Culture
Lotus Cars	S.A. Automobiles, Citroen
Mitsui Yamaha (UK)	Osel Mantis
Perry Oceanographics	Oceaneering International Services
Seiko Time (UK)	Normalair-Garrett Dive Helmets
Phillips Industries	Olin Skis
Tyrolia Bindings	Garmont Boots
Jewell Water Buggies	North Thames Gas Board
Scuba Pro Diving Equipment	Panavision, Technicolor, TVC Laboratories
Music recorded at the Music Centre.	Sound re-recorded at Pinewood Studio

NEVER SAY NEVER AGAIN (1983)

This is a remake of the film *Thunderball* (1965).

This film has a different cast and crew but the one constant is Sean Connery as Bond. Film producer Kevin McClory was awarded in a court settlement all film and TV rights to the story Thunderball, and entered an agreement with Eon Productions to produce *Thunderball* in return for a percentage of the profits. A contract stipulation prevented him from developing a new version of the film for ten years. McClory eventually sold all his rights to the project to Jack Schwartzman, an independent film producer, who brought it to the screen starring Sean Connery, and sporting a new title.

THE CAST

James Bond	Sean Connery
Largo	Klaus Maria Brandauer
Blofeld	Max Von Sydow
Fatima	Barbara Carrera
Domino	Kim Basinger
Leiter	Bernie Casey
Q Algy	Alec McCowen
M	Edward Fox
Miss Moneypenny	Pamela Salem
Small-Fawcett	Rowan Atkinson
Lady in Bahamas	Valerie Leon
Kovacs	Milow Kirek
Lippe	Pat Roach
Lord Ambrose	Anthony Sharp
Patricia	Prunella Gee
Jack Petachi	Gavan O'Herlihy
Elliott	Ronald Pickup
Italian Ministers	Robert Rietty & Guido Adorni
Culpepper	Vincent Marzello
Number 5	Christopher Reich
Captain Pederson	Billy J. Mitchell
General Miller	Manning Redwood
Kurt	Anthony Van Laast
Nicole	Saskia Cohen Tanugi
French Minister	Sylvia Marriott
Bouncer at Casino	Dan Meaden
Doctor at Shrublands	Michael Medwin
Nurse at Shrublands	Lucy Hornak
Porter at Shrublands	Derek Deadman
Cook at Shrublands	Joanna Dickens
Auctioneer	Tony Alleff
Ships Steward	Paul Tucker
Masseuse	Brenda Kempner
Receptionist at Health Spa	Jill Meager
Communications Officer	John Stephen Hill
Girl Hostage	Wendy Leech
Ships Captain	Roy Bowe

THE PRODUCTION STAFF

Art Directors	Michael White and Roy Stannard
Set Decorator	Peter Howitt
Property Master	Peter Hancock
Construction Manager	Bill Welch

2nd Unit Director/Photography	Paul Beeson B.S.C.
Aerial Photography	Peter Allwork B.S.C.
Production Manager (U.K.)	John Davis
Production Coordinator	Gladys Pearce
Script Supervisor	Pamela Mann Francis Petain
Production Accountant	Paul Tucker
Film Editor	Ian Crafford
Additional Editing	Peter Musgrave G.B.F.E.
Dubbing Editors	Norman Wanstall and John Poyner G.B.F.E.
Music Editor	Valerie Lesser
Assistant Directors	Roy Button, Carlos Gil, Greg Dark, Steve Harding
Production Manager/Bahamas	Malcolm Christopher
Production Manager/France	Jean Pierre Avice
Production Managers/Spain	Arnold Ross and Apolinar Rabinal
Camera Operators	Chic Waterson and Wally Byatt
Producer	Jack Schwartzman
Director	Irvin Kershner
Screenplay	Lorenzo Semple, Jr.
Based on an Original Story by	Kevin McClory, Jack Whittingham, Ian Fleming
Executive Producer	Kevin McClory
Associate Producer	Michael Dryhurst
Director / Photography	Douglas Slocombe B.S.C.
Production Designers	Philip Harrison and Stephen Grimes
Supervising Film Editor	Robert Lawrence
Music	Michel Legrand
Director, 2nd Unit	Michael Moore
Underwater Sequences	Ricou Browning
1st Assistant Director	David Tomblin
Consultant to Producer	Talia Shire Schwartzman
Costume Designer	Charles Knode
Casting	Maggie Cartier, Mike Fenton, Jane Feinberg (U.S.).
Optical Effects	Apogee Inc., Los Angelas
Supervisor of Special Visual Effects	David Dryer
Production Controller	Jack Smith
Production Supervisor	Ian Wingrove
Supervising Art Director	Leslie Dilley
Comedy Writers	Dick Clement, Ian LeFrenais
Motorcycle Stunts	Mike Runyard
Stunts	Roy Alon, Dickie Beer, Marc Boyle, EdwardGarcia, Frank Henson, Billy Horrigan, Wendy Leech
Underwater Consultant:	Scott Carpenter
Director / Photography Underwater	Bob Steadman
Underwater Camera Operators	Jordan Klein and Mike Ferris
Underwater Gaffer	Montie Taylor
Divemaster	Gavin McKinney
Boatmaster	"Moby" Griffin
Sound Recordist	Simon Kaye

Sound Mixer	David Allen
Sound Boom	David Sutton
Sound Maintenance	Taffy Haines
Assistant Film Editors	Wally Nelson, Jonathan Nuth, Nicholas Moore, Bill Barringer, Annie Negro
Dubbing Mixer	Bill Rowe
Dubbing Assistant	Ray Merrin
Music Mixer	Keith Grant
Unit Publicist	Sara Keene
Stills Photographer	Bob Penn
Standby Crew	Robert Betts, George Gibbons, Stephen Hargreaves, Allan Williams, Joe Dipple, Robert Hill
Focus Pullers	Robin Vidgeon and Keith Blake
Assistant Art Directors	Don Dossett, George Djurkovic, John Wood
Property Buyer	John Lanzer
Chief Make-up Artist	Robin Grantham
Make-up & Hairdresser to Mr. Connery	Ilona Herman
Chief Hairdresser	Stephanie Kaye
Hairdresser	Sue Love
Wardrobe Supervisor	Ron Beck
Assistant to Mr. Kershner	Anne Marie Stein
Associate to Mr. Schwartzman	Yvonne McGeeney and Anne Schwebel
Merchandising Coordinator	Jeff Freedman
Production Assistants	Linda Rabin, Jill Bender and Beatrice Geffriaud.
Unit Manager, 2nd Unit	Evzen Kolar
Location Consultant	Anne Glanfield
Special Effects Technicians	Trevor Neighbor, Roger Nicholls, David Beavis, David Harris, David Watkins
Electronics Graphics Supervisor	Rob Dickenson
Assistant Electronic Graphics	Ira Coleman
Stunt Coordinators	Glenn Randall and Vic Armstrong
Camera Grip	Brian Osborne
Electrical Gaffer	Martin Evans
Best Boy	Ray Meehan
Production Supervisor/ Optical Special Effects	Robert R. Shepherd
Optical Supervisor	Roger Dorney
Chief Camera Operator (Optical)	Douglas Smith
Technical Advisor	Guy Alimo
Lighting Equipment	Lee Electric, London
Additional Opticals	General Screen Enterprises
Re-recorded at	Thorn EMI Elstree Studios, Herts, England
Music	"Never Say Never Again" by Michael LeGrand.
Lyrics	Alan and Marilyn Bergman
Sung by	Lani Hall
Film Processing	Technicolor

Recorded in .... Dolby Stereo

ACKNOWLEDGEMENTS

Lee Electric, London
The Bahamas National Trust
Silver Springs, Florida
Universal Gym Equipment
Aiwa Audio Cassette Recorder
British Caledonia Airways, London
Nippon Electric, London
JVC
Khashoggi Foundation
Hetz, France
RCA Victor of Japan
Norark Engineering, London
Societe Des Bains De Mer-Monaco
Police Nationale

Robert A. Shaheen
The Nassau Beach Hotel
Furs & Leathers for Barbara Carrera by Fendi
Yamaha Motor Co., Ltd.
Atari
Morfax, London
Regie Renault, France
Princess Grace Foundation
Dacor
Harvey
Royal Small Arms Factory, Enfield, London
Pre-recorded at Thorn Emi Studios, Herts, England
Municipalite et Police De Villefranche, Sur Mer
Gendarmerie Nationale

Club De Vieux Manoir-Fort Carre D'Antibes
Foundation Rothchild-Saint Jean Cap-Ferrat
Chambre De Commerce Aeroport-Nice Cote D'Azur
Police Monegasque and Municiapalities of Antibes, Beaulieu
Mer, Menton, Monte Carlo, Nice Roquebrune-Cap Mann, Villefranche Sur Mer
All Sea Sequences Filmed in the Commonwealth of the Bahamas
Main & End Titles Designed & Produced By R.I. Greenberg Associates, Inc. N.Y.

OCTOPUSSY

A mad, ambitious Russian General Orlov wants to conquer all of Europe. To finance his scheme, he is raiding the Russian art treasury of its Faberge Eggs and selling them to the highest bidder. To cover his crime, he has an accomplice replacing them with counterfeit eggs. British agent 009 turns up dead with a fake Faberge egg in his hand as the original is being auctioned at Sotheby's. When General Orlov discovered the counterfeit had been lost, he has ordered Kamal Khan to recover the original at all cost so that his crime would not be discovered by an upcoming inventory.

Khan, of course, would be paid well for his services. British intelligence suspected the Russians of selling the eggs to finance covert spy operations in Europe. Bond is requested to investigate. Attending the auction and examining the egg, Bond switches the counterfeit for the original and unknowingly, Khan buys the fake for $500,000 pounds! Khan returns to India and Bond follows. At the hotel where Khan plays backgammon each day, Bond puts up the genuine egg as collateral for his wager of 200,000 rupees against Khan, and Khan's loaded dice beats him. Khan is furious and as Bond leaves the hotel, an attempt is made on his life. Now Khan sends his assistant, Magda, to retrieve the egg, which she does after sleeping with Bond.

But Khan is not satisfied with just getting the egg back. He captures Bond and is preparing to torture him when Bond escapes, and makes his way to the island home of Octopussy, a wealthy lady who has diverse business interests and also dealings with Khan. When Khan discovers that Bond is in her home he sends his hoods to assassinate Bond but Bond and Octopussy overpower them. Octopussy departs for Europe where her circus is playing at an air force base and Bond follows her. He discovers General Orlov's plot to detonate a nuclear device on the base which will turn the

European community against NATO and force them to disarm, leaving Europe wide open for invasion. However, General Gogol has discovered his plot and the Russians kill Orlov after he has set the timer to the device. Khan, who was also there, now leaves for India, hoping that the bomb will also destroy Bond and Octopussy. However, just before it is due to explode, Bond disarms it. Returning to India, Khan kidnaps Octopussy and Bond pursues them and manages to hang onto the tail of Khan's plane as it takes off.

The story reaches its climax as Bond rescues Octopussy, and they manage to leave the plane just before it crashes with Khan on board. Bond and Octopussy sail away in her private ship.

THE CAST

James Bond .... Roger Moore
Octopussy .... Maud Adams
Kamal.. Louis Jourdan
Magda .... Kristina Wayborn
Gobinda .... Kabir Bedi
Orlov... Steven Berkoff
Twin One .... David Meyer
Twin Two .... Tony Meyer
Vijay... Vijay Amritraj
Q .... Desmond Llewelyn
M.. Robert Brown
Gogog .... Walter Gotell
Minister of Defense .... Geoffrey Keen
Gwendoline... Suzanne Jerome
Midge .... Cherry Gillespie[1]
Sadruddin .... Albert Moses
Fanning .... Douglas Wilmer
009 .... Andy Bradford
Miss Moneypenny .... Lois Maxwell
Penelope Smallbone .... Michaela Clavell
Auctioneer .... Philip Voss
U.S. General .... Bruce Boa
U.S. Aide .... Richard Parmentier
Soviet Chairman .... Paul Hardwick
Kamp .... Dermot Crowley
Lenkin.. Peter Porteous
Rublevitch... Eva Rueber-Staier
Zec .... Jeremy Bullock
Bianca .... Tina Hudson
Thug with Yo-Yo .... William Derrick
Major Clive.. Stuart Saunders
British Ambassador .... Patrick Barr
Borchoi .... Gabor Vernon
Karl .... Hugo Bower
Colonel Toro .... Ken Norris
Mufti .... Tony Arjuna
Bubi .... Gertain Klauber

Schatzl .... Brenda Cowling
Petrol Pump Attendant .... David Grahame
South American V.I.P. .... Brian Coburn
South American Officer .... Michael Halphie

THE THUGS

Ray Charles	Sven Surtees
Michael Moor	Talib Johnny
Ravider Singh Reyett	Peter Edmund
Gurdial Sira	

THE CIRCUS

Ringmaster .... Roberto Germains
Francisco the Fearless .... Richard Graydon

The Hassani Troupe	The Flying Cherokees
Vera & Shirley Fossett	Barry Winship
Carol & Josef Richter	

THE GYMNASTS

Supervisor .... Suzanne Dando[2]

Teresa Craddock	Kirsten Harrison
Christine Cullers	Lisa Jackman
Jane Aldridge	Christine Gibson
Tracy Llewellyn	Ruth Flynn

THE OCTOPUSSY GIRLS

Mary Stavin[3]	Carolyn Seaward[4]
Cheryl Anne	Carole Ashby[5]
Jani-z	Julie Martin
Joni Flynn	Julie Barth
Kathy Davies	Helene Hunt
Gillian De Terville	Safira Afzal
Louise King	Tina Robinson
Allison Worth	Janine Andrews
Lynda Knight	

[1]A former dancer with Pan's People & regular appearances on British TV's "Top of the Pops".
[2]Former Captain of the British Women's Olympic Gymnastics team in Moscow.
[3]Former Miss Sweden and later Miss World in 1977.
[4]Former Miss England and runner-up in the Miss Universe contest.
[5]Former model and hostess of British TV's "Sale of the Century" quiz show.

THE PRODUCTION STAFF

Producer .... Albert R. Broccoli
Director .... John Glen
Screenstory and Screenplay .... George Macdonald Fraser, Richard Maibaum,
Michael G. Wilson
Executive Producer .... Michael G. Wilson
Associate Producer .... Thomas Pevsner
Music .... John Barry
Production Designer .... Peter Lamont

Main Title Designer .... Maurice Binder
Director / Photography .... Alan Hume
Supervising Editor .... John Grover
Special Effects Supervisor .... John Richardson
Director and Photographer, 2nd Unit .... Arthur Wooster
Costume Designer.. Emma Porteous
Casting .... Debbie McWilliams
Production Supervisor .... Hugh Harlow
Production Managers .... Philip Kohler, Barrie Osborne, Leonard Gmur,
Gerry Levy
Production Accountant .... Douglas Noakes
Production Controller .... Reginald A. Barkshire
Director of Publicity .... Charles Juroe
Assistant Director .... Anthony Waye
Camera Operator... Alec Mills
Sound Recordists .... Derek Ball
Continuity .... Elaine Schreyeck
Action Sequences arranged........................... Bob Simmons
Driving Stunts arranged .... Remy Julienne
Art Director.. John Fenner
Set Decorator .... Jack Stephens
Make–up Supervisor .... George Frost
Hairdressing Supervisor .... Christopher Taylor
Editors... Peter Davies and Henry Richardson
Sound Editor .... Colin Miller
Indian Production Advisor............................ Shama Habibullah
Location Managers .... Peter Bennett and Rashid Abassi
Assistant Director, 2nd Unit .... Gerry Gavigan
Additional Assistant Directors .... Baba Shaikh & Don French
Continuity, 2nd Unit .... Doreen Soan & Penny Daniels
Assistant Directors, 2nd Unit .... Terry Madden, Michael Zimbrich, Andrew Warren,
Tony Broccoli
Location Accountants .... Jane Meagher, Marge Rowland & Ursula Schlieper.
Production Assistants .... Iris Rose, Joyce Turner, Sheila Barnes, May
Capsaskis, Mohini Banerji
Executive Assistants .... Barbara Broccoli
Production Secretaries .... Mary Stellar, Joanna Brown, Eleanor Chaudhuri
U.S. Casting .... Jane Jenkins
Model Effects Supervisor .... Brian Smithies
Model Photography .... Leslie Dear
Additional Photography .... Jimmy Devis & Bob Collins
Camera Operators, 2nd Unit........................ Malcolm Vinson, David Nowell, Jack Lowin
Front Projection .... Charles Staffel
Wardrobe Master .... Tiny Nicholls
Costumes made by .... Bermans and Nathans
Additional Art Directors .... Michael Lamont, Ken Court, Ram Yedekar,
Jan Schlubach

Set Dresser (India) .... Crispian Sallis
Assistant Art Directors .... Ernie Archer, Jim Morahan, Fred Hole
Production Buyer .... Ron Quelch
Scenic Artists .... Ernest Smith and Jacqueline Stears
Boom Operator .... Ken Knightingall
Make–up .... Peter Robb-King and Eric Allwright
Hairdresser .... Jeannette Freeman
Effects Supervisor, 2nd Unit .... John Evans
Unit Publicist .... Geoff Freeman
Stills .... Frank Connor and George Whitear
Construction Manager .... Michael Redding
Electrical Supervisor .... John Tythe
Camera Grips .... Chunky Huse and Colin Manning
Property Master .... David Jordan
Stunt Engineers .... Dave Bickers and Dan Peterson
Boatmaster .... Michael Turk
Big Top by .... Supertents
Catering by .... The Location Caterers Ltd.
Helicopters .... Management Aviation Ltd.
Transport .... D & D & Location Facilities Reknown Freight Ltd,
                                                                        The Travel Company
Sound Effects .... Jean Pierre Lelong
Dubbing Editors .... Derek Holding and Michael Hopkins
Music Mixer .... John Richards
Re-recording Mixers .... Gordon McCallum and Ken Barker
Theme Song .... "All Time High" performed by Rita Coolidge
                                                                        Music by John Barry, lyrics by Tim Rice
Filmed in .... Panavision
Recorded in .... Dolby Stereo
Film Processing .... Technicolor
Sound re–recording .... Pinewood Studios
Music Recording .... The Music Centre
James Bond Theme .... Monty Norman

THE STUNT TEAM

Supervisors .... Martin Grace, Paul Weston, Bill Burton.

Dorothy Ford	Clive Curtis
Del Baker	Pat Banta
Bill Weston	Rocky Taylor
Jim Dowall	Wayne Michaels
Nick Hobbs	Jazzer Jeyes
Christopher Webb	Malcolm Weaver
Jack Sholomir	

THE AERIAL TEAM

Director .... Philip Wrestler
Coordinator .... Clay Lacy

Beech H18 .... B.J. Worth, Rande Deluca, Jake Lombard,
Joe Taylor

Bede Acro Star Jet .... 'Corky Fornof' and Rick Holley

ACKNOWLEDGEMENTS

The Senate of Berlin   The Royal Air Force, Northolt
Utah State Film Commission   Seiko Watches
Philips Indutrieis   Mont Blanc Simplo GmbH
Shrenni Maharana B.S. Mewar, Udaipur   Nene Valley International Steam Rail Way
The Ministry of Information & Broadcasting to the Government of India.

A VIEW TO A KILL

British intelligence has discovered the Russians to have the latest innovation in microchip technology which has proved impervious to intense magnetic pulse from nuclear explosions. This chip was developed by the British. But how did the Russians get it?

The chip was developed by Zorin Industries, but thorough investigation has revealed nothing. Bond learns that Zorin, also a horse breeder, is holding a horse sale at his Chateau in France. He and Lord Tibbett wrangle an invitation with Bond as Syngon Smythe and Tibbett as his chauffeur. They investigate Zorins stables at night but learn nothing.

Bond meets Stacey Sutton who has arrived to collect a check from Zorin for her mining property in California. Zorin becomes suspicious of them and has Tibbett killed. Knocked unconscious, Bond is placed in a Rolls-Royce and rolled into a lake to drown. Fortunately, he finds an air pocket and remains underwater until they leave. Bond's investigation then leads him to San Francisco where he learns of "Main Strike," Zorin's plan for flooding the Silicon Valley and destroying the microchip industry in the U.S. so that he will gain a monopoly in manufacture and distribution.

Bond meets Stacey again and they are captured by Zorin who kills a city hall official, forces them into an elevator, and sets fire to city hall. They manage to escape, steal a fire truck and make their way to Zorin's mine where he plans to detonate a bomb that will create the flood. Bond and May Day manage to place the bomb on a flat rail car but the brake release will not hold. May Day holds the release lever and rides the bomb into the tunnel until it explodes harmlessly, but killing herself.

Zorin has kidnapped Stacey in his airship but as it rises from the ground, Bond grabs a tie-line and holds on until it reaches the Golden Gate bridge where Zorn trys to knock him off. Bond wraps the line around a bridge brace which holds the airship in place. Bond and Zorin battle it out hand to hand on top of the bridge until Zorin slips and falls to his death as the airship explodes.

THE CAST

James Bond .... Roger Moore
Max Zorin .... Christopher Walken
Stacey Sutton .... Tanya Roberts
May Day .... Grace Jones
Tibbett .... Patrick Macnee
Scarpine .... Patrick Bauchau
Chuck Lee .... David Yip
Pola Ivanova .... Fiona Fullerton
Bob Conley .... Manning Redwood
Jenny Flex .... Alison Doody

Dr. Carl Mortner .... Willoughby Gray
Q .... Desmond Llewelyn
M .... Robert Brown
Miss Moneypenny .... Lois Maxwell
General Gogol.. Walter Gotell
Minister of Defense .... Geoffrey Keen
Aubergine .... Jean Rougerie
Howe .... Daniel Benzali
Klotkoff .... Bogdan Koninowski
Pan Ho .... Papillon Soo Soo
Kimberley Jones .... Mary Stavin
Butterfly Act Compere .... Dominique Risbourg
Whistling Girl .... Carole Ashby
Taiwanese Tycoon...................................... Anthony Chin
Paris Taxi Driver .... Lucien Jerome
U.S. Police Captain .... Joe Flood
Auctioneer .... Gerard Buhr
Venz .... Dolph Lundgren
Mine Foreman.. Tony Sibbald
O' Rourke .... Bill Ackridge
Guard I .... Ron Tarr
Guard II.. Taylor McAuley
Tycoon .... Peter Ensor
Helicopter Pilot .... Seva Novgorodtsev

Note on "A View To A Kill": Fleming took this phrase from the third verse of 'D' by Ken John Peel; a Cumberland hunting song written in 1820 by John Woodcock Graves.

THE PRODUCTION STAFF

Producer .... Albert R. Broccoli and Michael G. Wilson
Director .... John Glen
Screenplay.. Richard Maibaum and Michael G. Wilson
Associate Producer .... Thomas Pevsner
Music .... John Barry
Title Song Composed and Performed by ...... Duran Duran
Title Song Produced by .... Bernard Edwards
Production Designer .... Peter Lamont
Main Title Designer .... Maurice Binder
Director / Photography .... Alan Hume
2ⁿᵈ Unit Directed and
Photographed by .... Arthur Wooster
Ski Sequence Directed and
Photographed by .... Willy Bogner
Costumes Designer .... Emma Porteous
Casting .... Debbie McWilliams
Editor .... Peter Davies and John Groves
Sound Editor .... Colin Miller
Special Effects Supervisor .... John Richardson

The base of the Eiffel Tower where Bond commandered a taxi cab in his attempt to catch Mayday in *A View to A Kill*. (Society Novelle D'Exploration de la Tour Eiffel, Paris)

Production Supervisor	Anthony Waye
Production Managers	Philip Kohler, Serge Touboul, Leonard Gmur, Ned Kopp and Company, Jon Thor Hannesson
Third Assistant Director	Geoffrey Moore
Unit Manager	Iris Rose
Production Accountant	Douglas Noakes
Assistant Director	Gerry Gavigan
Camera Operator	Michael Frift
Sound Recordist	Derek Ball
Continuity	June Randall
Electrical Supervisor	John Tythe
Action Sequence Arranger	Martin Grace
Driving Stunts Arrnager	Remy Julienne
Art Director	John Fenner
Set Decorator	Crispian Sallis
Construction Manager	Michael Redding
Make-up Supervisor	George Frost
Hairdressing Supervisor	Ramon Gow
Production Controller	Reginald A. Barkshire
Director of Marketing	Charles Juroe
Location Managers	Nick Daubeny, Agust Baldursson, Stefan Zurcher, Jean-Marc Deschamps, Steph Benseman, Rory Enke
Assistant Director, 2nd Unit	Peter Bennett
Continuity, 2nd Unit	Peter Daniels and Daphne Carr
Additional Assistant Directors	Edi Hubschmid, Laurent Bregeat, Serge Menard, Terry Madden, Andrew Warren, Simon Haveland, Nick Heckstall-Smith, Barbara Broccoli
Location Accountants	Hazel Crombie, Mauricette Boisard, Jane Meagher, Christl Kirchner
Production Coordinators	May Capsaskis, Nathalie Farjon, Norma Garment, Sally Hayman, Maureen Murphy
Production Secretaries	Joanna Brown & Janine King
Mr. Moore's Assistant	Doris Spriggs
U.S. Casting	Jane Jenkins, Janet Hirshenson
U.S. Contracts	Mary Stellar and Tina Banta
Costume Supervisor	Tiny Nicholls
Costumes Made by	C & G Costumers Ltd.
Additional Wardrobe For Grace Jones	Azzedine Alaia
Additional Art Directors	Michael Lamont, Ken Court, Alan Tomkins, Serge Douy, Armin Ganz, Katharina Brunner
Assistant Art Directors	James Morahan, Ted Ambrose, Michael Boone
Assistant Set Decorator	Jille Brown
Sketch Artists	Roger Deer, Maciek Piotroski
Production Buyer	Ron Quelch
Scenic Artists	Ernest Smith, Jacqueline Stears
Computer Effects	Ira Curtis Coleman
Boom Operator	Ken Nightingall
Make-up	Eric Allwright and Bunty Phillips
Hairdressers	Vera Mitchell and Joan Carpenter

Unit Publicist .... Geoff Freeman
Special Effects .... John Morris, Joss Williams, Ken Morris,
                                                 Andre Trielli, Larry Cavanaugh, Willy Neuner
Publicity Assistant .... Jennifer Collen-Smith
Stills .... Keith Hamshere and George Whitear
Property Master .... John Chisholm
Model Photography .... Leslie Dear
Additional Photography .... Jan d'Alquen and Egil Woxholt
Camera Operators, 2nd Unit .... Malcolm Vinson and Robert Hillman
Focus .... Simon Hume and Michael Evans
Front Projection .... Charles Staffell and Roy Moores
Camera Grips .... Colin Manning and Ken Atherfold
Crowd Artists .... Central Casting
Eiffel Tower .... S.N.T.E.
Zorin's Stable .... Musee Vivant Du Cheval, Chantilly
Whitewood House .... Dunsmuir House, Oakland
Title Skiers .... British Ski Federation
Chateau Flowers .... Rene Veyrat
Speedboats .... Glastron and Chantiers Rocca
Cranes .... Lee Lifting Services
Ultraviolet lighting .... Thorn EMI
Cameras and Binoculars .... Nikon UK Ltd.
Special Properties .... The Sharper Image
Iceland Advisors .... Iceland Breakthrough, Tony Escritt
Travel and Transport .... Renown Freight Ltd, The Travel Company, D & D
                                                 International, Locations Ltd., Location Facilities
Sound Effects .... Jean-Pierre LeLong
Additional Editors .... John S. Smith and Henry Richardson
Assistant Editor .... John Nuth
Dubbing Editors .... Jack Knight, Nigel Galt, Stanley Fiferman
Assistant Dubbing Editor .... Bill Barringer
Music Editor .... Alan Killick
Orchestrations .... Nicholas Raine
Music Mixer .... Dick Lewzey
Re-recording Mixers .... Graham Hartstone and John Hayward
James Bond Theme .... Monty Norman

THE SNOW TEAM

| Peter Rohe | John Eaves | Thomas Sims |
| Steven Link | Joe Brown | Andrea Florineth |

THE HORSE TEAM

Olivier Victor-Thomas	Christian de Lagarde	Marcel Riou
Francois Nadal	Mario Luraschi	Brian Bowes
Anthony Fairbairn		

THE DRIVING TEAM

Michel Julienne	Dominique Julienne	Robert Blasco
Christian Bonnichon	Jean-Claude Lagniez	Jean-Claude Bonnichon
Jean–Claude Houbart		

THE STUNT TEAM

Supervisors	Jim Arnett, Bob Simmons, Claude Carliez
Stuntmen	Jason White, Mike Runyard, Tracey Eddon, Bill Weston, Elaine Ford, Doug Robinson, Pat Banta

THE AERIAL TEAM

Eiffel Tower Jump	B.J.Worth
Skyship 500	Nicholas T. Bennett
Helicopters	Helicopter Hire, Aerospatiale, Heliswiss, HeliFrance, Castle Air
Pilots	Marc Wolff, Rick Holley, Chuck Tamburro, Robert Liechti, Gerry Crayson
Camera	David Butler, Peter Allwork, Doug Milsome

THE GIRLS

Sian Adey-Jones	Samina Afzal	Celine Cawley
Nike Clark	Helen Clitherow	Maggie Defreitas
Gloria Douse	Caroline Hallett	Debrah Hanna
Josanne Haydon-Pearce	Ann Jackson	Terri Johns
Karen Loughlin	Angela Lyn	Patricia Martinez
Kim Ashfield Norton	Elke Ritschel	Lou-Anne Ronchi
Helen Smith	Jane Spencer	Paul Thomas
Mayako Torigai	Toni White	

Filmed in	Panavision, Technicolor
Prints in	Metrocolor
Title Opticals	National Screen
Sound Re-recording	Pinewood Studios

ACKNOWLEDGEMENTS

The Sheriff & People of Hofn	The Commune of Pontresina
The City of Paris	The Chateau of Chantilly
Renault Automobiles	Bollinger Champagne
Cartier	The Ascot Authority
Amberley Chalk Pits Museum	Airship Industries
Seiko Time (U.K.) Ltd.	Philips Electronics
Chevron U.S.A.	The Mayor and City of San Francisco

Note: The chase scene between fire truck and police took three weeks to film and destroyed 12 cars.

THE LIVING DAYLIGHTS

Bond is in Bratislava, Czechoslovakia to kill a Russian sniper who in turn, is out to kill a defecting Russian general. The sniper is a girl cello player from the local symphony orchestra. When Bond recognizes her from attendance at the theatre the night before, he purposely hits her rifle instead, preventing her from firing. Then, with the aid of Saunders, head of Station V, Vienna, they smuggle General Koskov out of the country and send him to England.

On the very same day Koskov is debriefed by the British, he is kidnapped by what 'M' thinks is Russian agents. Bond returns to Bratislava, finds the girl, examines her rifle and discovers it carries blank shells. The British and Kara had both been duped by Koskov, who had set-up his own defection. In Bond's Aston Martin Vantage, they flee, bound for Vienna. They are pursued by Russian military and forced to abandon their car after an exciting chase.

Arriving in Vienna, Bond meets again with Saunders, but Saunders is killed by Necros, a hood for Whittaker, who is an international arms dealer in partnership with Koskov. Bond's orders are to kill General Pushkin who is now in Tangiers.

After Bond's arrival there, he learns from Pushkin that he was about to arrest Koskov for stealing state funds to buy arms. Whittaker has ordered Pushkin killed but Pushkin and Bond have already devised a phony assasination of Pushkin.

Thinking him dead, Whittaker and Koskov go to Bond's room where Bond is drugged. He and Kara are taken prisoner by Koskov and flown to a Russian air base in Afghanistan. Arriving there they are to be jailed and sent to Russia, but Bond, using a device provided by 'Q', emits a stun gas and they overpower their jailers, free Kamran Shah, leader of the Afghan rebels, and flee the air base.

They are taken to Shah's headquarters and the following day return to the air base where Koskov's men are loading raw opium in a transport plane which he and Whittaker will sell for cash to buy guns which will be used against the rebels. Bond sneaks aboard the plane, kills Necros, and Kara then comes aboard. The rebels had stormed the base and are now fleeing across a bridge ahead of Russian troops. A bomb which Bond had originally intended to blow-up the plane, he now drops on the bridge, which prevents the Russians from pursuing the rebels. The plane runs out of gas.

Bond returns to Tangiers and kills Whittaker. General Pushkin sends Koskov off to exile in Russia. Then, after a symphony concert and reception for Kara, Bond and Kara are finally alone.

[1]Title and some aspects of this story derived from Ian Fleming's short story which originally appeared in the London Sunday Times, 1962.

THE CAST

James Bond	Timothy Dalton
Kara Milovy	Maryam d'Abo
General Georgi Koskov	Jeroen Krabbe
Brad Whitaker	Joe Don Baker
General Pushkin	John Rhys-Davies
Kamran Shah	Art Malik
Necros	Andreas Wisniewski
Saunders	Thomas Wheatley
Q	Desmond Llewelyn
M	Robert Brown
Minister of Defense	Geoffrey Keen
General Gogol	Walter Gotell
Moneypenny	Caroline Bliss
Felix Leiter	John Terry
Rubavitch	Virginia Hey
Col. Feyador	John Bowe
Rosika Miklos	Julie T. Wallace
Linda (Lady on the Boat)	Kell Tyler
Liz	Catherine Rabett

Ava .... Dulice Liecier
Chief of Security, Tangiers .... Nadim Sawalha
Koskov's KGB Minder .... Alan Talbot
Imposter .... Carl Rigg
Chief of Snow Leopard Brotherhood .... Tony Cyrus
Achmed .... Atik Mohamed
Kamran's men .... Michael Moor, Sumar Khan
Jailer .... Ken Sharrock
Gas Works' Supervisor .... Peter Porteous
Male Secretary .... Antony Carrick
002 .... Glyn Baker
004 .... Frederick Warder
Toastmaster, Tangiers Conference .... Richard Cubison

THE PRODUCTION STAFF

Producers .... Albert R. Broccoli, Michael G. Wilson
Director .... John Glen
Screenplay.. Richard Maibaum, Michael G. Wilson
Associate Producers .... Tom Pevsner, Barbara Broccoli
Music .... John Barry
Production Designer .... Peter Lamont
Main Title Designer .... Maurice Binder
Director / Photography .... Alec Mills
Director / Photography, 2nd Unit .... Arthur Wooster
Special Visual Effects .... John Richardson
Costume Designer....................................... Emma Porteous
Casting .... Debbie McWilliams
Editors.. John Grover, Peter Davies
Sound Editor .... Colin Miller
Production Supervisor .... Anthony Waye
Production Accountant .... Douglas Noakes
Director / Marketing .... Charles Juroe
Production Managers .... Philip Kohler, Sparky Greene, Arno Ortmair, Denis
                                                                          O'Dell, Leonard Gmur
Unit Manager .... Iris Rose
Assistant Director .... Gerry Gavigan
Camera Operator... Michael Frift
Aerial Cameraman .... Tom Saunders
Assistant Director, 2nd Unit .... Terry Madden
Additional Assistant Directors .... Crispin Reece, Terry Blyther, Callum McDougall,
                                                                          Nick Heckstall-Smith, Mohamed Hassini,
                                                                          Urs Egger, Ahmed Hatimi
Moroccan Production Liaison .... Zakaria Alaoui
Gibralter Production Liaison .... Joseph Viale
2nd Unit Continuity .... Jean Bourne
Sound Recordist.. Derek Ball
Continuity .... June Randall
Stunt Supervisor .... Paul Weston
Driving Stunts Arranger .... Remy Julienne

Aerial Stunts Arranger .... B.J. Worth
Horse Master .... Greg Powell
Electrical Supervisor .... John Tythe
Art Director .... Terry Ackland-Snow
Set Decorator .... Michael Ford
Construction Manager .... Anthony Graysmark
Dalton Stand-in .... Robert Grayson
Make-up Supervisor .... George Frost
Hairdressing Supervisor .... Ramon Gow
Production Controller .... Reginald A. Barkshire
Assistant Accountant .... Allan Davies
Location Accountants .... Jane Meagher, Christl Kirchner
Location Managers .... Driss Gaidi, Nick Daubeny, Stefan Zurcher, John Bernard, Arie Bohrer
Model Photography .... Leslie Dear
Scenic Artists .... Jacqueline Stears
Chief Sculptor .... Fred Evans
Sketch Artist .... Roger Deer
Location Transport Managers .... Andy Grosch, Arno Esterez
Production Coordinators .... May Capsaskis, Pam Parker, Dawn Severdsia, Janine Lodge, Brenda Ramos, Daniela Stibitz, Ihsanne Khalafaoui
Production Buyers .... Sid Palmer, Peter Palmer
Property Master .... Bert Hearn
Additional Construction Managers .... Ken Pattenden, Alfred Dobsak
Assistant Set Decorators .... Jille Brown, Christopher Kanter
Additional Art Directors .... Michael Lamont, Peter Manhard, Ken Court, Thomas Riccabona, Fred Hole, Bert Davey
Assistant Art Directors .... James Morahan, Dennis Bosher, Ted Ambrose
Secretary to Mr. Broccoli .... Sandra Frieze
Secretary to Mr. Wilson .... Joanna Brown
Secretary to Mr. Juroe .... Amanda Schofield
Location to Production Secretaries .... Sophie Koekenhoff, Sonja Beutura, Hind Hanif
U.S. Contacts .... Tina Banta, Mary Stellar
Additional Photography .... Phil Pastuhov, Tom Sanders
Camera Operator, 2nd Unit .... Malcolm Macintosh
Additional Camera Operators: .... Michael Anderson, Fred Waugh, Peter Rohe
Focus .... Frank Elliott, Horst Becker, Michael Evans, Dan McKinny, Nicholas Wilson
Camera Grips .... Chunky Huse, Ken Atherfold, Richard Haw
Video Effects Supervisor .... Richard Hewitt
Music Editor .... Alan Killick
Additional Sound Recordists .... Brian Marshall, Roby Guever
Additional Sound Editors .... Peter Musgrave, Derek Holding, Vernon Messenger
Front Projection .... Roy Moores
Boom Operator .... Ken Nightingall
Music Mixer .... Dick Lewzey

Assistant Sound Editors .... William Barringer, Mark Mostyn, Ross Adams
Robert Gavin
Assistant Editors .... Matthew Glen, John Nuth, Wayne Smith
Additional Sound Effects .... Jean-Pierre Lelong
Orchestrations .... Nicholas Raine
Re-recording Mixers .... Graham Hartstone, John Hayward
Costume Supervisor .... Tiny Nicholls
Wardrobe Master, 2ⁿᵈ Unit .... Don Mothersill
Make-up .... Naomi Donne, Eric Allwright, Edwin Erfmann
Hairdressers .... Helen Lennox, Barbara Sutton
Aerial Liaison .... Marc Wolff
Safety Climber .... Hamish MacInnis
Special Effects .... Chris Corbould, Willy Neuner, Joss Williams, Ken
Morris, Brian Smithies
Armourer .... Simon Atherton
Modelmaker .... Terence Reed
Unit Publicist .... Geoff Freeman
Publicity Assistant .... Rebecca West
Stills .... Keith Hamshere, George Whitear

THE GIRLS
Odette Benatar, Dianna Casale, Sharon Devlin, Femi Gardiner, Patricia Keefer, Ruddy Rodriquez, Moyte Sanchez, Cela Savannah, Karen Seeberg, Maris Walsh, Karen Williams.

THE STUNT TEAM
Doug Robinson, Michel Julienne, Nick Wilkinson, Simon Crane, Elaine Ford, Ray Olon, Del Baker, Jason White.

HORSE STUNTS
Brian Bowes, Graeme Crowther, Jorge Casares, Steve Dent, Nick Gillard, Joaquin Olias, Miguel Peoregosa, Jose Maria Serrano.

AERIAL STUNTS
Jake Brake, Garry Carter, Jake Lombard, Dan O' Brien.

DRIVING STUNTS
Christian Bonnichon, Jo Cote, Jean Claude Houbard, Dominique Julienne, Jean Claude Justice, Jean-Jacques Villain, Brigitte Magnin.

SNOW STUNTS
John Fallriner, Ida Huber, Rene Seiler, Herman Sporer.

ACKNOWLEDGEMENTS
Costumes made by .... Bermans & Nathans
Horses provided by .... La Societe R.E.H.A.
Travel and Transport .... Renown Freight, The Travel Company, D & D
International Locations, Location Facilities
Location Catering .... Rafael Hosteleria International , The Location
Caterers
CIA Boat .... Spectral Marine

Military Dioramas	Little Lead Soldiers
Floral Arrangements	Kenneth Turner Flowers
Hats	David Shilling
Swimwear	Gottex
Whitaker's Villa	Forbes Magazine, Palais El Mendoub, Tangiers.
Austrian Youth Symphony Orchestra	Conducted by: Gert Meditz; Cello: Stefan Kropfitsch
Sound re-recording	Pinewood Studios
James Bond Theme written by	Monty Norman
Title Opticals	Screen Opticals
Filmed in	Panavision, Technicolor
Sound	Dolby Stereo
Music Recorded at	C.T.S. London

The Mayor & City of Vienna

Cartier

Bollinger Champagne

Audi Ag

Aston Martin Lagonda Limited

The Providence of Karnten, Austria and the People of Weissensee

His Majesty King Hassan II and the Military & Civil Authorities of Morocco

The Nature Conservancy Council

The Government of Gibralter

Philips Electronics

The Ministry of Defense, London

LICENSE TO KILL

Felix Leiter, Drug Enforcement Agent (DEA) and his best man, James Bond, are on the seven Mile Bridge enroute to Key West where Leiter is scheduled to be married to Della Churchill. Moments later a giant Coast Guard helicopter sets down on the highway in front of them. Leiter is informed that Franz Sanchez, the Central American druglord has left his Isthmus City headquarters enroute to Cray Cay in the Bahamas. Leiter and Bond board the helicopter to Cray Cay, capture Sanchez and return to Key West where Leiter is married. Later however, Sanchez escapes authorities. In turn, his hoods kill Della Churchill and throw Leiter to the sharks where he is badly mauled but still alive.

Bond investigates the Ocean Exotica Wherehouse in Key West, owned by Milton Krest, a friend of Sanchez where Leiter was tortured and cocaine is stored for shipment. Later Bond is apprehended by British agents and taken to the Hemingway House where he is confronted by his boss 'M' who demands to know why he is not in Istanbul as ordered. He is told to leave Sanchez to the American authorities but Bond insists on seeking revenge for the assault on Leiter. 'M' demands his resignation and his weapon but Bond bolts over the veranda railing and escapes. Later, Bond disrupts a drug exchange between Milton Krest's yacht the "Wavekrest" and a seaplane. He destroys the cocaine and boards the seaplane as it is taking off.

In a vicious fight, Bond kills the two pilots, takes control of the plane and flies to Ballast Key where he sinks the plane. With the cash in two suitcases and the aide of a friend, he returns to Key West and Leiter's house. In Leiter's computer file Bond discovers a meeting date for the following day at the Barrelhead Saloon on Bimimi's West Island. It is there that Bond meets Pam Bouvier, Leiter's contact. They are confronted by Sanchez's men but manage to escape. Bond hires Bouvier, a former army pilot for Air America, to fly them to Isthmus City where they check into the El Presidente Hotel and deposit the five million dollars in drug money into the Banco de Isthmus, a bank owned by Sanchez! That evening they attend Sanchez's casino headquarters where Bond meets Sanchez face to face and develops a plot to kill him.

'M' sends 'Q' out to Isthmus City with a briefcase full of exotic equipment and weapons to give Bond support. However, Bond is captured and his plot foiled. Sanchez has developed a process whereby he can transport cocaine in gasoline tanker trucks, mixed in with the fuel undetected, and later retrieved intact. Sanchez has prepared a convoy of these trucks to deliver cocaine to the Chinese. Bond escapes with the aide of Pam Bouvier and her plane. They find the convoy and Bond is dropped onto one of the tankers. The story builds to climax as Bond battles Sanchez's men and destroys the tankers.

During a final vicious fight, Sanchez's clothes have become drenched with gasoline. On the verge of being killed, Bond manages to extract his cigarette lighter and ignite Sanchez's clothes, turning him into a human torch.

Back at the El Presidente Hotel, Bond and Pam Bouvier lock in a passionate embrace.

THE CAST

James Bond	Timothy Dalton
Pam Bouvier	Carey Lowell
Franz Sanchez	Robert Davi
Lupe Lamora	Talisa Soto
Milton Krest	Anthony Zerbe
Sharkey	Frank McRae
Felix Leiter	David Hedison
Killifer	Everett McGill
Dario	Benicio Del Tor
Perez	Alejandro Bracho
Della Churchill	Priscilla Barnes
M	Robert Brown
Q	Desmond Llewelyn
Heller	Don Stroud
Kwang	Cary-Hiroyuki Tagawa
Joe Butcher	Wayne Newton
William Truman-Lodge	Anthony Starke
Custom Agent	Robert Martinez
Miss Loti	Diana Lee–Hsu
Fallon	Christopher Neame
President Hector Lopez	Pedro Armendariz[1]
Moneypenny	Caroline Bliss
Hawkins	Grand L. Bush
Braun	Guy De Saint Cyr
Mullens	Rafer Johnson
Stripper	Jeannine Bisignano
Montelongo	Claudio Brook
Consuelo	Cynthia Fallon
Rasmussen	Enrique Novi
Oriental	Osami Kawawo
Doctor	George Belanger
Wavekrest Captain	Roger Cudney
Chief Chemist	Honorato Magaloni
Pit Boss	Jorge Russek

Bellboy .... Sergio Corona
Ninja .... Stuart Kwan
Tanker Driver .... Jose Abdala
Ticket Agent .... Teresa Blake
Della Churchill's Uncle .... Samuel Benjamin Lancaster
Casino Manager .... Juan Peleaz
Coast Guard Radio Operator .... Mark Kelty
Hotel Assistant Manager .... Umberto Elizondo
Sanchez's Driver .... Fidel Carriga
Barrelhead Waitress .... Edna Bolkan
Clive .... Eddie Enderfield
Warehouse Guards .... Jeff Moldovan, Carl Ciarfalio

[1]Son of Pedro Armendariz who portrayed Kerim Bey in the film *From Russia With Love*.

THE PRODUCTION STAFF

Producers .... Albert R. Broccoli and Michael G. Wilson
Director .... John Glen
Screenplay .... Michael G. Wilson
Story .... Richard Maibaum and Michael G. Wilson
Associate Producers .... Tom Pevsner and Barbara Broccoli
Production Designer: .... Peter Lamont
Director / Photography .... Alec Mills
Special Effects Supervisor .... John Richardson
Costume Designer .... Jodie Tillen
Editor .... John Grover
Action Sequence Supervisor .... Paul Weston
Score .... Michael Kamen
1st Assistant Editor .... Matthew Glen
Underwater Stills .... Michael G. Wilson
Unit Photographer .... Keith Hamshere
Main Title Designer .... Maurice Binder
Make-up .... George Frost
Hairdresser .... Trish Cameron
Song License to Kill .... Sung by Gladys Knight
Composed by .... Jeffrey Cohen, Walter Afanasieff and Narada
Michael Walden
Director/Photographer, 2nd Unit .... Arthur Wooster
Casting .... Jane Jenkins and Janet Hirshenson
Production Supervisor .... Anthony Waye
Underwater Scenes Director/Photographer .. Ramon Bravo
Production Accountant .... Douglas Noakes
Stunt Coordinator .... Paul Weston
Driving Stunts Arranger .... Remy Julienne
Music Consultant .... Joel Sill
Sketch Artist .... Roger Deer
Graphics .... Robert Walker
Sculptor .... Daniel Miller
Scenic Artist .... Gilly Noyes-Court

Camera Focus	Frank Elliott
Second Cameras (Mexico)	Donald Bryant and Tim Ross
Property Master	Bert Hearn
Production Buyer	Ron Quelch
Director / Publicity	Saul Cooper
Special Effects Supervisors	Laurence Cordereo and Sergio Jara
Special Effects (Unit 1)	Neil Corbould
Special Effects Technicians	Peter Pickering, Clive Beard, Nick Finlayson.
Make-up	Norma Webb
Wardrobe Master (Mexicali)	Enrique Villavicencio
Costume Supervisors	Barbara Scott and Hugo Pena
Boom Operator	Martin Trevis
Camera Grip	Chunky Huse
Music Editor	Andrew Glen
Assistant Editors	John Nuth, Wayne Smith, Ross Adams, Richard Fettes, Mark Mostyn, Rob Green
Additional Sound Effects	Jean-Pierre Lelong
Re-Recording Mixers	Graham Hartstone and John Hayward
Music Mixer	Dick Lewzey
Music Programming	Stephen McLaughlin
Music Performed by	The National Philharmonic Orchestra, London
Art Director	Dennis Bosher
Assistant Art Directors	Neil Lamont, Richard Holland, Andrew Ackland-Snow, Hector Romero
Sound Editors	Peter Musgrave and Mark Auguste
Editor (Mexico)	Carlos Puente
Assembly Editor	Matthew Glen
Assistant Accountant	Andrew Noakes
Accountants	Jane Meagher & Rosa Marie Gomez
Casting (Mexico)	Claudia Becker
Production Secretary	Ileana Franco
Aerial Stunt Supervisor	Corky Fornof
Director of Marketing	Charles Juroe
Production Supervisor (Mexico)	Hector Lopez
Production Manager	Philip Kohler
Unit Manager	Iris Rose
Assistant Directors	Miguel Gil and Miguel Lima
Camera Operator	Michael Frift
Sound Recordist	Edward Tise
James Bond Theme	Monty Norman
Continuity	June Randall
Electrical Supervisor	John Tythe
Art Director	Michael Lamont
Set Decorator	Michael Ford
Construction Manager	Tony Graysmark
Hairdressing Supervisor	Tricia Cameron
Sound Editor	Vernon Messenger
Production Manager	Efren Flores

Production Manager (Mexicali) .... Crispin Reece
Location Manager (Mexicali) .... Laura Aguilar
Production Coordinator .... Loolee Deleon
Production Coordinator (Mexicali) .... Georgina Heath
2nd Assistant Director .... Callum McDougall
Production Assistant .... Ignacio Cervantes, Marcia Perskie, Gerardo Barrera, Monica Greene
Stand-by Propman .... Bernard Hearn
Armourers .... Harris Bierman & Tony Didio
Transport Manager .... Arthur Dunne
Transport Captain (Mexico) .... Mauro Venegas
London Contact .... Amanda Schofield
Los Angeles Contact .... Linda Brown

SECOND UNIT

1st Assistant Directors .... Terry Madden, Sebastian Silva
2nd Assistant Director .... Marcia Gay
Continuity .... Sue Field
Camera Operator .... Malcolm Macintosh
Camera Focus .... Michael Evans
Camera Grip .... Ken Atherfold
Still Photographer .... George Whitear
Special Effects Supervisor .... Chris Corbould
Special Effects Technicians .... Andy Williams and Paul Whybrow
Make-up / Hair .... Di Holt
Stand-by Propman .... Rodney Pincott

FLORIDA

Production Supervisor .... Ned Kopp
Production Coordinator .... Patricia Madiedo
Location Manager .... Colette Hailey
Location Accountant .... Jack Descent
Second Camera .... John Elton
Art Director .... Ken Court
Set Decorators .... Richard Helfritz and Frederick Weiler
Special Effects Coordinator .... Larry Cavanaugh
Electrical Supervisor .... Norman Zuckerman
Key Grip .... Eddie Knott III
Costume Supervisor .... Robert Chase
Marine Coordinator .... Lorentz Hills
Transport Coordinator .... Joyce Lark

THE STUNT TEAM

Supervisors .... Gerardo Morerno, Marc Boyle, Art Malesci

Simon Crane	Jake Lombard	Steve Dent
David Reinhardt	Mark Bahr	Julian Bucio
Javier Lambert	Alex Edlin	Mauricio Martinez

THE DRIVING TEAM

Gilbert Bataille	Jo Cote	Didier Brule
Jean-Claude Houbart	Dominique Julienne	

THE AERIAL TEAM

Aerial Cameraman	Phil Pastuhov
Parachute Stunt Coordinator	B.J. Worth
Camera Helicopter	French Aircraft Agency
Helicopter Pilot	Ken Calman
U.S. Coast Guard Technical Advisor	Commander John McElwain
U.S. Coast Guard Helicopter Pilots	Lt. CDR. Randy Meade III, Lt. Neil Hughes, R.N., Lt. CDR. R. Allen

THE UNDERWATER TEAM

Coordinator	Rita Sheese
Location Managers	Nicole Kolin & Tony Broccoli
Camera Assistant	Pepe Flores
Special Effects	Daniel Dark
Divers	Emilio Magana, Juan Dario Corona, Alex Arnold, Jorge Cardenas, Manuel Cardenas

ACKNOWLEDGEMENTS

Special Consultants to the Producers	Sparky Greene, Jillian Palenthorpe
Camera Equiptment	Tratafilms (Mexico City), Cine Video Tech (Miami)
Film Stock	Kodak Mexicana
Lighting and Transport	Servicios Filmicos
Freight	Jose Vasques A. Vital International Freight Services, Renown Freight
Travel	Travel Shop International, The Travel Company
Catering	Alimentacion Filmica,Especializada
Medical Services	Lifestar International
Weapons	Stembridge Gun Rentals Inc.
Gun Holsters	Galco International
Animals by	Carlos Renero
Jewelry	Sheila Goldfinger
Filmed In	Panavision
Color by	Deluxe
Sound	Dolby Stereo
Title Opticals	General Screen Enterprises
Music Recorded at	C.T.S. London
Sound Re-Recorded by	Pinewood Studios

The Florida Film Bureau	The Key West Chamber of Commerce
United States Coast Guard	Cigarette Racing Team, Inc.
Pan American World Airways	Aerospatiale
Kenworth Truck Company	Philips Electronics
Furuno U.S.A., Inc.	Dacor Corporation
Mappin & Webb	Bollinger Champagne
Baron Enrico Di Portanova	The People and Government of Mexico

John H. Perry, Inc. & Submersible Systems Technology, Inc.
The Officials and People of the Lower Keys, Florida

GOLDENEYE

'M' ordered James Bond, 007, and Alec Trevelyn, 006, to destroy the Archangel Chemical Weapons facility in the USSR. During the operation, 006 was killed by a Colonel Ourumov, but 007's explosives destroy the facility and Bond gets out alive.

Driving the South coast of France, Bond is passed by a speeding red Ferrari. (In the book the Ferrari is yellow). In Monaco he discovers the Ferrari and the girl at the casino. Playing bacarat against her he wins 200,000 pounds. From M.I.6 he learns she is Xenia Onatopp with the Janus Crime Syndicate in the USSR. During the course of the following day she murders a US Admiral, two helicopter pilots and steals the latest French helicopter, the Tigre. Bond's efforts to stop her were not successful.

The scene is Severnaya radar station, USSR. Natalya Simonova, a computer technician manipulates a huge radio telescope dish locked onto a piece of Soviet space junk, in reality a fully operational satellite. She and co-worker Boris Grishenko are among a dozen men and women who work in a clean room far below the surface.

The Tigre lands at the station and out steps Xenia Onatopp and the now General Ourumov. They obtain the necessary codes, firing key and Goldeneye disc from the duty officer. They kill everyone in the station except Simonova who has hidden and Grishenko who disappeared. With the Goldeneye they proceed to arm the satellite, designating it to destroy the station, then leave.

Simonova survives the destruction, makes her way to St. Petersburg. Here she makes contact with Grishenko, who also survived and they agree to meet. Unfortunately, at their meeting, Grishenko is accompanied by Xenia Onatopp and is taken prisoner and drugged. Bonds meets with Jack Wade, CIA agent, who puts him in contact with an old nemesis of Bond's who can set him up to meet the head of the Janus Crime Sydicate. In the steam room of the Europa Hotel, Bond is attacked by Xenia Onatopp. He subdues her. Tied up, she agrees to take him to Janus in Statue Park. Out of the shadows steps Alec Trevelyn.

Bond is knocked unconscious and awakens to discover that he and Natalya Simonova are bound inside the Tigre helicopter, Its rockets have fired and are targeted to return. Bond hits the ejector switches with his nose and they are thrown clear, then taken prisoners by Russian Federal Intelligence. During interrogation by Viktor Mishkin, Minister of Defense, General Ourumov appears, and kills the Minister. Bond attacks Ourumov and escapes with Natalya. Natalya is again taken prisoner by General Ourumov, who flees the scene in a black sedan. Bond has commondeered a tank and pursues them. The chase takes them to the Strategic (Rail) Weapons Depot where General Ourumov, Janus, and Xenia board the train. Taking a shortcut, Bond straddles his tank on the rails. As the train approached, Bond fired the 100 mm gun with an Armor piercing shell. After the explosion, Bond boarded the train. He kept his gun on Xenia and Trevelyan. General Ourumov appears with a gun pointed to Natalya's head. She breaks free from the General and Bond kills him. Xenia and Trevelyn flee the car. Through the computer, Natalya learns that Grishenko is in Cuba. Bond contacts Jack Wade of the CIA. He arranges plane tickets to the states, clothes, and the right visa for Natalya. Traveling under disguises, they go first to Paris, then to Miami and on to Puerto Rico where they are met by CIA agent, Jack Wade. He leaves a Piper Archer airplane for them at the nearest airport.

Wade also has brought Bond a briefcase with 'Q''s latest gagetry. The following morning as they are looking for the antenna and dish, a 140 mm rocket suddenly shears off half of their port wing and the plane crashes. Hovering above them is a helicopter with a rope ladder extended. Xenia grabs Bond with her legs in a scissor lock. Bond manages to grab her machine pistol and fire it up towards the pilot. The helicopter surges forward, pulling the ladder after it. Xenia is caught in the trees, killed, and the helicopter crashes in a ball of fire.

Far below the lake, Boris Grishenko is working the computer, transferring billions of dollars from the Bank of England into private accounts in other foreign countries. Then, they would activate the satellite to destroy London.

Bond and Natalya watch as three tall masts and a dish rise from the lake. They start to climb, then slip on the wet metal to the bottom of the dish. At the base they enter a maintenance blockhouse, down another rung ladder to a catwalk circling the control room. Guards begin firing at them and Bond pushes Natalya away. She heads for the mainframe computer room. Bond had planted mines around the fuel tanks and they are activated. Bond is captured and brought to Trevelan, who examined all his personal effects. Natalya had succeeded in deflecting the course of the satellite. Shots ring out. Explosions are heard. The liquid coolants suddenly explode. Boris Grishenko is suddenly enveloped in a freezing white mist. He becomes a frozen statue inside the doomed building. Pursued by Trevelyn, Bond drops through a trapdoor with his hands on the bottom rung of a ladder. Trevelyan slips and falls, with Bond grabbing him by one wrist. As he pleads for Bond to save him, Bond shouts, "Go to hell!" and lets him go.

As Bond dangles from the bottom rung of the ladder, Natalya has forced the pilot of a helicopter gunship to maneuver closer and closer to Bond. He brings the port landing skid just below Bond who manages to grab it just as everything around him seems to be collapsing. The gunship brings him down gently.

As he and Natalya begin to make love, Jack Wade and the Marines appear from out of the bushes.

CAST

James Bond	Pierce Brosnan
Alec Trevelyan	Sean Bean
Natalya Simonova	Izabella Scorupco
Xenia Onatopp	Famke Janssen
Jack Wade	Joe Don Baker
M	Judi Dench
Valentin Zukovsky	Robbie Coltrane
Dimitri Mishkin	Tcheky Karyo
General Ourumov	Gottfried John
Boris Grishenko	Alan Cumming
Q	Desmond Llewelyn
Moneypenny	Samantha Bond
Bill Tanner	Michael Kitchen
Caroline	Serena Gordon
Severnaya Duty Officer	Simon Kunz
French Warship Captain	Pavel Douglas
French Warship Officer	Cmdt. Olivier Lajous
Admiral Chuck Farrel	Billy J. Mitchell
Computer Store Manager	Constantine Gregory

Irina .... Minnie Driver
Anna.. Michelle Arthur
MIG Pilot .... Ravil Isyanov
Croupier .... Vladimir Milanovich
Train Driver .... Trevor Byfield
Valentin's Bodyguard .... Peter Majer

PRODUCTION STAFF

Directed by .... Martin Campbell
Produced by .... Michael G. Wilson and Barbara Broccoli
Screenplay by .... Jeffrey Caine and Bruce Feirstein
Story by .... Michael France
Executive Producer .... Tom Pevsner
"Goldeneye" Theme Performed by .... Tina Turner
"Goldeneye" Theme Written by .... Bono and the Edge
"Goldeneye" Theme Produced by .... Nellee Hooper
Music by .... Eric Serra
Production Designer .... Peter Lamont
Director of Photography .... Phil Meheux B.S.C.
Editor .... Terry Rawlings
Costume Designer.. Linda Hemming
Associate Producer .... Anthony Waye
Financial Controller .... Douglas Noakes
Second Unit Director .... Ian Sharp
Second Unit Cameraman .... Harvey Harrison B.S.C.
Additional Unit Directed
and Photographed by .... Arthur Wooster B.S.C.
Special Effects Supervisor .... Chris Corbould
Miniature Effects Supervisor .... Derek Meddings
Stunt Coordinator .... Simon Crane
Casting .... Debbie McWilliams
Main Title Designed by .... Daniel Kleinman
Visual Effects Photography .... Paul Wilson B.S.C.
Supervising Sound Editor .... Jim Shields
Supervising Art Director .... Neil Lamont
Set Decorator .... Michael Ford
Construction Coordinator .... Tony Graysmark
Property Master .... Barry Wilkinson
Model Unit Art Director .... Michael Lamont
Modeller Head of Development .... Brian Smithies
Makeup Supervisor .... Linda Devetta
Hairdressing Supervisor .... Colin Jamison
Wardrobe Supervisor .... John Scott
Stills Photographer .... Keith Hamshere
Publicity and Marketing .... Gordon Arnell
Car Chase Stunts... Remy Julienne
Production Manager .... Philip Kohler
Unit Manager .... Iris Rose

Location Production Managers	Serge Touboul, Valery Yermolaev, Ellen Gordon, Leonhard Gmur, Stefan Zurcher
Assistant Director	Gerry Gavigan
Camera Operator	Roger Pearce
Sound Recordist	David John
Script Recordist	June Randall
Electical Supervisor	Terry Potter
Second Unit Assistant Director	Terry Madden

Produced and distributed by MGM/United Artists.

TOMORROW NEVER DIES

M.I.6 learned that Henry Gupta, a techno terrorist, has acquired an Atomic Clock Signal Encoding System (ACSES) of which there were supposedly only twenty-two in the world. This device hooked up to a Global Positioning Satellite System (GPS) could, among other things, send a ship off course. What they didn't know was that Gupta was employed by Elliot Carver, a man who had inherited his father's wealth through blackmail and murder. He loved power and discovered that by manipulating the news he could increase his company's earnings and his personal wealth. In the 90's the Carver Media Group Network was second only to CNN. Its communication satellite was currently over Southeast Asia.

The HMS Devonshire is off the coast of China when it is ordered by Chinese MIGs to put into the nearest port or be fired upon. Commander Day replies that his ship is in international waters and will defend itself if attacked. What Day doesn't know is that Sea Dolphin II, a stealth ship is following Devonshire. A device known as Sea-Vac, a jet engine drilling machine with rotary cutters for teeth and a video camera has been deployed. Fast forward as the Sea-Vac penetrates the hull of Devonshire, sinking it. Divers then enter the hull and remove one of its cruise missile. Sea Dolphin II then destroys one of the Chinese MIG's. What has developed here is an international crisis between Great Britian and China. It is a crisis engineered totally by Elliot Carver whose media slogan is "tomorrow's news today!"

M.I.6 learns that one of the CMGN satellites over China, a news satellite that never got permission to broadcast, did in fact send a signal on the very same night. Somehow, war between Great Britain and China has to be averted.

In the next scene, Bond is sent to Hamburg where CMGN is having a grand opening of its world headquarters. At Avis Rental Car 'Q' instructs Bond in the latest techno weapons, the new BMW 750 and the Walther P99.

At the party Bond meets Carver's wife who turns out to be an old flame. Here too he meets Wai Lin from Chinese intelligence. As the party progresses, Carter develops an instantaneous hatred toward Bond and tries to have him killed by sending his henchmen to lure and attack him. Bond dispatches them, then again runs into Wai Lin. Bond sets off the automated fire alarm which creates total chaos and they escape the building with the fleeing crowd. Wai Lin disappears.

In Bond's hotel room, Paris Carver and Bond meet, reminisce and end up making love. Bond leaves to return to CMGN to investigate while Carver's men find Paris in the room and murder her.

In Henry Gupta's office Bond discovers the missing ACSESn device. He flees the Carver building amid flying bullets. Back at the hotel Bond discovers Paris' body and tries to escape the parking garage in his exotic BMW but is forced to abandon it. However, by remote control, the BMW foils Carver's men. Bond directs the BMW to the rooftop and sends it flying into space, dropping six floors to the street below.

'M' orders Bond to Okinawa to meet with the CIA and find the Devonshire. To avoid Chinese radar Bond makes a high altitude, low opening (HALO) jump over the South China Sea where Devonshire went down. Finding the wreckage, he again discovers Wai Lin. Together they discover that none of the small missiles have been fired, which proves the Devonshire had not fired on the Chinese MIGs, and that one of the ship's cruise missiles had been taken. Upon reaching the surface, they are captured and taken to Carver's headquarters in Saigon. Needless to say, once again they make a dramatic escape and meet up at a bicycle repair shop, a front for Chinese Secret Service. Here they learn that Ha Long Bay is the logical location for the Carver stealth ship. Arriving at Ha Long Bay they discover Sea Dolphin II preparing to leave harbor to destroy the British ships.

The scene switches to Bond and Wai Lin boarding the ship from their inflatable raft. They plant limpet mines set for twenty minutes. Eventually they are discovered. Wai Lin is captured. Bond battles Stamper and his thugs, killing all of them. He rescues Wai Lin and they leave the ship in a raft just before the limpet mines and the HMS Bedford shells destroy Carver's ship.

CAST

James Bond	Pierce Brosnan
Elliot Carver	Jonathan Pryce
Wai Lin	Michelle Yeoh
Paris Carver	Teri Hatcher
Henry Gupta	Ricky Jay
Stamper	Gotz Otto
Wade	Joe Don Baker
Dr. Kaufman	Vincent Schiavelli
M	Judi Dench
Q	Desmond Llewelyn
Moneypenny	Samantha Bond
Robinson	Colin Salmon
Admiral Roebuck	Geoffrey Palmer
Minister of Defense	Julian Fellowes
General Bukharin	Terence Rigby
Professor Inga Bergstrom	Cecilie Thomsen
Tamara Steel	Nina Young
PR Lady	Daphne Deckers
Dr. Dave Greenwalt	Colin Stinton
Master Sergeant 3	Al Matthews
Stealth Boat Captain	Mark Spalding

HMS Chester:

Captain	Bruce Alexander
Firing Officer	Anthony Green

HMS Devonshire:

Commander Richard Day	Christopher Bowen
Lieutenant Commander Peter Hume	Andrew Hawkins
Lieutenant Commander	Dominic Shaun

Yeoman .... Julian Rhind-Tutt
Leading Seaman .... Gerard Butler
Sonar .... Adam Barker

HMS Bedford:
Admiral Kelly .... Michael Byrne
Captain .... Pip Torrens
Air Warfare Officer .... Hugh Bonneville
Principal Warfare Officer .... Jason Watkins
Yeoman .... Erin McCarthy
Leading Seaman............................ Brendan Coyle
First Sea Lord .... David Ashton
Staff Officer 1 .... William Scott-Masson
Staff Officer 2 .... Laura Brattan
Beth Davidson .... Nadia Cameron
Mary Golson .... Liza Ross
Jeff Hobbs .... Hugo Napier
Philip Jones .... Rolf Saxon
MIG Pilot .... Vincent Wang
General Chang .... Philip Kwok

PRODUCTION STAFF
Directed By .... Roger Spottiswoode
Produced by .... Michael G. Wilson and Barbara Broccoli
Screenplay by .... Bruce Feirstein
"Tomorrow Never Dies" Theme
    Performed by .... Sheryl Crow
    Written by .... Sheryl Crow and Mitchell Froom
    Produced by .... Mitchell Froom
Music by .... David Arnold
Production Designer .... Allan Cameron
Director of Photography .... Robert Elswit
Editors... Dominique Fortin and Michel Arcand
Costume Designer......................... Lindy Hemming
Production Supervisor .... Collum McDougall
Supervising Production Accountant .... Andrew Noakes
Production Executive .... David Pope
Assistant Director .... Gerry Gavigan
Camera Operator.......................... Ian Foster
Script Supervisor .... Angela Wharton
Sound Mixer .... Chris Munro
Supervising Sound Editor .... Martin Evans
Assistant Direct, 2nd Unit .... Terry Madden
Far East Production Supervisor .... Philip Kohler
Unit Manager .... Iris Rose
Production Manager .... Janine Modder
Makeup Supervisor .... Norma Webb
Hairdressing Supervisor .... Eithne Fennell

Wardrobe Supervisor	John Scott
Electrical Supervisor	John Higgins
Stills Photographer	Keith Hamshere
Publicity and Marketing	Gordon Arnell
Set Decorator	Peter Young
Construction Coordinator	Ray Barrett
Property Master	Tony Teiger
Location Production Managers	Terry Bamber, John Bernard, Leonhard Gmur, Neil Ravan
Casting	Debbie McWilliams
Stunt Supervisor	Dickey Beers
Director, 2nd Unit	Vic Armstrong
Special Effects Supervisor	Chris Corbould

Produced and distributed by MGM/United Artists.

FILM BUDGETS (IN MILLIONS OF DOLLARS)

Dr. No	1
From Russia With Love	2.2
Goldfinger	2.7 [1]
Thunderball	5.6
You Only Live Twice	7
On Her Majesty's Secret Service	8
Diamonds are Forever	8
Live & Let Die	10
The Man With the Golden Gun	12
The Spy Who Loved Me	13.5
Moonraker	30
For Your Eyes Only	30
Octopussy	31
Never Say Never Again	30
A View to a Kill	30
The Living Daylights	32
License to Kill	36
Goldeneye	60
Tomorrow Never Dies	110

[1]*Goldfinger* was the third highest grossing film of 1965 following *Mary Poppins* and *The Sound of Music*.

LENGTH OF BOND FILMS (IN MINUTES)

Dr. No	111
From Russia With Love	118
Goldfinger	111
Thunderball	129
You Only Live Twice	116
On Her Majesty's Secret Service	140

FILM LOCATIONS (PRINCIPAL)

DR. NO
Jamaica

Ocho Rios	Dunn's River Falls, Bauxite mine, Sans Siuci Hotel
Port Royal	Bauxite Mine
Falmouth	Mangrove swamp
North Shore	Beach Sequence (Laughing Water Estate)
Kingston	Palisades Airport, Morgan's Harbour, Kinsale street Afro–Chinese section, Queen's Club Government House
England	Pinewood Studios, Interiors

Location and principal photography completed March 30, 1962.
Premiere at the London Pavilion October 6, 1962.

GOLDFINGER

Fort Knox, Kentucky	U.S. Army Armor Center & gold bullion depository
Miami, Florida	Fontainbleau hotel & surrounding pool area Aerial views of Miami, Miami wrecking yard
Andermatt, Switzerland	Auto chase scenes on Swiss highways between Zurich and Lugano, Susten, Pass and Furka Pass
England	Stoke Poges Golf Course, Pinewood Studio; interior

Location and principal photography completed July 11, 1964.
Premiere at Odeon Theatre, Leicester Square, London, September 17, 1964.

FROM RUSSIA WITH LOVE

Istanbul, Turkey	1,000 year old Byzantine underground cistern
	St. Sophia, Blue, Suleiman & Dalmahahee mosques
	St. Sophia, Sirkeci and number three train stations
	Bosphorous ferry boat, gypsy girl fight & camp battle
	Orient Express
	Russian agent Krilencu's apartment[1]
Pendik, Turkey	Bay of Pendik background shots
Madrid, Spain	Interior of Byzantine cistern with live rats (set)
Crinan, Scotland	Speedboat chase
Lochgilphead, Scotland	Helicopter crash sequence
England	Pinewood studio. Interiors / Exteriors
	S.P.E.C.T.R.E. training camp on studio lawn

Location and principal photography completed August 23, 1963.
Premiere at the London Pavilion October 10, 1963.

[1]The trap door in the billboard in that Agent Krilencu crawled out of advertised Bob Hope & Anita Ekberg in *Call Me Bwana* produced by Eon Productions. In Fleming's novel it advertised *Niagra* with Marilyn Monroe, 20th Century Fox.

THUNDERBALL

France	Chateau D' Anet (40 miles west of Paris)
Paradise Island, Bahamas	Café Martinique
Nassau, Bahamas	Junkanoo parade
	Nicholas Sullivan summer estate (Palmyra)
	Surrounding Nassau harbor
	Underwater shots off Clifton Pier
England	Pinewood Studios, Interiors

Premiere at the London Pavilion December 29, 1965
Principal Photography begun February 16, 1965

YOU ONLY LIVE TWICE

Island of Kyushu, Japan	Extinct Volcano & Crater Lake. Helicopter sequences
Island of Aua	Ama Village
Kobe, Japan	Kobe docks
Torremolinas, Spain	Helicopter sequences
Tokyo, Japan	Himeji Castle, street scenes
Finmere, Scotland	Crash landing of Helga's Aero Commander
Gibralter	Bond's burial at sea from British destroyer, HMS Tenby
Bahamas	Rescue of Bond's body from bottom of the sea
England	Pinewood Studios, interiors

Principal photography begun July 4, 1966, completed March, 1967.
Premiere at the Odeon, Leicester Square, London, April 11, 1967.

ON HER MAJESTY'S SECRET SERVICE

Murren, Switzerland	Piz Gloria restaurant (top of Schilthorn Peak at 6900')[1]; action sequences and interiors
Lauterbrunnen, Switzerland	Monte-Carlo Rally sequence
Grinelwald, Switzerland	Ice skating rink sequence
Buckinghamshire, England	'M's' house
Guincho Beach, Portugal	Pre-title sequence, rescue of Tracy
Zambuljal, Portugal	Draco's birthday party (De Vinho estate)
England	Pinewood studio, interiors.

Principal photography completed June 23, 1969.
Premiere at the Odeon, Leicester Square, December 18, 1969.

[1]Piz Gloria was a five story complex that took six years to build. (1961 – 1967)

DIAMONDS ARE FOREVER

Los Angeles, California	Los Angeles Airport
Oceanside, California	Oil rig off the California coast
Palm Springs, California	Willard Whyte residence
North Hollywood, California (Universal Studio)	Parking lot car chase sequence
Las Vegas, Nevada	John Manville gypsum plant
	Las Vegas Visitors Bureau
	International Hotel
	Fremont street for high speed auto chase
	Interiors / exteriors
	Riviera Hotel[1]
England	Pinewood Studio, interiors

Other Film Locations	Germany, Netherlands, France

P & O Luxury liner the "Canberra" was featured in the ending sequence of the film.

[1]Bond and Tiffany Case make love on a plastic water bed filled with 3,000 tropical fish. The 7'x6' diameter bed was featured in the bridal suite of the Riviera Hotel.

Premiere at the Odeon, Leicester Square, London, December 30, 1971.

LIVE & LET DIE

New York City, NY	Street scenes
New Orleans, Louisiana	Railway station, Bourbon street scenes, International Airport, Lake Front Airport
Phoenix, Louisiana	Crawdad Bridge road jump, motor boat chase among the bayous, Treadway Estate, Baldwin estate
Slidell, Louisiana	Boatyard scene, Louisiana Hwy 11, car chase scene
Lake Pontchartain	Southern Yacht Club marina
Montego Bay, Jamaica	Crocodile farm, double-decker bus chase
Ocho Rios, Jamaica	Sans Souci Hotel, Runaway Caves, Eden Falls, alligator pond

North Coast, Jamaica .... Jetty
England .... Pinewood Studio, interiors

Principal filming begun October, 1972.
Premiere at the Odeon, Leicester Square, London, July 5, 1973.

THE MAN WITH THE GOLDEN GUN

Hong Kong, China .... Queen Elizabeth I, street scenes
Bangkok, Thailand....................................... Spiral car jump
Macao (Island) Khow-Ping-Kong, Thailand ... Amphibious stunts, Red Chinese listening post,
                                                              Scaramanga headquarters, beach duel
England .... Pinewood Studio, interiors

Principal photography begun in November, 1973.
Premiere at the Odeon, Leicester Square, London, December 19, 1974.

THE SPY WHO LOVED ME

Baffin Island, Canada .... Auquittug National Park, ski jump, Asgard Peak 3,
                                                              000' [1]
Bahamas.. Underwater sequences with Lotus Esprit,
                                                               supertanker, and Atlantis fortress
Cairo, Egypt .... Pyramids at Gizah, Egyptian temple, the Nile
Sardinia (Island).. Auto chase sequence, beach scenes
Other Film Locations .... Malta, Scotland, Okinawa, Switzerland
England .... Pinewood Studio, interiors

For this film Eon Productions built the "007" stage at Pinewood Studio at a cost of $1 million. Size: 374' length, 160' width, 53' high. It was christened December 5, 1976 in a ceremony attended by the British Prime Minister, Harold Wilson.

Premiere at the Odeon, Leicester Square, London, July 7, 1977.

[1] 1500 miles north of Montreal.

MOONRAKER

Los Angeles, California .... NASA test complex
Brazil .... Brazilian jungles, Rio de Janeiro and Iguacu Falls
Venice, Italy .... Piazza San Marco and gondola chase through
                                                       canals. Venice Glass Museum
France .... Chateau Vaux–le–Vicomte (50 miles outside Paris)
                                                       Boulogne, Éclair & Paris studios (interiors)
Other Film Locations .... Guatemala and jungles of Central America
England .... Pinewood Studio, interiors and special effects

Budget $30 million, nearly 30 times the cost of *Dr. No.*
Premiere at the Odeon, Leicester Square, London, June 26, 1979.

FOR YOUR EYES ONLY

Bahamas	Underwater sequences
Cortina d'Ampezza, Italy	Bobrun, skiing and motorcycle sequences
Corfu, Greece	Meteora Mountains
Kalambaka, Greece	600 year old Byzantine monastery
London, England	Pre–title sequence: opening helicopter scenes filmed at Becton Gasworks in London's Eastend
England	Pinewood Studio, interiors

Principal photography begun September, 1980.
Premiere at the Odeon, Leicester Square, London, June 24, 1981.

NEVER SAY NEVER AGAIN

Nice, France	The "French Riviera" and casino dance sequence
Saint Jean-Cap-Ferrat	Villa Rothschild
Villefranche	"The Citadelle"
Nassau, Bahamas	Underwater sequences, jungle scenes in island's center, Nassau Beach Hotel, British Colonial Hotel
England	Waddesdon Manor, Luton Hoo
Herts, England	Thorn, EMI Elstree studios, interiors
Other Film Locations	Spain

Principal photography begun September, 1982.

OCTOPUSSY

India	Udaipur, Lake Pichola, Jag Mandir palace, Monson palace, Taj Mahal
Germany	Checkpoint Charlies, Berlin Spandau prison, Potsdamer Platz, Brandenburg Gate
Cambridgeshire, England	Nene Valley Railway, between Wonsford and Orton Mere, near Peterborough, U.S. Air Force base at the Upper Heyford, Oxfordshire, the Royal Air Base at Northalt, Middlesex
England	Pinewood Studio, interiors

Principal photography begun August 16, 1982.
Premiere at the Odeon, Leicester Square, London, June 6, 1983.

A VIEW TO A KILL

Iceland	Glacier Lake, Hamlet of Hofn
Swiss Alps	Vadretta di Scerscen Inferiore glacier
Paris, France	Eiffel Tower, the River Seine, the "left bank" and the Pont Alexandre III
Chantilly, France	Zorin's stables Musee Vivant du Cheval, Chateau, race course, Piste d' Avilly, surrounding forests

San Francisco	Golden Gate bridge, Fisherman's Wharf, Potrero Hills, China Basin, cable cars, City Hall, streets of San Francisco
Oakland, California	Dunsmuir House
England	Royal Ascot racecourse, water–filled quarry at Wray Unry, Amberly Chalk Pits Museum, West Sussex
Pinewood Studio	Interiors: abandoned silver mine, East tower of Golden Gate bridge, Eiffel Tower restaurant, miniature submarine sequence

Premiere at the Odeon, Leicester Square, London, June 12, 1985.

THE LIVING DAYLIGHTS

Gibralter	Pre–title sequence
Tangier, Morocco	Exteriors: The Casbah and the Forbes Museum
Ouarzazate, Morocco	Ouarzazate Airfield
Austria	Lake Weissensee, Sachsenburg Tunnel, and the Sonnenalpe Nassfeld ski area
Vienna, Austria	Hotel Im Palais Schwarzenberg, the Weiner Prater Amusement Park, Sofiensale Theatre, and the Schonbrunn Palace and gardens
Thetford, England	Theatre
Pinewood Studios, England	Interiors
Other Film Locations	Italy, U.S.A.

Principal photography started September 29, 1986 and wrapped February 13, 1987.
World premiere, Odeon Leicester Square Cinema, London, June 29, 1987.

LICENSE TO KILL

Key West, Florida	Hemingway House, the Lighthouse, the Pier House, Harbor Lights Café, Singleton Party Ice Factory, Mallory Square, Garrison Bite Marina, Key West Airport, St. Mary's Catholic church, Seven Mile Bridge
Mexico City, Mexico	Churubusco Studios[1], Palacio de Bellas Ortes, Teatro de la Ciudad, Casino Espagnol, Gran Hotel Ciudad de Mexico. 50 miles outside of Mexico City, Otomi Ceremonial Center
Acapulco, Mexico	Beach residence near Las Brisas resort
Isla Mujeres (Island of Women) Mexico	Just off the Yucatan peninsula near Cancun. Underwater scenes
Mexicali, Mexico	50 miles west of the city on Rumorosa Road
Pinewood Studios, England	Interiors

Filming began July 18, 1988.

[1] Built in 1944 by Howard Hughes' RKO Studios.

GOLDENEYE

St. Petersburg, Russia .... The City
Principality of Monaco .... Monte Carlo Harbor, French Warship LaFayette
Puerto Rico, W.I. .... Caribbean, Radio Telescope, Arecibo
Switzerland .... Contra Dam, Lugano

TOMORROW NEVER DIES

France .... Peyresourde, French Pyrenees
Thailand .... Bangkok
Island of Phuket .... James Bond Island
Germany .... Hamburg International Airport
Mexico .... Fox Baja Studios, Rosarito Beach
USA .... HALO parachute jump off coast of Florida
United Kingdom .... North London, Brent Cross Shopping Centre
Portsmouth, Royal Navy Frigate
Miedenhall and Lakenheath: USAF Bases

Studio scenes: HMS Devonshire and HMS Bedford/ in studio tank.

FLEMING, IAN

AUTOMOBILES

PREWAR
1) Standard Tourer
2) Morris Oxford
3) 16-80 open Lagonda Stuebaker Avanti, 4 seater
4) Graham Paige convertible[1]
5) Opel (destroyed in the Blitz)

POSTWAR
6) Renault
7) Hillman Minx
8) 2 ½ litre Riley
9) Sapphire
10) Daimler, four litre Bentley
11) Thunderbird, two seater
12) Thunderbird, four seater
13) Studebaker Avanti, four seater

[1] Donated this car to the ambulance service.

CLOTHES (Typical Fleming Apparel)
Dark blue or white short sleeve shirt, black loafers, polka dot bow tie, dark blue suit. Fleming hated buttons, studs and laces.

CREATION OF BOND

James Bond was born on the third Tuesday of January in 1952 at Goldeneye, Jamaica. Fleming took the name Bond from James Bond, the author of *Birds of the West Indies*.

He finished Casino Royale six days before his marriage, using his twenty year old Imperial portable typewriter. When he saw that this book was going to be successful, he ordered a custom-made golden Royal and paid $174 for it.

BORN

May 28, 1908 at 27 Green Street, Mayfair, London

DIED

August 12, 1964 at Sandwich, England

EDUCATION

Eton, Sandhurst[1], private language tutoring school in Kitzbuhl, University of Geneva, University of Munich, Swiff Certificate in Anthropology, Foyer de Etudes Slaves, Paris. Fleming spoke fluent French, German, and Russian.

[1]Graduated from Sandhurst as a Second Lieutenant in the Black Watch but shortly thereafter resigned his commission.

EMPLOYMENT

Reuters News Service
Cul & Company merchant bankers
Rowe & Pitman's (partner) British stock brokerage firm
British Naval Intelligence (1939-1945)
The Book Collector (editor & owner)
Kemsley Newspaper chain

FAMILY

Ian Fleming was born into a wealthy family of London merchant bankers. His grandfather, Robert Fleming, was a millionaire investment banker and built the family home which he called "Nettlebed" near Henley-on-Thames. He had two sons Valentine and Philip who were educated at Eton and Oxford. Fleming's father, Major Valentine Fleming, was Commander of "C" Squadron of the Oxfordshire Hussars and was killed May 20, 1917 in France. He was posthumously awarded the D.S.O. Winston Churchill wrote Major Fleming's obituary for the London Times.

Fleming's mother, the former Evelyn St. Croix Rose, was often described as one of the most beautiful women in England and was a gifted hostess and musician. Fleming had three brothers; Peter, who became a distinquished explorer and writer, Robert, a London banker, and Michael, the youngest, who died of wounds as a prisoner of war, after Dunkirk.

Ian Fleming was buried at Sevenhampton, Gloucestershire, near his home at Warneford Place. A memorial service was held September, 1964 at St. Bartholomew the Great in Smithfield.

For the most comprehensive biography of Ian Fleming, we suggest *The Life of Ian Fleming*, by John Pearson. McGraw-Hill, 1966.

FAVORITE ACTIVITIES

Golf, bridge, scuba diving, skiing, fast cars, gambling. Fleming liked to go to Boodles private club to read, nap, or meet friends and to drink at El Vino's bar in Fleet Street, just behind his office which was located at 4 Old Mitre Street EC4.

FAVORITE DRINKS

Fleming liked clarets and champagne, but preferred martinis, brandy and ginger ale or bourbon and branch water.

MARTINI RECIPE

1) Fill shaker with ice   2) Pour in 6 parts gin   3) One part dry vermouth   4) "Shake until I say stop."

FAVORITE FOODS

Colchester & Whitstable oysters, all English fish, particularly Dover sole, Scottish smoked salmon, potted shrimp, lamb cutlets, roast beef, ham, English vegetables, especially asparagus and peas, English savouries and fruits.

RECIPE FOR DISTILLED COFFEE

1) Freshly ground coffee
2) Percolated over & over again with cold water until a thin black treacle is produced
3) 1/3 cup hot milk or water added

FAVORITE GOLF COURSE

The Royal St. George at Sandwich in Kent where Fleming was a six handicap

FAVORITE RESTAURANT

Scott's in Picadilly Circus. London

GOLDENEYE

Ian Fleming purchased his Jamaican property in 1944. He paid 2,000 pounds for 14 acres of land on the North Shore, close to Oracabessa. He built Goldeneye in 1946 also for 2,000 pounds. Goldeneye contained one vast living room with large windows, and slotted jalousies in place of glass. The house contained showers, but no hot water. It had three palin, four-square bedrooms and a low roof set with thick shingles.

Fleming's cook was Violet Cummings and "Felix" was his gardner. When living there Fleming preferred the local food and Violet would fix shrimp, fish, oxtail, liver, fish soup, black crab soup, calah soup, goat fish, bak soup,[1] conch soup, fried octopus tenacles with tartar sauce, papaya, scrambled eggs, and Blue Mountain coffee.

[1] A mixture made from crabs, yams, seafood and hot peppers.

HEROES

Sugar Ray Robinson and Jacques Cousteau

LITERARY AGENTS

First U.S. Agent	Curtis Brown, Ltd. (Naomi Burton)
First Film Agent	Bob Fenn (MCA)
Second U.S. Agent	Music Corp. of America
Literary	Phyllis Jackson

Film .... Lawrence Evans
Worldwide (Outside the US) .... Peter Janson-Smith

MARITAL STATUS

Fleming was a bachelor until he was 43. He married Lady Anne Rothermere, formerly Lady O'Neill on March 24, 1952 at 3pm in the town hall of Port Maria, Jamaica. Witnesses were Noel Coward who was a neighbor and Cole Leslie, Coward's secretary. They had one son, Caspar Robert Fleming.

PUBLISHERS

Jonathan Cape, Ltd. London.[1], Macmillan[2], Viking Press, New American Library, United States.

[1]First novel, *Casino Royale*, published April 13, 1953 by Jonathan Cape. First printing 4750 copies. Last novel, *The Man With The Golden Gun*, written during the winter of 1964.

[2]Al Hart edited the first six Bond books in America and became a close friend and companion to Fleming.

RESIDENCES

PRE-WAR

Batchelor mews in Mayfair, Carlton Hotel, new flat in Berkeley Square.

POST-WAR

Flat in Montagu Square, flat in Mayfair, flat in Carlyle Mansions, Chelsea, White Cliffs, Noel Coward's former house at St. Margaret's Bay, 16 Victoria Square, London, "Old Palace" Bekesbourne, near Canterbury in Kent, and Sevenhampton House near Swindon, in the Cotswold's. Office in Mitre Street, near Fleet Street, London.

WRITERS ADMIRED

Dashiell Hammett, Raymond Chandler, Eric Ambler, Graham Green, Edgar Allan Poe, E. Phillips Oppenehim, Sax Rohmer, Simenon, Somerset Maugham, Noel Coward.

WRITING HABITS

When Fleming took the job with the Kemsley newspaper chain, it was on the condition that his contract would include two months vacation a year. He spent this time at Goldeneye and wrote all the Bond novels there. He would rise at 7:30am, swim in his private cove, then have breakfast and relax until 10:00 am. He would write from 10 o'clock until noon; then sunbathe or snorkel, write for one hour in the afternoon, have dinner, visit with friends, and retire early.

His daily production was 2,000 words.

GAMBLING: BOND'S WINS & LOSSES (BOOK & FILM)

Casino Royale[1]	Baccarat. Won 70 million francs against Le Chiffre.
Moonraker	Bridge. Won 15,000 pounds against Sir Hugo Drax. (See Blades)
Diamonds Are Forever	Blackjack. Won $5,000 against the house. (Book) Roulette. Won $15,000 against the house. (Book) Craps. Won $ 50,000 against the house. (Film)
Thunderball	Chemin de fer. Winnings unknown against Largo.

Goldfinger	Golf. Won $10,000 against Goldfinger. (Book) Won 5,000 pounds against Goldfinger. (Film)
Role of Honor	Roulette. Won 150,000 Francs against the house.
On Her Majesty's Secret Service[2]	Chemin de fer. Lost four million francs against the house.
Octopussy	Backgammon. Won 200,000 Rupees against Kamal Khan. (Film)
Never Say Never Again	Game of "Domination." Bond won $267,000 from Largo. (Film)
Dr. No	Chemin de fer. Winnings unknown against the house. (Film)
For Your Eyes Only	Chemin de fer. Won one million Drachma against Bunky. (Film)
License to Kill	Blackjack. Won $250, 000 against the house.
Zero Minus Ten	Mahjong. Won approximately $41,200 from Thackeray.
Goldeneye	Baccarat. Won unspecified amount against Xenia Onatopp.
The Facts of Death	Baccarat. Won five million drachmas from Konstantine Romanos.

[1]At Royale–les–Eaux, against Le Chiffre. Others seated at the baccarat table: No. 1, Greek gambler, No. 2, Carmel Delane, American film star, No. 3, Lady Danvers, No. 4 & 5, Junius & Mrs. Dupont, No. 6, James Bond, No.7, Monsieur Sixte, No. 8, Indian Maharajah, No. 9, Lord Danvers, No. 10, Young Italian Signor Tomelli, and Banker Le Chiffre.

[2]This included a two million Franc loss of Tracy Vicenzo. Two million old Francs were equivalent to 20,000 new Francs. Bond was playing with the old Francs.

GARDNER, JOHN EDMUND

Born November 20, 1926, in Seaton Delaval, England; son of Cyril John (a priest of The Church of England) and Lena (Henderson) Gardner; married Margaret Mercer, September 15, 1952. Children: Alexis Mary, Simon Richard John.

Education: St. John's College, Cambridge, B.A., 1950, M.A., 1951; attended St. Stephen's House, Oxford, 1951 – 1952.

1943 – 1944	Magician with the American Red Cross, Entertainment Department
1944 – 1946	Royal Navy, Fleet Air Arm
1946	Royal Marine Commandos
1952 – 1958	Curate in Evesham, England. Ordained priest of Church of England, 1953
1959 – 1965	Herald, Stratford-upon-Avon, England. Theatre critic and arts editor

Glidrose Publications Board of Directors selected Gardner from among twelve authors to continue the James Bond novels after an absence of fourteen years. His first Bond novel, *License Renewed* was published in 1981. This was followed by fifteen additional Bond books. For the complete list of titles, refer to "Books and Short Stories: Casts and Synopses."

Mr. Gardner has written over thirty three novels and his books have been translated in more than fourteen languages.

GEOGRAPHIC LOCATIONS (BOOKS)

Casino Royale .... England, France
Live & Let Die .... England, US, Jamaica
Moonraker .... England
Diamonds Are Forever .... England, US, Africa
From Russia With Love .... England, Turkey, Italy, Greece, Yugoslavia, Switzerland, France
Dr. No .... England, Jamaica
Goldfinger... South America, England, France, Switzerland, US
Thunderball .... England, Bahamas
The Spy Who Loved Me .... Canada, England, US
On Her Majesty's Secret Service .... England, France, Switzerland, Germany
You Only Live Twice .... England, Japan
The Man With the Golden Gun .... England, Jamaica
Colonel Sun .... England, Greece
License Renewed.. Scotland, England, France
For Special Services .... England, US
Icebreaker .... Finland, England, Spain, Russia
Role of Honor .... England, Switzerland, Middle East
Nobody Lives Forever................................. England, France, Austria, US
No Deals, Mr. Bond .... England, Ireland, France, Hong Kong
Scorpius .... England, US
License to Kill... US & Central America
Win, Lose or Die .... Middle East, England, Sweden, Germany, at sea, France, Italy.
Broken Claw .... Canada & US
The Man From Barbarossa.......................... England, France, Russia
Death is Forever .... England, France, Germany, Italy
Never Send Flowers................................... England, Switzerland, Germany, France, Italy, Greece.
Seafire .... England, Spain, Israel, Germany, Puerto Rico
Coldfall .... England, USA, Italy, Switzerland
Goldeneye .... Soviet Union, Puerto Rico, Switzerland, French Riviera
Tomorrow Never Dies .... Saigon, England, Hamburg, Germany

GEOGRAPHIC LOCATIONS (SHORT STORIES)

A View to a Kill.. England, France
For Your Eyes Only .... Jamaica, England, Canada, US

GLOSSARY "A"

ACKEE. Jamaican fruit that is a deadly poison if not eaten at the right time.

AMTORG. Soviet trade organization.

A.T.A.C. Automatic Targeting Attack Communicator.

AWABI. Shells for which Kissy Suzuki dives.

BAST. The Brotherhood of Anarchy & Secret Terrorism.

BLADES. A private club of which 'M' is a member.

BLUE HARE. Russian ordnance depot near Alakurtii.

BOOK OF GOLDEN WORDS. Fleming's notebook of unusual words.

B.N.D. West German intelligence gathering organization.

B.T.R. –50. Russian tracked armored troop carrier.

B.T.V. West German equivalent of British M15.

BUREAU OF ALL–ASIAN FOLKWAYS. Cover name for Japanese Secret Police.

CCS. Communication Control Systems.

CHIGROES. Chinese blacks of the West Indies.

CIA. American Central Intelligence Agency.

CMG. Companion to the Order of St. Michael & St. George.

CMGN. Carver Media Group Network.

COAP. Covert Operations Accessory Pack.

COBRA. Cabinet office briefing room.

COLD. Children of the Last Days.

CRASH DIVE. SIS slang for bad news.

CUBAN G-2. Terrorist organization.

DAILY GLEANER. Newspaper of Jamaica.

DEUXIEME BUREAU. French Secret Service.

DGSS. Director General of the British Security Service.

DISCO VOLANTE. Ship owned by S.P.E.C.T.R.E.

DNI. Director of Navel Intelligence.

DOUBLE–O SECTION. Branch of British Secret Service to which Bond is a member.

EADY SUBSIDY PLAN. Allows certain productions filmed in the "Commonwealth" to have a portion of their costs underwritten.

EAUX-les-ROYALE. Casino on the north coast of France.

EMILY. KGB recruited operative, usually single girls.

EMP. Electro Magnetic Pulse.

EOKA. Greek guerrilla army.

EVA. Extra-vehicular activity.

EPOC FREQUENCIES. Emergency Presidential Order Communications.

F.A.L.N. Puerto Rican. The Armed Forces for National Liberation.

FOR YOUR EYES ONLY. Top secret. For agent's eyes only.

FRATERNITE INTERNATIONALE de la RESISTANCE CONTRE e' OPPRESSION. Former cover name for S.P.E.C.T.R.E. in Paris.

FROM A VIEW TO A KILL. From the third verse of 'D' by Ken John Peel. A cumberland hunting song written in 1820.

GLASER SAFETY SLUGS. Prefragmented bullet that contains several hundred no. 12 shot suspended in liquid teflon. Velocity over 1700 fps. Will penetrate body armor before blowing apart.

GOLDENEYE. WWII Operation for the defense of Gibraltar. Residence of Ian Fleming in Jamaica.

GPS. Global Positioning Satellite System

GRU. Secret arm of Russian intelligence.

GUTTERSNIPE SIGHT. Back-mounted with three triangular yellow walls that give instant target acquisition.

GWEILO. Ghost people

HVA. Eastern bloc intelligence organization.

I.D.S.O. International Diamond Security Organization.

ICE PALACE. Headquarters of the National Socialist Action Army.

I.P.I. Lightweight Classified Engine.

ISRAELI MOSSAD. Israel's equivalent to the CIA and the British SIS.

JUPITER 16. American space capsule.

HALO. High altitude, low opening parachute jump to avoid radar.

KGB. Soviet Secret Police.

KPG. Kensington Palace Gardens. No. 13 Russian Embassy.

LAW OF THE QUANTUM OF SOLACE. The death of common humanity. Equated to the amount of comfort, love, and friendship given to another human being.

LEATHERHEADS. Italian counter-terrorist unit.

LECTOR. Machine that held the coding key to Russian top secret diplomatic traffic.

METROPOLITAN POLICE SPECIAL BRANCH. A –11) Diplomatic protection group, C-13) Police anti–terrorist squad, C-7) Technical support branch, D-11) "Blue Berets," Scotland Yard's firearms dept.

MAGIC 44. A secret ciphering method developed by the Japanese Secret Service.

M.I.5. British Security Service.

M.I.6. British Secret Intelligence Service.

MOONRAKER. British Rocket owned by Sir Hugo Drax.

MOUSSELINE. A sauce applied over asparagus.

MR. SZASZ. A name Ian Fleming thought would be good for a villain.

NTSB. National Transportation Safety Board

"NOT FOR THE BROTHERHOOD." Not to be circulated to the CIA.

NSAA. National Socialist Action Army.

NSBS. Naval Special Boat Squadron.

NUB. Norrich Universal Bodyguards.

O.H.S. French Secret Army of the right wing.

PAW PAW. A Jamaican fruit.

PCHELA. Russian built hydrofoil.

PHELOPON. Japanese murder drug. Habit forming and induces the desire to commit murder.

PIZ GLORIA. Swiss mountain peak and revolving restaurant.

PREDATOR. Code name for James Bond.

PUSSY GALORE. Derived from the name of Ian Fleming's pet octopus who lived in Fleming's cove at Goldeneye, Jamaica.

'Q' British Secret Service Armorer.

REDSTAR. Top Secret file.

RAM. Random Access Memory.

RICIN. A deadly toxic nerve poison.

ROBINSON. A Russian sentenced to death who is used in combat training as a live target.

R.N.V.R. Royal Naval Volunteer Reserve.

RV. Rendezvous point.

SALAMAGUNI. A mixture of raw herring, onions and spices.

SARIN. A deadly nerve agent.

SCATTER. The "deepest" hiding place for a service agent in London. A safehouse.

SCOTCH WOODCOCK. A Fleming favorite. Scrambled eggs topped with anchovies.

SHAMELADY. Jamaican name for a sensitive plant whose leaves curl up when touched.

SHAPE. Supreme Headquarters for Allied Powers in Europe. A branch of NATO.

SMERSH. Now Dept. VIII of Directorate S. of the KGB.

SPECIAL BRANCH. London Metro Police.

S.P.E.C.T.R.E. The Special Executive for Counterintelligence, Terrorism, Revenge, and Extortion.

SOR et lumiere. Devices installed to steal both conversations and video recordings.

SOLITAIRE. A bird. A thrush of magnificent song. Blue, black, and gray plumage with hazel eyes and a copper-tinged tail. Native to the high cool mountains of central Jamaica.

SPETSNAZ. Red Army Special Forces.

SVOJELUPOLIISI (SUPO). Finnish Intelligence & Security Agency.

"THE EYES." Mr. Big's team of spies.

UNION CORSE. French Mafia.

URGENT CODE ONE. Serious accident.

WARTSKI. World's greatest Faberge dealer. 138 Regent St. London.

WASP. White Anglo Saxon Protestant.

JAPANESE GLOSSARY "B"

A list of Japanese words with English translation which Bond was exposed to in Japan while on assignment in *You Only Live Twice*.

AWAHI SHELLS. Japanese abalone.

BAKYARO. Bloody Fool.

BLACK DRAGON SOCIETY. Powerful secret society.

BOJUTSU. Fighting with the stave.

BONDO-SAN. James Bond.

BON-SAN. Priest.

BUSHIDO. Ways of the warrior.

CHIMBO. Masculine.

DEMOKORASU. Democracy.

FUGU. Japanese blow or puffer fish[1.]

FUTON. Bedding.

FUT SUKA-YOI. Honorable hangover.

GAIJIN. Foreigner.

HAI. Yes.

HAIKU. Classical forms of Japanese verse.

JISATSU. Suicide.
JIZO. God who protects children.
KAMI-KAZE. Divine Wind.
KANGEI. Welcome aboard.
KEMPEITAI. Japanese Gestapo.
KONCHIKISHO. You animal.
MASHOS. Antiseptic gauze mask.
MONKO. Feminine.
NINJA. Stealers-in.
MINJUTSU. The art of stealth or invisibility.
O-furo. Honorable bath.
PANCHINKO. Japanese game of balls.
POSIDONIA. Seaweed.
RONIN. Bodyguards.
SAMSARA. Wine & Women.
SEPPUKU. Hari-kiri or belly cutting.
SHIKIRINAOSHI. Making you wait.
SHIMATTA. I have made a mistake.
SHOCHU. Raw gin.
SOSAKO. Japanese C.I.D.
SOSHI. Unemployed Samurai.
SUKIYAKI. National dish of beef stew.
TANKAS. Profound statement.
TODOROKI. Thunder.
TORII. Rough Stone.
TSUMBO DDEOSHI. Deaf and dumb.
YUKATO. Wrap-around robe.

[1]FUGU is the Blow- fish or Puffer fish native to Japan. The U.S. is the only country outside of Japan to import it. There are 15 kinds of Fugu, all prepared from Puffer fish. The liver, ovaries and entrails contain tetrodotokin, a deadly poison. If not cleaned properly, this poison will bring death instantaneously! Removal of the dangerous organs in Japan is done by chefs with a minimum of 15 years experience and all restaurants who serve it are licensed.

It now appears on the menus of numerous New York restaurants. James Bond and Tiger Tanaka had Fugu for dinner one evening in Brppu, Japan, on the island of Kyushu, while he was on assignment in *You Only Live Twice*.

GLOSSARY "C"

DELTA 9. A lethal nerve gas Goldfinger was planning to use in the course of assaulting Fort Knox.
GAMMA GAS. Used in *Thunderball* to murder Major Derval and the crew of a British Vulcan bomber.
GOLDEN BULLETS. Twenty-three Karat gold with traces of nickel. Used by Scaramang in *The Man With The Golden Gun*.
INTERNATIONAL BROTHERHOOD FOR STATELESS PERSONS. A front for S.P.E.C.T.R.E. headquarters in Paris.
LE CERCLE, LES AMBASSADEURS CLUB, MAYFAIR, LONDON. The club where Bond is first introduced on screen in *Dr. No*.
M1. Admiral Sir Miles Messervy's personal submarine.

MR. KISS, KISS, BANG, BANG. Italian nickname for 007.

KISS KISS CLUB. Bahamian nightclub in *Thunderball*.

NINJAS. Tiger Tanaka's secret force of hand to hand combat warriors.

ORCHIDACEAE NEGRA. A very rare orchid which is the essential element in a lethal nerve gas produced by Hugo Drax to kill the world's population in *Moonraker*.

RPM CONTROLLER. A 'Q' invention for stopping the rotating cylinders in a slot machine so that it pays off each time, as seen in *Diamonds Are Forever*.

SAKI. Traditional Japanese drink. According to Bond, must only be drunk at 98.4 degrees fahrenheit.

SECTION 26, PARAGRAPH 5. "Need to know" basis only.

SOLEX AGITATOR. A device to convert solar radiation into electricity on an industrial basis.

VIRUS OMEGA. Developed by Blofeld at his alpine clinic, Piz Gloria, In *On Her Majesty's Secret Service*. It is intended for use in destroying the world's crops and livestock.

GLOSSARY "D"

ASP. Armament Systems & Procedures.

BND. German Intelligence Service.

DGSE. French Secret Intelligence Service.

GIGN. French Anti–Terrorist Unit.

GSG-9. German Counter-Terrorist Unit.

IFF. Identification Friend at Fal.

IZL. Irgun Zenoi Levmi (Jewish Right Wing Terrorist Group).

JANUS. Russian Crime Syndicate.

KNOUT. Russian flogging investment.

MISCHA. Russian satellite designed as space junk.

SAYARET MATKAL. Israeli Anti-Terrorist Military Unit.

SOJ. Scales of Justice.

ST. KYRIL OF ANTIOCH. Old Orthodox Monastary.

2 PLOSCHAD DZERZHINSKOGO. Postal Address of KGB Moscow Headquarters.

HELICOPTERS FEATURED IN BOOK & FILM

From Russia With Love [1]	F
Thunderball	F
You Only Live Twice [2]	F
On Her Majesty's Secret Service	B & F
Diamonds Are Forever [3]	B & F
The Spy Who Loved Me [4]	F
Moonraker	F
For Your Eyes Only [5]	F
Never Say Never Again	F
Octopussy	F
A View to a Kill [6]	F
License to Kill	B & F
The Living Daylights	F
License Renewed	B
For Special Services	B

[1]Bond wounds Smersh co-pilot with AR-7 survival rifle causing him to drop live grenade which destroys helicopter and both occupants. (F)

[2]Flying "Little Nellie," Bond destroys four of Blofeld's helicopters, each carrying one pilot. (F)

[3]Bond shoots down helicopter with a Bofors 40mm. artillery gun, killing Jack Spang. (B)

[4]Bond destroys Stromberg's helicopter and girl pilot with rocket fired from underwater in the Lotus Esprit.

[5]Bond flying M.I.6 helicopter dumps Blofeld down smoke stack. (F)

[6]Bond fires a red flare gun into Russian helicopter causing it to crash into the side of the mountain killing both pilots. (F)

[7]Bond fired a Stinger missile that destroyed a Huey VH-1. It plummeted 10,000 feet and crashed into the sea. Four of the victims were women. (B)

INJURIES BOND HAS INCURRED (BOOK)

CASINO ROYALE:
Genitals mutilated by carpet beater, right hand damaged by Smersh agents, superficial shock from camera bomb blast, superficial injuries from wrecked Bentley.

LIVE & LET DIE:
Barracuda bite to shoulder, back and legs cut on coral reef, little finger of left hand fractured.

MOONRAKER:
Contusions from cliff fall, cuts and bruises from beating by Drax, second degree burns from steam hose, superficial injuries from wrecked Bentley.

DIAMONDS ARE FOREVER:
Abrasions from being kicked by thugs, stab wound from fight with Wint and Kidd.

FROM RUSSIA WITH LOVE:
Superficial injuries from fight with Red Grant, nerve poisoning from stab wound by Rosa Klebb.

DR. NO:
Left forearm lacerated from being struck with gun butt, electric burn to palm on hand, superficial burns from obstacle course, superficial injuries to abdomen from giant squid.

GOLDFINGER:
Bruised right hand from fight with Mexican drug dealer, knocked unconcious by Goldfinger's hoods, superficial injuries from fight with Goldfinger.

THUNDERBALL:

Spear wound to Bond's stomach, battle fatigue from underwater combat, superficial shock and contusions inflicted by traction machine, superficial head injuries from butt on CO2 gun.

THE SPY WHO LOVED ME:

Large gash just below the hairline from being hit by TV set thrown by Sluggsy.

ON HER MAJESTY'S SECRET SERVICE:

Fatigue from ski escape down Piz Gloria, superficial injuries from bobsled chase.

YOU ONLY LIVE TWICE:

Amnesia resulting from head wound, deep depression from murder of Tracy, superficial wound to ribs by Blofeld's sword.

THE MAN WITH THE GOLDEN GUN:

Gunshot wound to left shoulder, nerve poisoning from bullet dipped in snake venom.

COLONEL SUN:

Drugged at Quarterdeck by 'M's' abductors, knocked unconcious by Sun's men, tortured with probing device to the ears and mouth, superficial injuries from fight with Von Richter.

LICENSE RENEWED:

Superficial injuries from fighting Franco and Caber, tortured with sound waves, injected with drugs.

FOR SPECIAL SERVICES:

Drugged and brainwashed by S.P.E.C.T.R.E.

ICEBREAKER:

Gunshot wound to upper chest, shock and frostbite from immersion in freezing water, stab wound to right shoulder.

ROLE OF HONOR:

Bullet wound to right hip, superficial shock and deafness from stun grenades.

NOBODY LIVES FOREVER:

Superficial shock and deafness from explosion.

NO DEALS MR. BOND:

Arm lacerated by German Shepherd bite, left arm shattered by mace, hands cut by barbed wire.

SCORPIUS:

Shoulder ripped by glass shard.

LICENSE TO KILL:

Knocked unconcious from rifle butt, lacerations from fight with Sanchez & his men.

WIN, LOSE OR DIE:

Lacerations and deafness from bomb blast, kicked in groin by British Wren.

BROKEN CLAW:

Open wounds to back and shoulder caused by steel pegs.

BARBAROSSA:

Injury to right shoulder, drugged unconcious and knocked unconcious.

DEATH IS FOREVER:

Broken nose, knife wounds.

NEVER SEND FLOWERS:

None.

SEAFIRE:

None.

ZERO MINUS TEN:

Knife wound to left arm, beating on bare buttocks with cane stick, and injury to head and left leg.

THE FACTS OF DEATH:

Bond suffers injury to forehead on the right side, and to face on the left side. Cut shoulder, painful knife cut to palm of left hand. Sliced knuckles.

INJURIES BOND HAS INCURRED (SHORT STORIES)

FROM A VIEW TO A KILL:

Hit hard on side of head by Russian boot.

RISICO:

Knocked unconcious by the butt of Luger pistol.

THE LIVING DAYLIGHTS:

Hot lead splashed on Bond's hand from bullet.

INJURIES BOND HAS INCURRED (FILM)[1]

SUPERFICIAL ABRASIONS FROM FIGHTS, FALLS, & CAR CRASHES:

Dr. No, From Russia With Love, Goldfinger, You Only Live Twice, On Her Majesty's Secret Service, Diamonds Are Forever, Live & Let Die, The Spy Who Loved Me, Moonraker, Octopussy, Never Say Never Again, A View to a Kill, The Living Daylights, License to Kill

GUNSHOT WOUND TO LEFT LEG:

Thunderball

KNOCKED UNCONSCIOUS

Goldfinger, Diamonds Are Forever, A View to a Kill, License to Kill, Broken Claw, Coldfall

INJURIES THAT HAVE HOSPITALIZED BOND (BOOK)

Casino Royale   *Dr. No*

From Russia With Love   *Icebreaker*

Live & Let Die   *No Deals, Mr. Bond*

The Man With the Golden Gun   *Thunderball*

Broken Claw   *Death is Forever*

Cold Fall

[1]Bond spent six months in hospital prior to assignment in *Dr. No.*

ISLANDS (BOOK & FILM)

Dr. No	Jamaica and Crab Key
From Russia With Love	Spectre Island
Thunderball	Bahamas, Dog Island
You Only Live Twice	Ama, Matsu, Kuro, Kyushu
Live & Let Die	Jamaica, Isle of Surprise, San Monique
The Man With the Golden Gun	Jamaica, Kao-Ping-Kan, Phuket, Scaramanga's Isle
The Spy Who Loved Me	Sardinia, Ile d' Orleans
For Your Eyes Only	Greek Islands, Jamaica, Crete
Colonel Sun	Vrakonisi
Octopussy	Jamaica
The Hildebrand Rarity	Seychelles, Chagrin
Quantum of Solace	Bahamas and Jamaica
Role of Honor	Corfu
Nobody Lives Forever	Shark
No Deals Mr. Bond	Cheung Chau
Scorpius	Hilton Head
License to Kill	Cray Cay, Ballast Key, Bimini
Icebreaker	Madeira
Win, Lose or Die	Ischia, off the Italian coast
Broken Claw	Vancouver Island
Death is Forever	Venitian Islands
Seafire	Puerto Rico
Goldeneye	Puerto Rico
Zero Minus Ten	Victoria, Jamaica
The Facts of Death	Cyprus, Chios, Samos

KEEN, GEOFFREY

Actor. Born in England in 1916. Distinctive versatile character player of British films and stage. The son of Malcolm Keen. Portrays the Minister of Defense, Sir Frederick Gray, in the later James Bond films.

FILMOGRAPHY

1946 .... *Riders of the New Forest*
1947 .... *Odd Man Out*
1948 .... *The Fallen Idol*
1949 .... *The Third Man, Hour of Glory*
1950 .... *Treasure Island, It's Hard to Be Good, Seven Days to Noon, The Yellow Cloud*
1951 .... *Chance of a Lifetime, High Treason, Cheer the Brave, Green Grow the Rushes*
1952 .... *His Excellency, The Stranger in Between, Cry the Beloved Country, Lady in the Fog, Angels One Five*
1953 .... *The Long Memory, Rob Roy, Genevieve*
1954 .... *Face the Music, Turn the Key Softly, The Maggie, Doctor in the House, The Divided Heart*
1955 .... *A Town Like Alice, Zarak, Loser Takes All, The Man Who Never Was, The Long Arm, The Spanish Gardner, Sailor Beware*
1957 .... *The Scamp, The Birthday Present, Doctor at Large, Town on Trial, The Secret Place, Yield to the Night, Triple Deception, Fortune is a Woman*
1958 .... *Nowhere to Go*
1959 .... *The Scapegoat, Horrors of the Black Museum, Beyond This Place, Deadly Record, The Boy and the Bridge, Devil's Bait*
1960 .... *The Dover Road Mystery, Sink the Bismarck, The Angry Silence*
1961 .... *The Malpas Mystery, No Love For Johnnie, Spare the Rod, The Silent Weapon, Raising the Wind*
1962 .... *Live Now, Pay Later, The Spiral Road, A Matter of Who, The Inspector, The Prince and the Pauper, The Mind Benders*
1963 .... *The Cracksman, Return to Sender, Dr. Syn Alias the Scarecrow*
1964 .... *Torpedo Bay*
1965 .... *Dr. Zhivago*
1966 .... *The Heroes of Telemark, Born Free*
1967 .... *Berserk!*
1968 .... *Thunderbird 6*
1970 .... *Cromwell*
1971 .... *Taste the Blood of Dracula*
1972 .... *Sacco & Vanzetti, Living Free*
1973 .... *Doomwatch*
1974 .... *QB VII*
1977 .... *The Spy Who Loved Me*
1979 .... *Moonraker*
1981 .... *For Your Eyes Only*
1983 .... *Octopussy*
1985 .... *A View to a Kill*
1987 .... *The Living Daylights*

TELEVISION
Crown Court, Churchill & The Generals, Cribb & Strangers, The Troubleshooters

THEATRE
The Winter's Tale, King Lear

LAZENBY, GEORGE (BOND NUMBER TWO)

Actor. Born Goulburn, Australia on September 5, 1939. Former Mercedes Benz automobile salesman in Australia. Moved to Europe in 1964 to become a model.

A tall, 6'2" handsome actor whose first screen role was that of James Bond in *On Her Majesty's Secret Service* (1969). Other films include *Universal Soldier, Stoner, The Man From Hong Kong, Operation Regina*. TV credits include Return of *The Man From Uncle* (1983), *Evening in Byzantium* (1978) and *Cover Girls* (1977). Since then however, he has faded into obscurity.

His salary for *On Her Majesty's Secret Service* was a flat 22,000 pounds. Perks included a furnished flat in London and a limousine. He appeared in Australian and British TV commercials.

1969	*On Her Majesty's Secret Service*
1971	*Universal Soldier*
1975	*The Man From Hong Kong*
1977	*The Kentucky Fried Movie*
1979	*Saint Jack*
1986	*Never Too Young to Die*
1987	*Hell Hunters*

LEE, BERNARD

Actor. Born January 10, 1908 in London. Died January 16, 1981. Noted British actor of stage, and screen and TV. Educated at the Royal Academy of Dramatic Art (RADA). Served in the British Army 1940-1945. Best known for his role as 'M', Chief of British Secret Service (M.I.6) in the James Bond films.

1934	*The Double Event*
1935	*The River House Mystery*
1936	*Rhodes of Africa (aka Rhodes-US)*
1937	*The Black Tulip*
1938	*The Terror*
1939	*The Frozen Limits, Murder in Soho (aka Murder in the Night US 1940)*
1940	*Spare a Cooper, Let George Do It*
1941	*Once a Crook*
1946	*This Man is Mine*
1947	*Dusty Bates, The Courtney's of Curzon Street (The Courtney Affair-US)*
1948	*Quartet*
1949	*The Fallen Idol*
1950	*The Third Man, Elizabeth of Ladymead, Odette, Morning Departure, Last Holiday, Cage of Gold, The Blue Lamp*
1951	*Appointment with Venus, The Adventurers, Mr. Denning Drives North, Calling Bulldog Drummond, White Corridors*
1952	*The Yellow Balloon, The Gift Horse*
1953	*Beat the Devil, Sailor of the King*
1954	*Seagulls Over Sorrento, The Rainbow Jacket, The Detective, The Purple Plain*
1955	*Out of the Clouds, The Ship That Died of Shame*

1956	*Pursuit of the Graf Spee, The Spanish Gardener*
1957	*Fire Down Below, Across the Bridge*
1958	*The Key, The Man Upstairs, Dunkirk, Nowhere to Go*
1959	*Breakout, Beyond This Place*
1960	*The Clue of the Twisted Candle, The Angry Silence, Kidnapped, Cone of Silence*
1961	*The Secret Partner, Whistle Down the Wind, Partners in Crime, Clue of the Silver Key, Fury at Smugglers Bay*
1962	*The L-Shaped Room, The Share Out, Vengeance, Dr. No, From Russia With Love, Two Left Feet, Ring of Treason, A Place to Go*
1964	*Dr. Terror's House of Horrors, Saturday Night Out, Who Was Maddox, Goldfinger*
1965	*The Amorous Adventures of Moll Flanders, Thunderball, The Legend of the Young Dicken Turpin, The Spy Who Came In From the Cold*
1967	*You Only Live Twice, Operation Kid Brother*
1969	*On Her Majesty's Secret Service, Crossplot*
1970	*10 Rillington Place, The Raging Moon*
1971	*Dulcima, Diamonds Are Forever, Danger Point*
1973	*Live & Let Die, Frankenstein and the Monster From Hell*
1974	*The Man With the Golden Gun*
1977	*The Spy Who Loved Me*
1978	*It's Not the Size that Counts*
1979	*Moonraker*

LEITER, FELIX (CIA)[1]

Featured in the following books:

Diamonds Are Forever	*License to Kill*
The Man With the Golden Gun	*Seafire*
Thunderball	*The Facts of Death*
Live & Let Die	*Casino Royale*
Goldfinger	*For Special Services*

Featured in the following films:

Dr. No	*Goldfinger*
Thunderball	*Diamonds Are Forever*
Live & Let Die	*The Living Daylights*
License to Kill	*Never Say Never Again*

[1]Leiter lost an arm and leg in Florida to a shark owned by Milton Krest. After retiring from the CIA, he worked for several years for the Pinkerton Detective Agency, then several years with the DEA. Now he is in private practice and living in Austin, Texas.

LLEWELYN, DESMOND

Actor. Born in Newport, Wales. In British films since 1939 when he made his movie debut in a Will Hay film. Trained at the Royal Academy of Dramatic Art (RADA). His most noted role of course is as 'Q' in sixteen James Bond films, beginning with *From Russia With Love* (1963) through *Tomorrow Never Dies* (1998).[1]

After working extensively in repertory theatre, Desmond's first television appearance was in 1939. He appeared is As You Like It in 1946 and went on to record more television at the Alexandra Palace including The Good Companions, Trilby, and The Scarlet Pimpernel for producer Fred O' Donovan as well as many children's plays for television.

He played Mr. Hyde in the first production out of Lime Grove Studios, *Dr. Jekyll and Mr. Hyde*, again for Fred O' Donovan. Plays for Welsh televison included *How Green Was My Valley*, *Moulded In Earth*, *The Rescuers*, *Poison Pen* and many others. For the BBC, work includes *Doomwatch* for Darrol Blake, *Dixon of Dock Green* and *The Onedin Line* for Raymond Menmuir, *Some Mothers Do 'Ave Them* for Michael Mills, *The Happy Autumn Fields* for Peter Hammond, *The Speed King* for Ferdy Fairfax, *A Walk With the Lions* for Ronald Wilson, *After the Party* for Charles Sturridge, *Lloyd George* and *Jekyll and Hyde* for Alastair Reid.

Desmond played the Colonel in Yorkshire's long-running series *Follyfoot*. He also appeared in many other television shows from *Emergency Ward 10* and *Hazel* to *The Tommy Cooper Show*.

ADDITIONAL FILMOGRAPHY
Ask a Policeman, 1939, *They Were Not Divided*, 1950, *Bunty Wins A Pup*, 1953, *Sword Of Sherwood Forest*, 1960, *Cleopatra*, 1962, *The Silent Playground*, 1963, *Operation Kid Brother*, 1967, *The Nine Tailors*, *Warhead*, 1980.

While serving with the Royal Welsh Fusiliers he was captured at Dunkirk on May 27, 1940 and remained a prisoner of war until Easter, 1945. He served in German prisoner of war camps in Lauten, Warburg, and Rotenburg.

[1]The two Bond films Desmond Llewelyn did not appear in were *Dr. No* and *Live and Let Die*.

MAXWELL, LOIS (MISS MONEYPENNY)

Born Lois Hooker in 1927 in Canada. First film: *That Hagen Girl*, 1947 with Shirley Temple.

1947	*That Hagen Girl*
1948	*Corridor of Mirrors, The Decision of Christopher Blake, The Ark Past*
1949	*Women of Twilight, The Crime Doctor's Diary, Kazan*
1950	*Brief Rapture, Tomorrow is Too Late*
1952	*Scotland Yard Inspector, The Woman's Angle*
1953	*Aida, Mantrap*
1955	*Passport to Treason*
1956	*The High Terrace, Satellite in the Sky*
1957	*Kill Me Tomorrow, Town Without Pity*
1959	*Face of Fire*
1960	*The Unstoppable Man*
1962	*Lolita, Dr. No*
1963	*Come Fly With Me, The Haunting, From Russia With Love*
1964	*Goldfinger*

1965 .... *Thunderball*
1967 .... *Operation Kid Brother, You Only Live Twice*
1969 .... *On Her Majesty's Secret Service*
1970 .... *The Adventurers*
1971 .... *Endless Night, Diamonds Are Forever*
1973 .... *Live & Let Die*
1974 .... *The Man With the Golden Gun*
1977 .... *The Spy Who Loved Me*
1979 .... *Moonraker*
1980 .... *Mr. Patman*
1981 .... *For Your Eyes Only*
1983 .... *Octopussy*
1985 .... *A View to a Kill*

MESSERVY, ADMIRAL SIR MILES K.C.M.G. ALIAS 'M' (NOW RETIRED)

Chief of British Secret Service, head of the Double-0 section.

HEADQUARTERS:
Top floor of the large, grey building overlooking Regents Park.

CODE NAME:
Mailed-fist

MEMBER:
Blades and "The Senior," military service club.

TYPICAL DRESS:
Dark grey suit, white shirt, blue bow tie, rimless glasses for reading only.

APPEARANCE AND AGE:
Grey eyes, grey hair. Late fifties or early sixties.

FAVORITE DRINKS:
Scotch and soda, Mouton Rothschild, Algerian wine.

SMOKES:
Two cigars a day. Smokes a pipe. Uses matches. Holds tobacco in a brass 14 pounder shell casing.

HOBBIES:
Fishing, collecting butterflies, water color painting of only the wild orchids of England.

CHILDREN:
One daughter, two grandchildren (boy and girl), son-in-law a professor at Cambridge.

RESIDENCE:
A small Regency manor house on the edge of Windsor[1] Forest and a small flat in London.

HOUSEKEEPER:

Mrs. Hammond [3]

BUTLER:

Former Chief Petty Officer (retired) Hammond.[3]

CHAUFFEUR:

Ex-leading stoker, Smith.

AUTOMOBILE:

Old black Silver Wraith Rolls-Royce.

[1] 'M' calls his Windsor residence "Quarterdeck". A retired Naval Admiral whose last command was as Captain of the battle cruiser "Repulse." At Quarterdeck he exhibits a 1/144 scale model of this ship and his front doorbell is the brass bell of a defunct battle cruiser. M's residence has only been viewable to us in one film, *On Her Majesty's Secret Service.*

[2] Retired CPO Hammond and Mrs. Hammond were both murdered during Bond's assisgnment in *Colonel Sun.* Former CPO Davison and Mrs. Davison have assumed the duties of the Hammonds at Quarterdeck.

There is some confusion as to the exact location of M's office in the tall building overlooking Regents Park.[1]

Casino Royale	Top floor
Live & Let Die	Top floor
Moonraker	Ninth floor
From Russia With Love	Top floor
Dr. No	Eighth floor
Goldfinger	Eighth floor
Thunderball	Eighth floor
The Man With the Golden Gun	Eighth floor
The Property of a Lady	Eighth floor
License Renewed	Ninth floor
For Special Services	Ninth floor
Icebreaker	Ninth floor
Role of Honor	Ninth floor
No Deals Mr. Bond	Eighth floor
Scorpius	Eighth floor
Broken Claw	Ninth floor
Death is Forever	Fifth floor
Zero Minus Ten	Eighth floor

[1] Location is not mentioned in other stories. M.I.6 has since moved to another location.

MOORE, ROGER (BOND NUMBER THREE)

Actor. Born Roger George Moore in London, October 14, 1927. Served as a Lieutenant in the British Army in Germany. Married to the former actress Luisa Mattioli. Three children.

Film debut in *Perfect Strangers,* stage debut in Androcles and the Lion. U.S. Film debut in *The Last Time I Saw Paris.* Starred in the television series *Ivanhoe, The Alaskans,* and *Maverick,* but aside from James Bond, probably best known for his role as *The Saint* (1962-1968).

FILMOGRAPHY

1945 .... *Perfect Strangers, Caesar & Cleopatra*
1946 .... *Gaiety George, Piccadilly Incident*
1948 .... *The Fuller Brush Man*
1949 .... *Paper Orchid, Trottie True*
1954 .... *The Last Time I Saw Paris*
1955 .... *Interrupted Melody, The King's Thief*
1956 .... *Diane*
1959 .... *The Miracle*
1961 .... *The Sins of Rachel Cade, Gold of The Seven Saints*
1962 .... *No Man's Land, Rape of The Sabines*
1968 .... *Vendetta For The Saint*
1969 .... *Crossplot*
1970 .... *The Man Who Haunted Himself*
1973 .... *Live & Let Die*
1974 .... *Gold, The Man With The Golden Gun*
1975 .... *That Lucky Touch*
1976 .... *Shout At The Devil, Street People, The Sicilian Cross, Sherlock Holmes In New York*
1977 .... *The Spy Who Loved Me*
1978 .... *The Wild Geese*
1979 .... *Moonraker, Escape To Athena, Folkes*
1980 .... *The Sea Wolves, Sunday Lovers*
1981 .... *The Cannonball Run, For Your Eyes Only*
1983 .... *Octopussy*
1984 .... *The Naked Face, Curse Of The Pink Panther*
1985 .... *A View To A Kill*
1987 .... *The Magic Snowman* (Voice Only)
1990 .... *Bullseye*
1991 .... *Fire, Ice & Dynamite*
1992 .... *Bed & Breakfast*
1994 .... *The Man Who Wouldn't Die*
1995 .... *The Quest*

Author of the *James Bond Diary.* Fawcett Publications, 1973.
Narrator: *Happy Anniversary 007,* 1988 (TV).
Moore's favorite Bond film is *The Spy Who Loved Me.*

MUSIC (FILMS)

DR. NO:
Music composed by Monty Norman. Orchestrated by Burt Rhodes. James Bond theme played by the John Barry Orchestra. Conducted by Eric Rodgers.

James Bond (Roger Moore) and Rosie Carver (Gloria Hendry) in a scene from *Live & Let Die.* This was Moore's first film as Bond. Thought to be a CIA agent, Rosie Carver actually was employed by badman Mr. Big. (Rex USA Ltd.)

FROM RUSSIA WITH LOVE:
Orchestral music composed and conducted by John Barry. Title song written by Lionel Bart. "From Russia With Love" sung by Matt Monro. "James Bond Theme" written by Monty Norman.

GOLDFINGER:
Music composed and conducted by John Barry. Title song lyrics by Leslie Bricusse and Anthony Newley. Sung by Shirley Bassey.

THUNDERBALL:
Music composed and conducted by John Barry. Title song lyrics by Don Black. Sung by Tom Jones.

YOU ONLY LIVE TWICE:
Music composed and conducted by John Barry. Title song lyrics by Leslie Bricusse. Sung by Nancy Sinatra.

CASINO ROYALE:
Music composed and conducted by Burt Bacharach. Title song by Herb Alpert and the Tijuana Brass. "The Look of Love" sung by Dusty Springfield.

ON HER MAJESTY'S SECRET SERVICE:
Music composed and conducted by John Barry. Song "We Have All The Time In The World" lyrics by Hal David. Sung by Louis Armstrong.

DIAMONDS ARE FOREVER:
Music composed, conducted, and arranged by John Barry. Title song lyrics by Don Black. Sung by Shirley Bassey.

LIVE & LET DIE:
Music score by George Martin. Title song written by Paul and Linda McCartney. Sung and performed by Paul McCartney and Wings.

THE MAN WITH THE GOLDEN GUN:
Music composed, conducted, and arranged by John Barry. Title song lyrics by Don Black. Sung by Lulu.

THE SPY WHO LOVED ME:
Music by Marvin Hamlisch. "Nobody Does It Better" lyrics by Carole Bayer Sager. Sung by Carly Simon.

MOONRAKER:
Music by John Barry. Title song lyrics by Hal David. Sung by Shirley Bassey.

FOR YOUR EYES ONLY:
Music by Bill Conti. Title song lyrics by Michael Leeson. Sung by Sheena Easton.

OCTOPUSSY:
Music composed and conducted by John Barry. Song "All Time High" Lyrics by Tim Rice. Sung by Rita Coolidge.

NEVER SAY NEVER AGAIN:
Musical score by Michael Legrand. Title song and lyrics by Alan and Marilyn Bergman. Sung by Lani Hall.

A VIEW TO A KILL:
Music composed and conducted by John Barry. Title song composed and sung by Duran Duran.

THE LIVING DAYLIGHTS:
Music composed by Pal Waataar and John Barry. Title song performed by A-ha.

LICENSE TO KILL:
Music composed by Michael Kamen. Title song sung by Gladys Knight. Produced and arranged by Narada Michael Walden in association with Walter Afanasieff. Written by Narada Michael Walden, Jeffrey Cohen and Walter Afanasieff.

GOLDENEYE:
Music by Eric Serra. Title song produced by Nellee Hooper, written by Bono and The Edge, and performed by Tina Turner.

TOMORROW NEVER DIES:
Music by David Arnold. Title song produced by Mitchell Froom, written by Sheryl Crow and Mitchell Froom, and performed by Sheryl Crow.

MUSIC FROM THE BOND NOVELS

CASINO ROYALE:
La Vie en Rose. (Looking at Life Through Rose Colored Glasses)

DIAMONDS ARE FOREVER:
Feuilles-Mortes. (Autumn Leaves), J'attendrai. (I'll Be Yours), La Vie en Rose, Avril au Portugal. (April in Portugal), Je n'en Connais pas la fin. (The Song That Haunts My Heart)

FROM RUSSIA WITH LOVE:
Prologue from "Boris Godounov" (Moussorsky)

DR. NO:
Take Her To Jamaica Where The Rum Comes From, Kitch, Don't Touch Me Tomato, Marion

THUNDERBALL:
Java Jive (The Ink Spots)

THE SPY WHO LOVED ME:
Someone's Rocking My Dreamboat (The Ink Spots), Ain't She Sweet and Paper Doll (The Ink Spots), Tales of the Vienna Woods

ON HER MAJESTY'S SECRET SERVICE:
Zither music, Skater's Waltz, Auld Lang Syne

YOU ONLY LIVE TWICE:
Music on a three-stringed samisen, Ride of the Valkyries (Wagner)

THE MAN WITH THE GOLDEN GUN:
After You've Gone, Linstead Market, Belly Lick, Iron Bar

LIVE & LET DIE
Voodoo drums

THE LIVING DAYLIGHTS:
Overture to "Boris Godounov" (Moussorsky).

LICENSE RENEWED:
As Time Goes By from *Casablanca,* Piano Music, Mozart & light opera overtures, Thus Sprach Zarathustra by Richard Strauss.

FOR SPECIAL SERVICES:
Aunt Hagar's Blues by Art Tatum.

ICEBREAKER:
The Horst Wessel song.

ROLE OF HONOR:
Rolling Home, By the Light of the Silvery Moon
He Shakes My Ashes, Freezes My Griddle, Churns My Butter, Stokes My Pillow
My Man is Such a Handy Man

NOBODY LIVES FOREVER:
There's a Hole in Daddy's Arm, Where All the Money Goes, Bewitched.

SCORPIUS:
Walk in the Light with Aretha Franklin & Detroit's New Bethel Baptist Church Choir
Bridal March, New Bo-Weevil Blues by Gertrude "Ma" Rainey, a 1927 recording with unnamed jazz group, throbbing ethereal electronic music

LICENSE TO KILL:
The Bridal Chorus from Lohengrin, music from Mozart

WIN, LOSE, OR DIE:
Drake's Drum, My Way, Have Yourself a Merry Little Christmas, Bing Crosby, There Was A Lady Sweet and Kind, For They Are Monarchs of the Sea.

BROKEN CLAW:
None.

THE MAN FROM BARBAROSSA:
Chopin Prelude from Swan Lake.

DEATH IS FOREVER:
Medley from "Cats," variations from "Phantom Of The Opera", "Shanty" music by Benjamin Britten.

NEVER SEND FLOWERS:
Wagner's "Siegfried".

SEAFIRE:
None.

GOLDENEYE:
Memories, Raining in Baltimore.

MUSICAL SCORES OTHER THAN TITLE SONG (FILM)

DR. NO:
Three Blind Mice, Underneath the Mango Tree, Jump Up Jamaica, Jamaica Jump Up. Performed on screen by the Bryon Lee Chinese band.

THUNDERBALL:
Mr. Kiss Kiss Bang Bang (Whistle Whistle Boom Boom). Music by John Barry, words by Leslie Bricusse.

YOU ONLY LIVE TWICE:
The Wedding, Mountains & Sunsets, Twice is the Only Way to Live, Fight at Kobe Docks, Drop In The Ocean.

ON HER MAJESTY'S SECRET SERVICE:
Do You Know How Christmas Trees are Grown? Music by John Barry, lyrics by Hal David. Goldfinger, whistled by midget janitor.

LIVE & LET DIE:
Oh For A Closer Walk With Thee, Live & Let Die (the Fillet of Soul Sequence). The Olympia Brass Band, B.J. Arnau.

THE MAN WITH THE GOLDEN GUN:
After You've Gone.

MOONRAKER:
The Magnificent Seven theme, and melody from *Close Encounters of the Third Kind*.

THE SPY WHO LOVED ME:
Theme music from *Lawrence of Arabia*. The Mojave Club. Laras Theme from *Dr. Zhivago*.

A VIEW TO A KILL:
California Girls written by Brian Wilson and sung by Gidea Park. Vivaldi's The Four Seasons performed by Trevor Pinnock and the English Concert.

THE LIVING DAYLIGHTS:
Where Has Everybody Gone and If There Was a Man. Performed by the Pretenders. Music by John Barry, lyrics by Chrissie Hynde, produced by John Barry and Paul O' Duffy.

LICENSE TO KILL:
Wedding Party performed by Ivory. Produced & written by Jimmy Duncan and Phillip Brennan. Dirty Love performed by Tim Feehan, produced by Tim Feehan and David White, written by Steve Dubin & Jeff Pescetto. If You Asked Me To performed by Patti LaBelle, produced by Stewart Levine, arranged by Aaron Zigman, written by Diane Warren.

GOLDENEYE:
"The Experience of Love". "Stand By Your Man", composed by Billy Sherrill and Tammy Wynette. Performed by Minnie Driver.

TOMORROW NEVER DIES
"Surrender", sung by k.d. lange. "Back Seat Driver", sung by David Arnold and Alex Gifford. "It Had To Be You", sung by Simon Greenaway.

MUSICAL COMPOSERS

BURT BACHARACH

Composer, songwriter. Born May 12, 1929 in Kansas City, MO. Became internationally known as conductor-arranger of Marlene Dietrich's worldwide concert tour. Won two Oscars in 1969 for scoring the film *Butch Cassidy & the Sundance Kid* and for "Raindrops Keep Falling On My Head."

Other songs he is noted for are "Alfie," "I'll Never Fall in Love Again," "What's New Pussycat?" and "Do You Know the Way to San Jose?". He was the musical composer for score and songs in the James Bond film *Casino Royale* (1967).

JOHN BARRY

Composer. Born November 3, 1933 in York, England. He began film work in the late fifties. He gained international recognition for his scores of Bond films. He won four Academy Awards for his music in 1) *The Lion in Winter*, 1968, 2) *Born Free* (two Oscars) and 3) *Out of Africa*, 1985. His Bond credits include: *Dr. No* (1962); *From Russia With Love* (1963); *Goldfinger* (1964); *Thunderball* (1965); *You Only Live Twice* (1967); *On Her Majesty's Secret Service* (1969); *The Man With the Golden Gun* (1974); *Diamonds Are Forever* (1971); *Moonraker* (1979); *Octopussy* (1983): *A View to a Kill* (1985); *The Living Daylights* (1987).

MARVIN HAMLISCH

Composer, arranger. Born June 2, 1944, in New York City. The first individual ever to win three Oscars in one night (1974). Two of the Oscars he received were for his work on *The Way We Were*, starring Robert Redford and Barbra Streisand. He received his third Oscar for *The Sting*. He composed the score for *A Chorus Line,* for which he received the Tony Award, the New York Drama Critics Award, the Theater World Award, and the Pulitzer Prize. He has composed the scores of over thirty-eight films including "Nobody Does it Better," from *The Spy Who Loved Me* (1977).

MICHAEL LEGRAND

Composer. Born in 1932 in Paris. A musical prodigy at eleven. A former bandleader, singer, and songwriter. He began composing for films in the 50's. His score for the film *The Umbrellas of Cherbourg* in 1964 gained him international recognition. He has won two Academy Awards: "Windmills of Your Mind" (from the *Thomas Crown Affair*, 1968) and *Summer of '42* (1971). He has also won four Grammys and an Emmy for "Brian's Song", 1972. He did the musical score for *Never Say Never Again*, 1983.

NOVELS (LENGTH IN HARD OR SOFTCOVER)

By Ian Fleming

Casino Royale	238
Live & Let Die	159 [1]
Moonraker	175 [2]
Diamonds Are Forever	215
From Russia With Love	228
Dr. No	206 [3]
Goldfinger	270 [4]
Thunderball	188 [5]
The Spy Who Loved Me	113

SHORT STORIES by Ian Fleming

[1] Working title: The Undertaker's Wind.

[2] Working title: Mondays are Hell-Hell is Here. First published in the U.S. as "Too Hot To Handle."

[3] Originally a filmscript for Henry Morganthou III for a prospective TV series.

[4] Working title: The Richest Man in The World.

[5] Based on screenplay "Longitude 78 West" Written by Ian Fleming, Kevin McClory and Jack Whittingham.

[6] Working title: The Belles of Hell.

[7] Working title: Death Leaves An Echo.

By John Gardner

By Robert Markham (Kingsley Amis)

By Raymond Benson

OPERATION CODE NAMES (BOOK OR FILM)

Moonraker	Orchid
Diamonds Are Forever	Passover
Goldfinger	Rockabye Baby & Grand Slam
On Her Majesty's Secret Service	Bedlam & Corona
Octopussy	Trove
Thunderball	Omega & Thunderball
For Your Eyes Only	Undertow
The Living Daylights	'Smiert Spionen' & Extase
License Renewed	Meltdown
For Special Services	Heavenly Wolf
Icebreaker	Icebreaker
Role of Honor	Down Escalator
Nobody Lives Forever	Headhunt
No Deals Mr. Bond	Seahawk & Cream Cake
Scorpius	Last Enemy & Cobra
A View to a Kill	Mainstrike
Win, Lose or Die	Landsea 89 & Win, Lose, Sleeping Beauty
Broken Claw	Curul, Jericho
The Man From Barbarossa	Barbarossa / Fallen Timbers
Death is Forever	Cabol
Never Send Flowers	None
Seafire	Apocalypse
Cold Fall	Blizzard & Antifreeze
Goldeneye	Cowslip
Tomorrow Never Dies	None
Zero Minus Ten	None
The Facts of Death	None

00 AGENTS OF THE BRITISH SECRET SERVICE

001	Unknown
002	Killed in 1969, in Beirut, by Scaramanga.[1]
003	Killed by a Russian agent and buried in the ice of Siberia.
004	Died on Gibralter from a fall caused by a Russian agent.
005	Stuart Thomas. Became head of Station 'G', Greece and then was murdered by Colonel Sun's men.
006	Alec Trevelyan, ex-Royal Marine Commando, killed by Bond.
007	James Bond
008	Escaped from East Berlin and recovered in military hospital at Wahnerheide. Served as backup to Bond during the Goldfinger assignment.
009	Killed by a midget knife thrower in West Berlin.
0010	Unknown
0011	Disappeared in Singapore in 1955. Never replaced.

[1] Bill Fairbanks. (Agent 002 who replaced him, parachuted into Gibralter with 007 during the Living Daylights assignment.)

DIRECTOR OF PHOTOGRAPHY

Dr. No	Ted Moore, B.S.C.
From Russia With Love	Ted Moore
Goldfinger	Ted Moore
Thunderball	Ted Moore
You Only Live Twice	Freddie Young
Casino Royale	Nicolas Roeg
On Her Majesty's Secret Service	Michael Reed
Diamonds Are Forever	Ted Moore
Live & Let Die	Ted Moore
The Man With the Golden Gun	Ted Moore, Oswald Morris
The Spy Who Loved Me	Claude Renoir
Moonraker	Jean Tournier
For Your Eyes Only	Alan Hume
Octopussy	Alan Hume
Never Say Never Again	Douglas Slocombe
A View to a Kill	Alan Hume
The Living Daylights	Alec Mills
License to Kill	Alec Mills
Goldeneye	Phil Meheux
Tomorrow Never Dies	Robert Elswit

PHOTOGRAPHERS

TED MOORE
Director of Photography. Born 1914 in South Africa. A decorated WWII combat pilot in the RAF. Entered the British film industry in the late 40's and won an Academy Award in cinematography for *A Man For All Seasons* in 1966. Considered Britain's most accomplished color and widescreen cinematographer.

OSWALD MORRIS
Director of Photography. Born November 22, 1915 in Ruislip, England. Entered the film industry in 1931 at age 16. A RAF bomber pilot in WWII. One of Britain's leading cinematographers. Won an Academy Award in cinematography for *Fiddler on the Roof* in 1971. Collaborated on photography for *The Man With The Golden Gun* in 1974.

CLAUDE RENOIR
Director of Photography. Born December 4, 1914 in Paris. Noted for the sensual effects of his color photography. Director of Photography for *The Spy Who Loved Me* in 1977.

NICOLAS ROEG
Director of Photography, Director. Born in 1928 in London, England. Entered the film industry in 1950. His work over the past thirty five years has shown the industry that he is one of the most gifted cinematographers in the world today. Director of Photography for *Casino Royale* in 1967.

DOUGLAS SLOCOME

Director of Photography. Born in London, February 10, 1913. He had a previous career in journalism and feature writing. Former photo-journalist for *Life* and *Paris Match* magazines. British Academy Award for *The Servant* in 1963, *The Great Gatsby* in 1974, and *Julia* in 1978. Director of Photography for *Never Say Never Again* in 1983.

FREDERICK A. YOUNG

Director of Photography. Born in 1902 in England. Winner of three Academy Awards in cinematography for *Lawrence of Arabia* in 1962, *Doctor Zhivago* in 1965, and *Ryan's Daughter* in 1970. Director of Photography for *You Only Live Twice* in 1967.

PRODUCERS

Dr. No	Albert R. Broccoli and Harry Saltzman
From Russia With Love	Albert R. Broccoli and Harry Saltzman
Goldfinger	Albert R. Broccoli and Harry Saltzman
Thunderball	Kevin McClory for Eon Productions
You Only Live Twice	Albert R. Broccoli and Harry Saltzman
Casino Royale	Charles K. Feldman
On Her Majesty's Secret Service	Albert R. Broccoli and Harry Saltzman
Diamonds Are Forever	Albert R. Broccoli and Harry Saltzman
Live & Let Die	Albert R. Broccoli and Harry Saltzman
The Man With the Golden Gun	Albert R. Broccoli and Harry Saltzman
The Spy Who Loved Me	Albert R. Broccoli
Moonraker	Albert R. Broccoli
For Your Eyes Only	Albert R. Broccoli
Octopussy	Albert R. Broccoli
Never Say Never Again	Jack Schwartzman
A View to a Kill	Albert R. Broccoli and Michael G. Wilson
The Living Daylights	Albert R. Broccoli and Michael G. Wilson
License to Kill	Albert R. Broccoli and Michael G. Wilson
Goldeneye	Albert R. Broccoli, Barbara Broccoli, Michael J. Wilson
Tomorrow Never Dies	Michael G. Wilson, Barbara Broccoli

PRODUCERS, BIOGRAPHIES

ALBERT R. BROCCOLI

Born April 5, 1909 in New York City.[1] Educated at City College of New York. Entered the film industry in 1938 as an Assistant Director with 20th Century-Fox. In England, during the early 50s he co–founded Warwick Pictures with Irving Allen. In the early 60s he began co–producing the James Bond films with Harry Saltzman. Saltzman sold out his interest to United Artists in 1976. Broccoli continued to produce the Bond series in conjunction with MGM/UA studios until his death in 1997.

CHARLES K. FELDMAN

Born Charles Gould, April 26, 1904 in New York City. Died 1968. Educated at the University of Michigan and USC. Opened a law practice in Los Angeles in 1928. In 1932 he became President of

Famous Artists talent agency, representing prominent producers, directors, and actors. He became a producer in the early 40's turning out fourteen films including *Casino Royale* in 1967.

HARRY SALTZMAN

Born October 27, 1915 in St. John, Canada. He entered the film industry in 1946. In the 60s he and his partner Albert R. Broccoli started co–producing the Bond series after obtaining the film rights from Ian Fleming. Saltzman left the partnership and moved on to other film projects.

JACK SCHWARTZMAN

Born in New York and educated at UCLA, graduating as a tax attorney. Schwartzman started his own firm in 1965 and by 1978 was considered a leading authority in entertainment law. That same year he joined Lorimar Film Productions as Executive Vice President. In 1980 he left Lorimar to become an independent producer. He produced *Never Say Never Again* in 1983.

[1] March, 1982, received the Irving G. Thalberg Award from the American Academy of Motion Picture Arts & Sciences. Roger Moore presented the award.

PRODUCTION CAST (FREQUENCY OF APPEARANCE IN BOND FILMS)

DIRECTOR[1]

Terence Young	3
Guy Hamilton	4
Lewis Gilbert	3
Peter Hunt	1
John Glen	5
Irwin Kershner	1
Martin Campbell	1
Roger Spottiswoode	1

SCREENWRITERS[2]

Richard Maibaum	13
Michael Wilson	4
Tom Mankiewiez	3
Lorenzo Semple, Jr.	1
George Macdonald Fraser	1
Christopher Wood	2
Michael Sayers	1
John Law	1
Wolf Mankowitz	1
Roald Dahl	1
John Hopkins	1
Paul Dehn	1
Berkeley Mather	1
Johnna Harwood	1
Michael France	1
Jeffrey Caine	1
Bruce Firstein	2

MUSICAL COMPOSERS

John Barry 11
Burt Bacharach 1
George Martin 1
Marvin Hamlisch 1
Bill Conti 1
Michael Legrand 1
Monty Norman[1] .... -
Michael Kamen 1
Eric Serra 1
David Arnold 1

DIRECTOR OF PHOTOGRAPHY

Ted Moore 7
Alan Hume 3
Alec Mills 2
Douglas Slocombe 1
Jean Tournier 1
Claude Renoir 1
Oswald Morris[2] 1
Michael Reed 1
Nicolas Roeg 1
Frederick Young 1

[1] Monty Norman composed the James Bond theme music which is played in every film.
[2] Co-director

PRODUCTION DESIGNER

Ken Adam 7
Peter Lamont 7
Syd Cain 3
Peter Murton 1
Philip Harrison 1
Stephen Grimes 1
Allan Cameron 1

MAIN CREDITS DESIGNER

Maurice Binder 14
Robert Brownjohn 2
Leslie Dilley 1
Daniel Kleinman 1

[1] Does not include "Casino Royale" which had five directors, each doing a few scenes.
[2] Some of these were co-screenwriters.

RIGG, DIANA

Actress. Born July 20, 1938 in Yorkshire and trained for the stage at the Royal Academy of Dramatic Art. After appearing in repertory in Chesterfield and in York, she joined the Royal Shakespeare Company, Stratford-on-Avon in 1959 and made her first appearance in London at the Aldwych in January 1961 where in repertory she played Philipe Trincante in *The Devils*, Gwendolyn in *Beckett*, Bianca in *The Taming of the Shrew*, and Madame de Tournel in *The Art of Seduction*. Returning to Stratford in April 1962, she played Helena in *A Midsummer Night's Dream*, Lady Macduff in *MacBeth*, Adriana in *The Comedy of Errors*, and Cordelia in *King Lear*.

After a year of appearing as Emma Peel in *The Avengers*, she rejoined the RSC at Stratford in June 1966 to play Viola in *Twelfth Night*. She played Heloise in *Abelard and Heloise* (Wyndhams and New York, 1970) and joined the National Theatre in March 1971 to play Dottie in Tom Stoppard's *Jumpers*, Lady Macbeth, and Celimene in *The Misanthrope*. She played Eliza Doolittle in *Pygmalion* (Albery Theatre, May 1974), returned to the National Theatre in 1976 to play Phaedra in *Phaedra Britannica*, appeared in Tom Stoppard's *Night and Day* (Phoenix Theatre, 1978), *Heartbreak House* (Haymarket Theatre, 1983), *Little Eyolf* (Lyric Theatre Hammersmith, 1985), *Wildfire* (Phoenix), *All for Love*, (As Cleopatra), (Almeida Theatre, 1991).

Television credits include "Little Eyolf" (BBC TV), "This House of Brede" (American TV), "Hedda Gabler" (Yorkshire TV), "King Lear" (Granada TV), "Witness for the Prosecution" (American TV), "Bleak House" (BBC TV), as presenter for "Held in Trust" (Scottish TV), "Worst Witch" (Central TV) and "Snow White" (Cannon Films), "A Hazard of Hearts" (Gainsborough Film and TV Pictures), "Follies", Cameron Mackintosh Limited, Shaftesbury Theatre, and "Unexplained Laughter" (BBC TV), "Mother Love" (PBS) and "Mystery Theatre" (PBS) as presenter.

In the film *On Her Majesty's Secret Service*, 1969, she portrayed La Comtesse Teresa (Tracy) di Vicenzo, the only woman ever to marry James Bond.

Diana Rigg was awarded the Order of the British Empire (OBE) by Queen Elizabeth and is a Dame of the British theatre.

FILMOGRAPHY

1968	*The Assassination Bureau*
1969	*On Her Majesty's Secret Service*
1970	*Julius Caesar* (as Portia)
1971	*The Hospital*
1973	*Theatre of Blood*
1977	*A Little Night Music*
1981	*The Great Muppet Caper*
1982	*Evil Under the Sun*
1989	*Snow White*
1994	*A Good Man in Africa*

THE SACRIFICAL LAMBS (FILM)

Dr. No .... Quarrel
From Russia With Love .... Kerim Bey

Diana Rigg as Tracy Di Vincenzo, the only woman to ever marry James Bond in *On Her Majesty's Secret Service* (London Management)

Goldfinger	Jill and Tilly Masterson
Thunderball	Paula Caplan, Fiona Volpe
You Only Live Twice	Aki, Helga Brandt
On Her Majesty's Secret Service	Shaun Campbell
Diamonds Are Forever	Plenty O'Toole
Live & Let Die	Rosie Carver
The Man With the Golden Gun	Andrea Anders
The Spy Who Loved Me	Stromberg's assistant, Naomi
Moonraker	Corinne Dufour
For Your Eyes Only	Contessa Lisl, McGregor
Octopussy	Vijay
Never Say Never Again	Nicole
A View to a Kill	Tibbett
The Living Daylights	Saunders
License to Kill	Della Churchill
Goldeneye	Xenia Onatopp
Tomorrow Never Dies	Paris Carver

SCREENWRITERS

Dr. No	Richard Maibaum, Johanna Harwood, Berkeley Mather
From Russia With Love	Richard Maibaum
Goldfinger	Richard Maibaum, Paul Dehn
Thunderball	Richard Maibaum, John Hopkins
You Only Live Twice	Roald Dahl
Casino Royale	John Law, Wolf Mankowitz, Michael Sayers
On Her Majesty's Secret Service	Richard Maibaum
Diamonds Are Forever	Richard Maibaum, Tom Mankiewicz
Live & Let Die	Tom Mankiewicz
The Man With the Golden Gun	Richard Maibaum, Tom Mankiewicz
The Spy Who Loved Me	Christopher Wood, Richard Maibaum
Moonraker	Christopher Wood
For Your Eyes Only	Richard Maibaum, Michael G. Wilson
Octopussy	George Macdonald Fraser, Richard Maibaum, Michael G. Wilson
Never Say Never Again	Lorenzo Semple, Jr.
A View to a Kill	Richard Maibaum
The Living Daylights	Richard Maibaum, Michael G. Wilson
License to Kill	Richard Maibaum & Michael G. Wilson
Goldeneye	Jeffrey Caine & Bruce Feirstein
Tomorrow Never Dies	Bruce Feirstein

SCREENWRITERS: SHORT BIOGRAPHIES

ROALD DAHL
Born in Norway, 1916. Screenwriter for *Chitty Chitty Bang Bang* and *You Only Live Twice* in 1967.

PAUL DEHN
Screenwriter, lyricist, playwright, film critic. Born November 5, 1912 in Manchester, England. Educated at Oxford University. Won an Oscar for original story *Seven Days to Noon* in 1951 and British film Academy Award for script *Orders To Kill* in 1958.

RICHARD MAIBAUM
Screenwriter, producer. Born May 26, 1909 in New York City. Director of the Army's combat film division in WWII. Returned to Paramount as a producer and screenwriter.

TOM MANKIEWICZ
Screenwriter, producer, director. Born in Los Angeles, California on June 1, 1942. Educated at Exeter Academy and Yale University. The son of Joseph Mankiewicz.

WOLF MANKOWITZ
Novelist, playwright, screenwriter. Born November 7, 1942 in London, England. Masters degree from Cambridge University.

SECURITY DEVICES

The following is a list of sophisticated electronic equipment available not only to 'Q' and James Bond, but to the general public as well.

Bugs[1]	Chemical Detectors
Bug Detector	Tracers
Scrambler for Fax Machines	Portable Ground Radar
Voice Stress Analyzer	Bomb Detectors
Letter Bomb Detectors	Lie Detectors
Infrared Night Viewers	Tape Recorder Detector
Seismic Intrusion Detector	Bullet Proof Cars
Acoustic Sensors	

Flights With Magnesium Flash Bulbs (These cause temporary blindness)
Telephone Electronic Guard (A system to help track down kidnap victims)

[1] To tap a telephone or bug a room in the U.S. is a felony crime. Bugs are illegal in the U.S. but can be purchased over the counter in most foreign countries. Many can also be assembled from parts sold at domestic shops.

SELECTED STUNTS

NEVER SAY NEVER AGAIN:
The cliff jump on horseback was filmed in France on Paradise Island by stunt coordinator Vic Armstrong who doubled for Connery and Wendy Leech, stunt lady, who doubled for Kim Basinger. Actual height of the jump was 35 feet into 12 feet of water.

FOR YOUR EYES ONLY:

Rick Sylvester, doubling Roger Moore, had to climb the mountain on which the St. Cyril monastery is situated and then purposely lose his footing to fall 100 feet, hanging by a single rope. A special sandbag pulley system was devised to cushion his fall but Sylvester had no idea how or where he would land and even if the rope would support him.

During the bobsled sequence in the same film, where Bond chases a bobsled and where a motorcyclist chases Bond, one of the stuntmen was killed.

A VIEW TO A KILL

The Eiffel Tower was built by the French engineer, Alexandre Gustave Eiffel and opened to the public March 31, 1889. At the time, it was the world's tallest structure; standing 1,024 feet above the street. It took Eiffel two years, two months, and two days to complete what has become the very symbol of France. The tower spans two and one-half acres at its base and, despite its height, sways no more than four and one half inches in strong winds. Built of 9,700 tons of iron, 2.5 million rivets, and 40 tons of paint, the tower distributes its weight so evenly that its four legs exert no more pressure on the ground per square inch than does a man sitting in a four-legged chair.

The tower contains three floors and three restaurants. At the 187 foot level there are two restaurants, a post office, and an auditorium featuring a sound and light show on the tower's history. One hundred and ninety feet further up on the second level is one of Paris' finest restaurants, the Jules Verne. It offers a five-star view; forty miles on a clear day.

On just such a clear day, James Bond, who was investigating Zorin Industries, was having lunch with a Mr. Aubergine in the Jules Verne. Bond was hopeful that Aubergine could shed some light as to why Zorin's horses always won their races. Unfortunately, Mr. Aubergine fell victim to a poisonous fish hook cast by Zorin's girlfriend May Day. She then fled up the steps of the Eiffel Tower with Bond in pursuit, whereupon she jumped, parachuting in descent.

Stuntman, B.J. Worth, doubling for May Day, made this dramatic jump from the 800 foot level of the tower. The chute opened and Worth skillfully guided himself down to land on the upper deck of the Bateau Mouche, on the river Seine, on the first take, just as it was called for in the script.

MOONRAKER:

In the chase scene where Bond is pursued by Jaws, he drives a Glastron / Carlson 23' Hardtop which had been modified to extend back to the transom. This boat was also capable of firing rockets and laying mines.

Technical Data of the Glastron/Carlson 23' Hardtop

LOA	23'-4-3/4"
Beam	91.5"
Transom Width	85"
Depth	50"
Capacity	1200 lbs.
Engine	260 Mercruiser

LIVE & LET DIE:

In a sensational speedboat chase across Louisiana lakes and bayous, James Bond, in a fifteen-foot Glastron GT-150 powered by an Evinrude 135 hp Starflite Outboard engine, leaps fourteen feet out of the water and 110 feet over two automobiles parked on a gravel roadway to land safely back into the Louisiana bayou. In all, twenty-six boats were used in the spectacular chase. The stunt was completed by Jerry Comeaux and at the same time, set a new world record of 110 feet. Comeaux also jumped the "Bond Bad-Guy" boat.

To make the jumps, the boats were modified by moving all the weight towards the center. Other stunts involved skidding jet boats across grass, into a swimming pool, and through a garden wedding.

The film company bought 26 boats from Glastron, including two built in England by Norman Fletcher, Ltd. for studio close–ups, and multiple extra parts. Boats for the "heavies" were trimmed in black.

In addition to destroying seventeen of the twenty-six Glastrons, the production company totalled out ten airplanes, a dozen autos, and LST, and a yacht.

Maurice Patchett, a London bus driver, drove the Leyland R.T. double-decker bus in all the chase scenes. It was originally from London's number 19 bus route. The top half of the bus was sawn off and placed on rollers and re-attached to the lower half so it would slide off easily when it hit the trestle bridge at exactly 30 miles per hour. This scene was shot December 7, 1972 outside of Montego Bay, Jamaica on highway A1 to Lucea.

THE SPY WHO LOVED ME:

Rick Sylvester, for $30,000, ski jumped off Baffin Island's 3,000 foot Asgard Peak in Canada and parachuted to safety.

THE MAN WITH THE GOLDEN GUN:

Bond drives a 1974 American Motors Hornet Hatchback in a chase scene with Scaramanga. The jump scene stunt was programmed by a Hal 2000 computer at Cornell University Aeronautic Laboratory. Modifications were made to the Hornet and it had to hit the ramp at the precise speed. The stunt was performed by Bumps Willard and completed in fifteen seconds on one take.

The spiral car jump required 1) a specific speed, 2) a custom designed automobile, and 3) take-off and landing ramps specifically designed so that the machine would turn in mid-air properly and land on all four wheels. Modifications of the car included: 1) adjusting the weight factors, 2) redesigning the chassis, and 3) shortening and widening various parts of the body.

GOLDENEYE:

Stuntman Wayne Michaels makes an incredible bungee jump of 800 feet off the top of the Contra Dam near Lugano, Switzerland.

Near the end of the jump, Michaels had only split seconds to pull a gun out of his pocket to fire a piton into the concrete below. When the bungee cord had played out to its normal length, Michaels had to pull himself hand over hand on the line anchored to the ground below by the piton. If the piton had failed, he would have been hurled back up the face of the dam by the bungee cord.

TOMORROW NEVER DIES

1) Motorcycle chase scene with Bond and Wai Lin handcuffed together. She operates the clutch and he the throttle. They leap the bike from one roof, across the street over a hovering helicopter and onto another roof. The chase scene starts in Bangkok, then moves to the backlot where various rigs, harnesses, etc. were utilized.

2) Chase scene with Bond's BMW 750 IL. The BMW employed little multi-rocket launchers, self-inflating tires, a cable cutter, metal tire spikes, and gas emission from under the car. All of these gadgets were operated by Bond from the back seat of the car with a mobile phone display. Bond uses a remote-control touch pad with a liquid crystal view screen. Ex-world motor-cross champion Cavid Bickers, was employed to complete this stunt, and drove the newly designed camera car in speeds up to sixty miles an hour within the Brent Cross shopping center in North London.

SHIPS IN BOOK AND FILM

LIVE & LET DIE:
Mr. Big's yacht the "Secatur." Black with grey super structure. Speed 20 knots. Built 1947. General Motors twin diesels, steelhull, latest electric gear. The "Point Spencer" Coast Guard Cutter. Speedboats.

MOONRAKER:
HMS "Merganzer", naval security patrol. Gondola, speed boats. Unnamed Russian submarine.

DIAMONDS ARE FOREVER:
Luxury Liner "Queen Elizabeth I" in actuality the P&O luxury liner "Canberra." Hovercraft.

FROM RUSSIA WITH LOVE:
Fairey Huntsmen patrol-style pleasure boats. Bosphorous ferry boat. S.P.E.C.T.R.E. yacht.

DR. NO:
Small launch owned by Quarrel. Tanker SS "Blanche." HMS "Narvik."

GOLDFINGER:
Unnamed Soviet cruiser of the Sverdlovsk class.

THUNDERBALL:
"El Capitan" and "San Pedro" sunk in 1719. M.V. "Mercurial," U.S.S. "Manta," nuclear powered submarine. George Washington class. Four thousand tons, crew of 100. Cost: 100 million. Range 100,000 miles. 16 vertical launching tubes. Two banks of eight for the Polaris solid-fuel missile, range 1200 miles, Catamaran Tropic Rover. Hydrofoil.

The "Disco Volante", 110 foot length. Formerly the "Flying Fish" hydrofoil built by Leopoldo Rodriques of Messina, Italy. Powered by two Daimler–Benz four–stroke Diesels, supercharged by twin Brown–Boveri turbo superchargers, hull of aluminum and magnesium alloy. Restored by Allied Marine of Miami, Florida for 200,000 pounds. Weight 100 tons, speed 50 knots, cruising range 400 miles.

THE SPY WHO LOVED ME:
Super tanker "Liparus," USS "Wayne and HMS Ranger", submarines. Nile river boat, Ark Royal British aircraft carrier.

ON HER MAJESTY'S SECRET SERVICE:
Bombard rescue boats.

YOU ONLY LIVE TWICE:
Tanker "Ning-Po," British submarine M1, "Murasaki Maru," 3,000 tons, British destroyer HMS "Tenby." Hydrofoil.

THE MAN WITH THE GOLDEN GUN:
Southeast Asian skiff, Chinese junk, speedboats, "Thunder Bird," a big Chris Craft, Queen Elizabeth I. Hydrofoil.

COLONEL SUN:
"Cynthia", 24 feet belonging to G. Ionide and "Altair," 50' wide diesel belonging to Niko Litsas.

FOR YOUR EYES ONLY:
British electronic surveillance and fishing trawler the "St. George." Melina Havelock's yacht "Triana," and "Neptune," Havelocks two-person submarine. Unnamed 50 foot Chris Craft owned by Major Gonzales, motorboat.

THE HILDEBRAND RARITY:
The "Wavekrest" 100 feet long, 200 tons.

RISICO:
"Colombina" owned by Colombo.

SCORPIUS:
"Vladem I" owned by Scorpius. Powered by two 3, 000 HP marine diesels.

THE LIVING DAYLIGHTS:
128 foot "Moonmaiden II", 65 foot Catamaran "Spectral Marine 2:20"

A VIEW TO A KILL:
Un-named Bateau Mouche on the River Seine. Iceberg camouflaged launch.

NOBODY LIVES FOREVER:
40 foot power cruiser.

NEVER SAY NEVER AGAIN:
"The Flying Saucer" is in reality the "Nabila" which was owned by Adnan Khashoggi. This custom-designed yacht is 285 feet long, 43 feet wide and built at a cost of 29 million. Its five decks comprise the height of a three-story building. It contains three elevators, helicopter pad, movie theatre, two saunas, swimming pool, a discotheque, jacuzzi, game room, eleven guest suites with private baths and one master suite of four rooms. All fittings are gold. The bridge is fitted with all the most modern electric technology. The "Nabila" is capable of 18 knots. S.P.E.C.T.R.E. fishing boat, submarine.

LICENSE TO KILL:
150 foot "Wavekrest" yacht owned by Milton Krest. Coast Guard Cutter "Dauntless." Pa Ja Ma fishing boat.

WIN, LOSE OR DIE:
"Son of Takashani" a Japanese oil tanker. "Estado Novo", a freighter. "HMS Invincible" a British aircraft carrier, 677 feet long, and weighing 19,500 tons.

BROKEN CLAW:
US Aircraft Carrier, Nimitz Class, nuclear.

SEAFIRE:
"Golden Bough", "Mare Nostrum", Submarine Type VII, "Caribbean Prince."

COLD FALL:
Clay Pigeon.

TOMORROW NEVER DIES:
"HMS Devonshire", "HMS Bedford", Sea Dolphin II.

ZERO MINUS TEN:
Viking 66 Sports Cruiser, Taitai, Peacock, Statesman.

GOLDENEYE:
Manticore-La Fayette.

THE FACTS OF DEATH:
Yacht "Persephone".

SOTHEBY'S

London & New York. Founded 1744. Sotheby's has been featured in a James Bond film (*Octopussy*) and a Bond short story (*The Property of a Lady*).[1]

SOTHEBY'S (NEW YORK)

June 28, 1986. Sale of James Bond's Aston Martin DBV ($275,000) and Goldfinger's Phantom III Rolls-Royce ($121,000).

[1] *The Ivory Hammer: The Year at Sotheby's*. (Holt Rheinehart and Winston, 1964). Contains the James Bond story *The Property of a Lady* concerning an auction at Sotheby's. Sotheby's specially commissioned Ian Fleming to write the story for their publication.

STATION HEADS FOR M.I.6

Commander Damon	Station "A", USA
Tangueray	Station "B", West Berlin
Capt. Paul Sender, #2	Station "B", West Berlin
Commander Strangways	Station "C", Caribbean[1]
Alec Hill	Station "C", Caribbean
Wing Commander Rattray	Station "F", France
Stuart Thomas	Station "G", Greece[2]
Dickson	Station "H", Hong Kong
Sadruddin	Station "I", India
Commander Ross	Station "J", Jamaica[3]
Lt. Commander Savage	Station "M", Munich[4]
Clifford Dudley	Station "S", Sweden
Darko Kerim	Station "T", Turkey[5]
Saunders	Station "V", Vienna[6]
Hier Muir	Station "Z", Zurich
Shaun Campbell, #2	Station "Z", Zurich[7]
T.Y. Woo	Station "H", Hong Kong[8]

[1] Killed by Dr. No's men [2] Killed by Col. Sun's men [3] Killed by Scaramanga [4] Best man at Bond's wedding
[5] Killed by Smersh agents [6] Killed by Whitaker's men [7] Killed by Blofeld's men [8] Replaced Dickson, killed by General Wong

STUDIOS

Pinewood Studio, Ltd.
Pinewood Road, Iver Heath
Buckinghamshire SLO ONH

Managing Director: Cyril Howard.

Studios—New Headquarters

Leavesden Aerofrome, Herts, England
EON Studios, Frogmore, Herfordshire

TIGER TANAKA

Chief of the Koan-Chosa-Kyoku Japanese Secret Service. Educated at Trinity College & Oxford University. Black belt in Karate. Assistant Naval Attache, Japanese London Embassy prior to WWII. Personal aide to Admiral Ohnishi during WWII. Trained as kamikazi pilot at ending of WWII.

HEADQUARTERS, JAPANESE SECRET SERVICE

Sign on dull, grey building reads "Bureau of All Asian Folkways." These are the doors you must pass through to reach Tiger Tanaka.

1) Coordination Department, 2) International Relations, 3) Visual Presentation Bureau, 4) Documentation, 5) Walk behind wall of book shelves to door marked "Proposed Extension To Documentation Department, Danger! Construction Work In Progress" 6) Walk across "Nightingale" floor of squeaks and groans, 7) Small facing door, a spy-hole, through this door into small room whose entire floor was a lift, 8) down, deep into the ground, then out and through an arch marked "Exit", 9) into a waiting room and outer office, 10) and through a door into Tiger Tanaka's office.

UNDERWATER ACTIVITIES

FEATURED IN THE FOLLOWING BOOKS & FILMS:

Goldfinger	*The Spy Who Loved Me*
For Your Eyes Only	*A View to a Kill*
Moonraker	*Thunderball*
Live & Let Die	*Dr. No*
The Hildebrand Rarity	*Octopussy*
Colonel Sun	*Nobody Lives Forever*
You Only Live Twice	*License to Kill*
The Man From Barbarossa	*Seafire*
Goldeneye	*Tomorrow Never Dies*
The Facts of Death	

VILLAINS (BOOKS)

Casino Royale	LeChiffre
Live & Let Die	Mr. Big
Moonraker	Hugo Drax
Diamonds Are Forever	Spang brothers
From Russia With Love	Rosa Klebb, Red Grant
Dr. No	Dr. No
Goldfinger	Auric Goldfinger
Thunderball	Blofeld, Largo
The Spy Who Loved Me	Horror and Sluggsy
On Her Majesty's Secret Service	Blofeld and Bunt
You Only Live Twice	Blofeld and Bunt
The Man With The Golden Gun	Scaramanga
Colonel Sun	Colonel Sun
License Renewed	Anton Murik
For Special Services	Nena Bismaquer
Icebreaker	Konrad Von Gloda
Role Of Honor	Tamil Rahani
Nobody Lives Forever	Tamil Rahani
No Deals Mr. Bond	General Chernov
Scorpius	Scorpius
License To Kill	Franz Sanchez
Win, Lose Or Die	Bassam Baradj
Broken Claw	Brokenclaw

The Man From Barbarossa .... General Yuskovich
Death Is Forever .... Wolfgang Weisen
Never Send Flowers .... David Dragonpol
Seafire .... Maxwell Tarn
Cold Fall .... General Brutus Clay, Tempesta Brothers
Goldeneye .... Alec Trevelyan, Xenia Onatopp
Tomorrow Never Dies .... Elliot Carver
Zero Minus Ten .... Guy Thackeray
The Facts of Death .... Konstantine Romanos, Hera Volopoulos,
Melina Papas, Dr. Ashely Anderson

VILLAINS (SHORT STORIES)

From A View To A Kill .... Russian spy group
For Your Eyes Only .... Von Hammerstein
Risico .... Kristatos
The Hildebrand Rarity .... Milton Krest
Octopussy .... Major Dexter Smythe
The Living Daylights .... "Trigger"
The Property Of A Lady .... Piotr Malinowski and Maria Freundenstein

VILLIANS (FILM) AKA "THE BAD GUYS"

Joseph Wiseman as Dr. Julius No in *Dr. No*, 1962
Robert Shaw as Red Grant in *From Russia With Love*, 1963
Gert Frobe as Auric Goldfinger in *Goldfinger*, 1964
Adolfo Celi as Emilio Largo in *Thunderball*, 1965
Donald Pleasance as Ernst Stavro Blofeld in *You Only Live Twice*, 1967
Telly Savalas as Ernst Stavro Blofeld in *On Her Majesty's Secret Service*, 1969
Charles Gray as Ernst Stavro Blofeld in *Diamonds Are Forever*, 1971
Yaphet Kotto as Mr. Big, alias Dr. Kanaga in *Live and Let Die*, 1973
Christopher Lee as Scaramanga in *The Man With The Golden Gun*, 1974
Curt Jurgens as Stromberg in *The Spy Who Loved Me*, 1977
Michael Lonsdale as Hugo Drax in *Moonraker*, 1979
Julian Glover as Kristatos in *For Your Eyes Only*, 1981
Louis Jourdan as Prince Kamal Khan in *Octopussy*, 1983
Christopher Walken as Max Zorin in *A View to a Kill*, 1985
Joe Don Baker as Whitaker in *The Living Daylights*, 1987
Klaus Maria Brandauer as Largo in *Never Say Never Again*, 1983
Robert Davi as Franz Sanchez in *License to Kill* , 1989
Sean Bean as Alec Trevelyan in *Goldeneye*, 1995
Jonathan Pryce as Elliot Carver in *Tomorrow Never Dies*, 1997

VILLAIN'S DEMISE (BOOK)

Le Chiffre .... Killed by Smersh gunshot

Mr. Big	Devoured by shark
Hugo Drax	Died in Moonraker explosion
Jack Spang	Died in helicopter explosion
Red Grant	Stabbed to death by Bond
Dr. No	Buried under bat guano by Bond
Goldfinger	Choked to death by Bond
Largo	Killed by Domino with speargun
Sol Horowitz and Sluggsy Morant	Shot to death by Bond
Ernst Blofeld	Choked to death by Bond
Irma Bunt	Stabbed to death with stave by Bond
Scaramanga	Shot to death by Bond
Colonel Sun	Stabbed to death by Bond
Anton Murik	Shot to death by Bond
Nena Bismaquer	Crushed to death by giant Python
Konrad Von Gloda	Shot to death by Bond
Tamel Rahani	Killed by Bond with explosive charge
Scorpius	Died from snake bites
Franz Sanchez	Burned to death
Bassam Baradj	Shot to death by Beatrice da Ricci
Brokenclaw	Shot to death with bow and arrow by Bond
The Man From Barbarossa	Killed by explosion
Wolfgang Weisen	Electrocuted by Bond
David Dragonpol	Killed by explosion
Maxwell Tarn	Killed by Bond with flare gun
Brutus Clay	Drowned with the aid of Bond
Alec Trevelyan	Fell to his death with the aid of Bond
Elliot Carver	Drowned
Guy Thackeray	Drowned with the aid of Bond
Konstantine Romanos	Shot to death

VILLAIN'S DEMISE (SHORT STORIES)

Russian Spy Group	Killed and captured
Von Hammerstein	Killed by Judy Havelock with bow and arrow.
Major Gonzales	Killed by Bond with rifle fire
Kristatos	Shot to death by Bond
Milton Krest	Strangled by having fish stuffed in his mouth.
Major Dexter Smythe	Drowned by Octopussy
Maria Freudenstein	Killed by Smersh agents

VILLAIN'S DEMISE (FILM)

Dr. No	Falls into core of nuclear reactor
Red Grant	Choked to death by Bond
Rosa Klebb	Shot to death by Tatiana Romanova
Goldfinger	Sucked out of plane window
Oddjob	Electocuted by Bond

Count Lippe	Murdered by Volpe
Fiona Volpe	Killed by Spectre agents
Emilio Largo	Killed by Domino with speargun
Blofeld	Killed by Bond with Crane
Mr. Big	Killed by Bond
Scaramanga	Shot to death by Bond
Karl Stromberg	Shot to death by Bond
Hugo Drax	Pushed out into space by Bond
Kristatos	Killed by Columbo
Kamal Khan	Dies in plane crash
Max Zorin	Falls to his death from airship
Whitaker	Crushed to death by heavy object
Sanchez	Burned to death
Alec Trevelyan	Fell to his death off tower
Elliot Carver	Drowned

VILLAIN'S IMPAIRMENTS / ODDITIES

Dr. No	Steel pincers for hands. Heart on right side of chest.
Ernst Stavro Blofeld	No earlobes. Right nostril eaten away from syphilis.
Sir Hugo Drax	Skin grafts to face and neck.
Oddjob	Ridges of bone-like tissue on hands from karate.
Mr. Big	Enlarged head, hairless, no eyebrows, no eyelashes.
Scaramanga	A third mammary gland located on his chest.
Karl Stromberg	Webbed fingers.
General Brutus Clay	Prosthetic legs
Alec Trevelyan	Disfigured face

VILLAINS (OCCUPATION)

Le Chiffre	Treasurer & Paymaster for communist-controlled French Union
Mr. Big	Powerful Black businessman, member of Smersh
Hugo Drax	Wealthy & respected national hero
Jack Spang	Head of spangled mob syndicate
Rosa Klebb	Head of Smersh executions
Red Grant	Paid assassin
Dr. No	Prominent engineer
Goldfinger	Wealthy industrialist
Blofeld	Leader of S.P.E.C.T.R.E.
Largo	Adventurer
Horror & Sluggsy	Small time gangsters
Scaramanga	Freelance assassin
Colonel Sun	Red Chinese terrorist
Anton Murik	Nuclear scientist
Nena Bismaquer	Head of S.P.E.C.T.R.E.

Konrad Von Gloda .... Leader / National Socialist Action Army
Tamil Rahani .... Leader of S.P.E.C.T.R.E.
General Chernov .... Head of Smersh
Scorpius .... International terrorist
Franz Sanchez .... Druglord
Bassam Baradj .... Terrorist
The Man From Barbarossa .... Russian General
Wolfgang Wiesen .... East German Agent
David Dragonpol .... Retired Actor
Maxwell Tarn .... Industrialist
Brutus Clay .... Retired General
Alec Travelyn .... Terrorist
Elliot Carver .... Media Executive
Guy Thackeray .... Business Executive
Konstantine Romanos .... Terrorist

VILLAIN'S OCCUPATIONS (SHORT STORIES)

Russian Spy Group .... Professional spies
Von Hammerstein .... Paid assassin and ex-nazi
Kristatios .... Head of drug smuggling operation
Milton Krest .... Wealthy, sadistic entrepreneur
Major Dexter Smythe .... Retired army officer
"Trigger" .... Russian executioner & musician
Maria Freudenstein .... Double agent

VILLAIN'S ORGANIZATIONS

	BOOK	FILM
Casino Royale	Smersh	-
Live & Let Die	Smersh	Smersh
Moonraker	USSR	Independent
Diamonds Are Forever	Syndicate	S.P.E.C.T.R.E.
From Russia With Love	USSR	S.P.E.C.T.R.E.
Dr. No	USSR	S.P.E.C.T.R.E.
Goldfinger	Smersh	Freelance
Thunderball	Spectre	S.P.E.C.T.R.E.
The Spy Who Loved Me	Independent	Independent
On Her Majesty's Secret Service	Spectre	S.P.E.C.T.R.E.
You Only Live Twice	Independent	S.P.E.C.T.R.E.
The Man With the Golden Gun	Independent	Castro / USSR
Colonel Sun	Red Chinese	-
License Renewed	Independent	-
For Special Services	S.P.E.C.T.R.E.	-
Icebreaker	NSAA[1]	-
Role of Honor	Spectre	-
Nobody Lives Forever	Spectre	-
No Deals Mr. Bond	Smersh	-
Scorpius	Independent	-
License to Kill	Independent	Independent

Win, Lose or Die .... Bast[2] -
Brokenclaw .... Independent -
The Man From Barbarossa .... USSR -
Death is Forever .... Independent -
Never Send Flowers .... Independent
Seafire .... Tarn International -
Coldfall .... Children of the Last Days (COLD)
Goldeneye .... Janus Crime Syndicate
Tomorrow Never Dies .... Carver Media Group
Zero Minus Ten .... EurAsia Enterprises
The Facts of Death .... New Pythagorean Society

[1] National Socialist Action Army   [2] Brotherhood of Anarchy and Secret Terrorism.

VILLAIN'S ORGANIZATION (SHORT STORIES)

From A View to a Kill .... USSR
Quantum of Solace .... None
Risico .... Independent
The Hildebrand Rarity .... Independent
The Property of a Lady .... USSR
For Your Eyes Only .... Independent
Octopussy .... Independent
The Living Daylights .... USSR

WATER CRAFT OPERATED BY BOND (FILM)

NEPTUNE MINI-SUBMARINE
Bond operated this machine in his attempt to locate the ATAC aboard the wreckage of The St. George. This two-man submarine could stay underwater for hours and dive fairly deep. It was designed by Peter Lamont for the film *For Your Eyes Only.*

MOTORIZED ALLIGATOR SUBMARINE
This vehicle was used by Bond to approach Octopussy's island headquarters undetected in India.

UNDERWATER SLED
Bond used one of these to good advantage in the film *Thunderball* when he was chasing Largo and his men in the Bahamas.

WETBIKE HYDROFOIL
This one-man hydrofoil can attain speeds up to 40 mph. Bond used this machine to carry him out to Stromberg's Atlantis complex in *The Spy Who Loved Me.*

GIANT SILVER PLASTIC BALL
Bond pedaled out to Blofeld's oil rig headquarters inside of this ball which just skims along on the surface of the water in *Diamonds Are Forever.*

WATER CRAFT OPERATED BY BOND ON ASSIGNMENT (FILM)

Dr. No	Small motorboat
From Russia With Love	Fairey Huntsmen patrol styled pleasure boat
Thunderball	Disco Volante
Live & Let Die	Glastron speed boat
The Spy Who Loved Me	Wetbike and Lotus Esprit sports car converted into a submersible
Moonraker	Bondola-Gondola, motor-launch and hovercraft. Glastron speed boat
Octopussy	Alligator submarine
The Man With the Golden Gun	Southeast Asian long tail-boat skiff, Chinese junk
License to Kill	Small rubber Seriel dinghy
Goldeneye	Speedboat
Tomorrow Never Dies	Chinese fishing junk
Zero Minus Ten	Sampan

WEAPONS USED BY BOND (BOOK)

Casino Royale	.25 Beretta & .38 Colt Police Positive.
Live & Let Die	.25 Beretta, .38 Colt Detective Special, Champion harpoon gun, Limpet mine, steel-capped shoes.
Moonraker	.25 Beretta, .45 Collt Army Special, long-barrel nuclear missile.
Diamonds Are Forever	.25 Beretta, Bofors Artillery gun.
From Russia With Love	.25 Beretta, Wilkinson knives, Red Grant's gun in book.
Dr. No	Walther PPK 7.65mm, .38 Smith & Wesson Centennial, Airweight, steak knife, spear, crane with load of bat guano.
Goldfinger	Walther PPK, daggers concealed in shoe soles, bazooka.
Thunderball	Walther PPK, knives & spears.
The Spy Who Loved Me	Walther PPK, Smith & Wesson Police Positive.
On Her Majesty's Secret Service	Plastic bombs, ski poles, Rolex watch used as brass knuckles.
You Only Live Twice	Walther PPK, Bare hands, stave.
The Man With the Golden Gun	Walther PPK, cyanide gun.
Colonel Sun	Walther PPK, knife, Mills grenades, Thompson sub-machine gun.
License Renewed	Antique dueling pistol, tear gas, cigarette lighter with knockout gas, Colt Python .357 Magnum, crossbow, 9mm Browning automatic, Ruger Super Blackhawk .44 Magnum MBA Gyrojet rocket pistol.

For Special Services .... Armalite AR18 machine gun, gasoline bomb, Ruger Super Blackhawk .44 Magnum, .38 Cal. Pistol, Winchester pump shotgun, Sykes-Fairbairn throwing Knives, Heckler & Koch VP70 automatic.

Icebreaker .... Sykes-Fairbairn commando dagger, stun grenades, L2A2 hand bombs, Ruger Super Redhawk .44 Magnum, Lapp reindeer knife, Heckler and Koch P7 automatic, steel telescopic baton.

Role of Honor .... Smith & Wesson ASP 9mm automatic, steel telescopic baton[1].

Nobody Lives Forever .... [1]Smith & Wesson ASP 9mm automatic, Uzi machine pistol, Stetchkin automatic pistol, steel telescopic baton.

No Deals Mr. Bond .... ASP 9mm automatic pistol, steel telescopic baton, Luger 9mm, Uzi machine pistol.

Scorpius .... Steel telescopic baton, Browning 9mm automatic pistol, ASP 9mm automatic pistol, Ruger P-85 pistol, .38 Cal. S&W Police Positive, XL65E5 rifle.

License to Kill .... Walther P38k, Browning 9mm pistols, 9mm signature rifle. This rifle has a five round magazine, fires teflon glaser slugs, telescopic sight, accurate up to 1,000 yards. Microchips programmed to Bond's palm and fingerprints. Will not fire for anyone else. Chip operates an optical skin reader, FN 9mm automatic pistol, pocket version.

Win, Lose, or Die .... 9mm Browning automatic pistol, Sykes–Fairbairn knife and his bare hands.

Brokenclaw .... ASP, 9mm. Automatic, 9mm. DA140 Browning automatic, bow & arrow.

The Man From Barbarossa .... ASP, 9mm, automatic, Wather P6, 9mm with silencer. Russian PRI 5.45mm Automatic with silencer.

Death is Forever .... ASP 9 mm Automatic gold and silver pens containing lethal & mace gases, Fairburn Commando Dagger.

Never Send Flowers .... 45 Colt Automatic, 10mm Browning automatic, 9mm AsP Automatic with guttersnipe sight and Glaser slugs.

Seafire .... ASP 9mm Automatic.

Cold Fall .... Sykes-Fairbairn command knife, ASP 9 mm automatic.

Goldeneye .... T-55 Tank, ASP 9 mm pistol.

Tomorrow Never Dies .... Walther PPK 7.65 mm.

Zero Minus Ten .... Walther PPK 7.65 mm.

The Facts of Death .... Walther PPK & P99.

WEAPONS USED BY BOND (SHORT STORIES)

From A View to a Kill	.45 Calibre Colt Long–Barrel, Walther PPK.
For Your Eyes Only	Walther PPK pistol, Savage 99f with Weatherby 6x62 scope rifle.
Risico	Walther PPK pistol.
Hildebrand Rarity	Champion harpoon gun.
Quantum of Solace	None.
The Property of a Lady	None.
Octopussy	None.
The Living Daylights	.308-calibre International Experimental Target rifle, Winchester, with sniperscope.

[1] The ASP, 9mm automatic pistol is not a production model but rather a customized weapon.

WEAPONS USED BY BOND (FILM)

Dr. No	Walther PPK with silencer.
From Russia With Love	Walther PPK, AR-7 Survival rifle, throwing knife, tear gas. Red Grant's garrote wire.
Goldfinger	Timing device with plastic explosive, Walther PPK, Aston-Martin DBV with Browning .50 Cal. machine-guns, 220 volt power-line, electric heater.
Thunderball	Aston Martin DB 5, Walther PPK, spear gun, fireplace poker. Two compressed-air missiles with explosive heads.
You Only Live Twice	Walther PPK, cigarette with rocket-powered dart, "Little Nellie" gyrocopter with machine guns, rockets, flame-throwers, aerial mines, heat-seeking air-to-air missiles.
On Her Majesty's Secret Service	New Aston-Martin DB6, Armalite machine gun. Walther PPK, ski poles, hands.
Diamonds Are Forever	Walther PPK, scalpels, fire–extinguisher.
Live & Let Die	Walther PPK, sharkgun, gas pellet, gasoline.
The Man With the Golden Gun	Walther PPK, karate, Nikon camera which causes subject to explode when photographed.
The Spy Who Loved Me	Ski pole rocket gun, Walther PPK, Lotus Esprit equipped with surface to air missile launcher, underwater rockets, and mine laying capability.
Moonraker	Wristgun which fired poisonous and armor piercing darts, dagger, bare hands. Motorboat with mine-laying capabilities and homing torpedo.
For Your Eyes Only	Helicopter, Walther PPK, pinion spikes, wooden plank.
Octopussy	Bede Accrostar, Walther PPK, bare hands, knife, rifle.

WEAPONS USED BY BOND, DESCRIPTION OF

50 Calibre BROWNING MACHINE GUN

Two of these (air cooled), were mounted on the Aston Martin DBV which Bond drove on assignment in *Goldfinger* and used to good advantage.

WINCHESTER MODEL 12 GAUGE PUMP SHOTGUN

18.5mm. Bond used such a weapon on assignment *For Special Services*. (Book)

CIGARETTE ROCKET

This lethal jet-propelled bullet was developed by the Japanese Secret Service who demonstrated it to Bond. He in turn used it effectively on S.P.E.C.T.R.E. agents. (Book)

DUNHILL HALOTHANE LIGHTER

Halothane is a potent, quick acting drug which renders a person unconscious instantly. In *License Renewed* Bond used this to good advantage in his fight with Caber.

SKI POLE ROCKET

Bond had to use this one-shot weapon of considerable power to kill a Russian agent during a dramatic chase scene in *The Spy Who Loved Me*.

SHAVING CANNISTER FLAMETHROWER

Bond ignited his aerosol can, converting it to a flamethrower in order to kill a snake in *Live & Let Die*. 'Q' provides Bond with an ingenious "wrist–gun" which fires poisonous or armour–piercing darts. He and Holly Goodhead were saved from instant cremation with this device in *Moonraker*.

SHARK GUN WHICH FIRES COMPRESSED AIR PELLETS

In his final fight with Mr. Big, Bond pushed one of these into Mr. Big's mouth which caused him to swell up like a balloon and explode.

MBA GYROJET ROCKET PISTOL

Although not of a very reliable nature, Bond used this weapon in *License Renewed* to kill Anton Murik, the Laird of Murcaldy, as he was attempting to flee in his helicopter. (Book)

FOUNTAIN PEN WHICH FIRES EXPLOSIVE CARTRIDGES

Bond used this weapon to kill the seductive Fatima Blush in *Never Say Never Again.*

Bond has also used a poison ball point pen in *Moonraker* and a Champion harpoon gun in *Thunderball* and the *Hildebrand Rarity.* Bond fired a Stinger missile to destroy Huey helicopter in *The Facts of Death.* (Book)

THE BERETTA MODEL 418, .25 Calibre PISTOL

Bond carried this weapon for fifteen years but in *From Russia With Love* it nearly cost him his life when his silencer caught in his soft chamois holster. Thereafter, "M" insisted that Bond carry a Walther PPK, 7.65mm. (Book)

BERETTA MODEL 418: 6.35mm

Weight	11.72 ounces (with alloy frame)
	14.87 ounces (with steel frame)
Length	4.56 inches
Barrel Length	2.36 inches
Magazine Capacity	8 rounds

Pietro Beretta SPA is an Italian armaments firm who manufacture designs of semi-automatic pistols. Total production of the Model 418 was 140,000 pieces. Production run years were 1949 thru 1958. Bond used this weapon in the first five Ian Fleming novels: *Casino Royale*, *Live & Let Die*, *Moonraker*, *Diamonds Are Forever* and *From Russia With Love.*

BROWNING 9MM HIGH POWER SINGLE Action SEMI-AUTOMATIC PISTOL

Used by Bond on the firing range and in *License Renewed*, *Scorpius* and *License to Kill* (Book).

System of Operation	Recoil, semi–automatic
Overall Length	7.75"
Barrel Length	4.75"
Weight	32 ounces
Magazine	Box-type, double-line staggered, 13 round capacity.
Muzzle Velocity	1040 to 1500 fps depending on type and manufacture of ammunition.
Sights	Low profile fixed blade front with drift Adjustable rear. Adjustable: Fixed blade front with screw adjustable rear sight.

John M. Browning (1855-1926) was a major designer of pistols, rifles, and machine guns, most of which are still in use. Some of his products bear his name, while others were designed for the Colt, FN., Remington, and Winchester firms.[1]

[1] FN. Initials of the Belgian arms manufacturer Fabrique Naationale d' Arms de Guerre, one of the world's foremost arms producers.

The Colt Python 357. Bond used this weapon on assignment in *License Renewed*. (Colt Industries, Hartford CT)

THE COLT PYTHON

Bond used this weapon on assignment in *License Renewed*. (Book)

Technical Data

Type	I Frame, Double Action revolver
Calibre	357 Magnum
Barrel Length	2 1/2", 4", 6", 8"
Height	5-5/8"
Weight	38 ounces with 4" barrel
Overall Length	9 1/4" with 4" barrel
Cylinder Capacity	6 rounds
Front Sight	Ramp type
Sight Radius	5-5/8"-4" barrel
Grips	Checkered service stocks for 2 ½". Checkered TGT stocks for 4", 6", 8".
Safety	Safety bar blocks hammer
Rifling	6 groove, left-hand twist, one turn in 14"

THE COLT 45 LONG-BARREL REVOLVER

Bond used this revolver with great effectiveness on assignment in *Moonraker* and *A View To A Kill*. Bond also kept this weapon in a special compartment in his automobile. (Book)

Technical Data

Calibre	Chambered for 357 Magnum, 45 Colt & 44 Special.
Operation	Manual, single action.
Barrel Length	7.5 or various other lengths.
Overall Length	13 inches with 7.5" barrel.
Weight	43 ounces with 7.5" barrel.
Sights	Open, fixed
Cylinder Capacity	6 rounds

This weapon has been produced for over 100 years and is known as "the gun that won the West."

THE COLT DETECTIVE SPECIAL / POLICE POSITIVE

Bond has used these weapons on various assignments including *Casino Royale* and *Live & Let Die*, often times keeping the revolver under his pillow at night.

Technical Data

Calibre	.38
Overall Length	7"
Weight	22.5 ounces with steel frame
Weight (Cobra)	16-5/8 ounces with aluminum frame
Capacity	6 rounds
System / Operation	Double-single action with swing-out cylinder

THE COLT MODEL 1911A1

Bond used this weapon often on the firing range to keep up his proficiency.

System / Operation	Recoil, semi–automatic
Overall Length	8.62"
Barrel Length	5"
Feed Device:	7-round, in-line, detachable box magazine
Sights	front. Blade rear. Square notch.
Weight	2.43 lbs.
Muzzle Velocity	830 fps

Samuel Colt (1814-1862) was an American designer of firearms and pioneer of modern mass-production. Famous mainly for his inexpensive, reliable revolvers. The company he established in 1836 still produces many of the older models as well as the latest military weapons. Colt Industries. Hartford, Conn.

THE HECKLER & KOCH VP70Z AUTOMATIC PISTOL

Manufactured by Heckler & Koch GMBH, D-7238 Oberndorf / Neckar, Federal Republic of Germany. This weapon was used effectively by Bond in the novel *For Special Services*. (Book)

Calibre	9mm Parabellum
System of Operation	Recoil operated
Weight W/O Magazine	11.1 ounces (315g)
Weight W/18 Rounds	29.0 ounces (820g)
Length Overall	8.01" (204mm)
Barrel Length	4.56" (116mm)
Height	5.59" (142mm)
Width Across Grips	1.25" (32mm)
Feed Device	18-round, detachable, staggered row
Sights	Front. Blade Rear. Square notch
Sight Radius	6.90" (175mm)
Muzzle Velocity	1180 fps (360 m/s)
Feed	Straight magazine for 18 rounds

THE HECKLER & KOCH P7M13

Manufactured by Heckler & Koch GMBH, D-7238 Oberndorf / Neckar. Federal Republic of Germany. This weapon was used by Bond in *Icebreaker*.

The Colt Detective Special/Police Positive. Bond used these weapons on various assignments including *Casino Royale* and *Live & Let Die,* often keeping the revolver under his pillow at night. (Colt Industries)

Operating Principle	Recoil operated
Action	Retarded inertia bolt
Feed	Straight magazine for 13 rounds
Calibre	9mm Parabellum
Muzzle Velocity	Approx. 351 m/ sec. V
Mode of Fire	Single fire
Overall Length	6.65 (169mm)
Height Of Pistol	5.30 (135 mm)
Width Across Grips	1.30 (33m)
Length Of Barrel	4.13" (105mm)
Sight Radius	5.83 (148mm)
Pistol w/o Magazine	29.98 ounces (850g)
Pistol w/Empty Magazine	34.42 ounces (975g)
Magazine w/ 13 Rounds	10.06 ounces (285g)

THE RUGER SUPER BLACKHAWK

Bond used this weapon on assignment in *License Renewed* and *For Special Services.* (Book)

Technical Data

Calibre	.44 Magnum
Length	7.5" barrel, 13-3/8" overall (blued). 10.5" barrel, 16-3/8" overall (blued). The same dimensions are available in stainless steel.
Weight	(7.5" barrel) 48 ounces. (10.5" barrel) 51 ounces

Sights .... Front ramp type. Rear fully adjustable
Capacity .... 6 rounds

Wide, deeply serrated hammer spur, long walnut grip panels and dragon style grip frame of steel.

RUGER P-85 9mm AUTOMATIC PISTOL

Bond used this weapon on assignment in the novel *Scorpius*. (Book)

Technical Data

Calibre 9mm
Method / Operation .... Recoil operated, semi-automatic
Breech Locking Mode .... Tilting barrel, link actuated
Action .... Double-action
Ammunition .... Cal. 9 x 19mm
Magazine Capacity .... 15 rounds
Weight, Magazine Empty .... 2.0 lbs.
Weight, Magazine Loaded .... 2.38 lbs.
Barrel Length .... 4.50 inches
Height .... 5.63 inches
Width .... 1.125 inches
Overall Length .... 7.84 inches
Sight Radius 6.12
Sights .... Fixed square notch rear adjustable for windage, square post front. Front and rear have white dot inserts

RUGER SUPER REDHAWK

Bond used this revolver on assignment in *Icebreaker.* (Book)

Technical Data

Calibre .... 44 Magnum
Cylinder Capacity .... 6 rounds

RUGER. NEW MODEL SUPER BLACKHAWK.

Catalog No. KS47N

Sturn, Ruger of Southport, CT and Prescott, AZ. Legendary manufacturers of pistols, rifles and shotguns. Most notable are the 22 calibre auto-loading pistols, the Super Blackhawk, Super Redhawk and the P-85. Bond used the Blackhawk on assignment in *License Renewed* and *For Special Services.* (Sturn, Ruger)

Weight	Empty 3.5 lbs. (7.5" barrel). 3.10 lbs. (9.5" barrel)
Length Overall	13" (7.5" barrel). 15" (9.5" barrel)
Sight Radius	9.5" (7.5" barrel). 11 ¼" (9.5" barrel)
Sights	Front ramp front sight base with Redhawk interchangeable insert sight blades are standard. Rear adjustable rear sight with a white outline square notch blade.

Sturm, Ruger & Company. Southport, Conneticut and Prescott, Arizona. Bill Sturm and William B. Ruger. Legendary manufacturers of pistols, rifles, and shotguns. Most notable are the 22 calibre auto loading pistol, the Super Blackhawk and Super Redhawk, and the P-85.

SMITH & WESSON POLICE POSITIVE

Calibre	.38 S & W Special
Frame	K
Capacity	6 shot cylinder
Front Sight	Serrated Ramp
Rear Sight	Fixed square notch
Barrel Length	2" (5.1cm). 4" (10.2cm)
Overall Length	6-7/8" (17.5cm) With 2" barrel. 9-5/16" (23.6cm) With 4" barrel
Weight	28 ounces with 2" barrel. 30.5 ounces with 4" barrel

Bond carried and used this weapon to kill a Russian agent and two hoods in the novel *The Spy Who Loved Me* (Book).

SMITH & WESSON CENTENNIAL AIRWeight

Bond carried this weapon on assignment in the novel *Dr. No* (Book).

Technical Data

Calibre	.38
Operation	Manual, double or single action
Overall Length	6-3/8
Barrel Length	2"
Weight	14.5 ounces (aluminum alloy frame)
Sights	Open, fixed
Cylinder Capacity	5 rounds

Smith & Wesson. Horace Smith (1808-1893) and David Wesson (1825-1906) were the founders in 1857 and held patent to the breech–loading revolvers. Springfield, MA.

WALTHER PPK, 7.65mm

Starting with his assignment in *Dr. No*, Bond carried this weapon at all times.

Technical Data (expressed in millimeters & grams)

Calibre	7.65mm
Overall Length	155mm
Height	100mm
Width	25mm
Barrel Length	83mm

Weight, empty, steel frame 590g
Weight, empty, light metal 470g
Magazine Capacity .... 7 rounds
Muzzle Velocity .... 308 m / s
Muzzle Energy .... 220 Joule
Zero Range 25mm

WALTHER MODEL P5

Bond has used this weapon on numerous assignments beginning with *A View To A Kill.*

Technical Data (expressed in millimeters & grams)

Calibre .... 9mm & 19 Parabellum
Mechanical System .... Locked-breech recoil loader
Breech-Locking Mode .... Tilted locking piece
Trigger Function .... Double action
Overall Dimensions .... 180 x 129 x 32 mm
Barrel Length 90mm
Sight Radius.. 134mm
Width Of Sights
Front / Rear 3, 5/3, 9mm
Frame .... Light metal
Weight, empty .... ca. 795g
Weight, loaded .... ca. 885g
Magazine Capacity .... 8 rounds
Muzzle Velocity .... ca. 350 m/s
Muzzle Energy .... ca. 500 Joule

WALTHER WA2000 RIFLE

Bond used this rifle against the Russian sniper in *The Living Daylights.* (Production discontinued)

The Ruger P-85™ is a 9mm, double-action, semi-automatic pistol equipped with a 15-shot magazine. The P-85 is the result of Ruger's relentless pursuit of perfection. The slide is heat-treated chrome-molydenum steel and the frame is investment cast in light weight aluminum alloy which is hard coated for toughness. Simple to operate and maintain. Features include an ambidextrous safety, grooved hammer spur, left and right hand magazine latches, oversized trigger guard and a lanyard loop.

Catalog Number P-85™

Ruger P-85 9mm Automatic Pistol. Bond used this weapon while on assignment in the novel *Scorpius.* (Sturn, Ruger)

Walther PPK 7.65mm. Bond has carried this through most of his career starting with *Dr. No.* (Carl Walther, Ulm, Germany)

Technical Data

Calibre	.300 Win. Mag. / 308 Win
Function Principle	Gas operation
Bolt Type	Rotating
Magazine Capacity	5/6
Overall Length	975mm
Barrel Length	650mm
Weight: (excl. scope)	7.6 kg
Trigger Pull Weight	1200-1500g
Trigger Type	Two–stage
Buttplate Adjustment Height	+30mm

Carl Walther GmbH. D-7900, Ulm, Federal Republic of Germany. German manufacturer of firearms famous especially for the P38, P5, P88, P99, and PP / PPK semi-automatic pistols, referred to as "Walther's." The initials PPK stand for Polizei Pistole Kriminal, which indicated its intended use.

AR-7 SURVIVAL RIFLE

Calibre	.22 rimfire, long rifle, standard & high velocity
Action	Semi-automatic
Magazine	Detachable box type, capacity eight rounds
Barrel	16 inch precision high grade steel rifling
Stock	Full pistol grip, recessed to stow barrel, action and magazine. High quality Cycolac plastic
Safety	Convenient thumb safety at rear of receiver. Locks trigger

Sights	Square-blade front, adjustable for windage by tapping; aperture rear adjustable for elevation
Weight	2.75 lbs.
Overall Length	34.5"
Length When Stowed	16.5"
Finish	Anodized black aluminum alloy & parkerlubed steel. Bolt & charging handle chrome-plated to resist corrosion. This weapon floats.

ARMALITE AR-18 COMBAT RIFLE

This rifle was never manufactured in the U.S.A., but rather by the Sterling Armament Co. in Dagenham, England. The guns were stamped "Costa-Mesa-California, USA." They also had the word "Sterling" in a block. They were then sent to the USA where they were sold by Armalite Inc. all over the world. In July 1988 Sterling Armament Co., Ltd. was acquired by Royal Ordinance Plc and the business which had been in Dagenham for 90 years was moved to Nottingham and amalgamated with the Guns & Vehicles Division of Royal Ordnance Plc. This rifle was used by Bond on assignment in *For Special Services*. (Book)

Technical Data
Selective Fire, Auto / Semi-Auto

Calibre	5.56mm (.223 cal.)
Mag. 20 rd, loaded	11 ounces
Barrel Length	18 ¼"
Sighting Radius..	20 7/8"
Overall Length	38"
With Butt Stock Folded	28 3/4"
Rate of Fire	Approx. 750 rounds per minute
Weight (empty)	6.7 lbs.
With Telescopic Sight	7.7 lbs.
Muzzle Velocity	990 meters 3250 fps
Max. Range	3045 meters 3333 yds.

Ruger Super Redhawk .44 Magnum. Bond used this revolver while on assignment in *Icebreaker*. (Sturn, Ruger)

Walther P5, 9mm. Bond used this weapon on numerous assignments beginning with
A View to A Kill. (Carl Walther)

Sights .... Rear: Peep-adjustable for windage.
Front: Post-adjustable for elevation.
Action .... Gas operated with piston and cylinder and operating rod mounted above barrel.

Armalite, Inc. Costa Mesa, California. This company was sold in 1984 to Elisco Tool Company of the Philippines. Prior to that, it manufactured in the U.S.A., as the AR-7 Survival Rifle. This rifle was carried by Bond in his special attache case on assignment in *From Russia With Love.* Bond fired this weapon, wounding the co-pilot of a S.P.E.C.T.R.E. helicopter. He in turn dropped a live grenade inside the helicopter which exploded, destroying the machine and the pilots.

THE BOFORS L / 70 ANTI AIRCRAFT GUN

First introduced in 1947, and to the British Army in 1953. It was manufactured by AB Bofors, Bofors, Sweden. Utilizing a British Bofors L / 70, Bond shot down Jack Spang's helicopter in the novel *Diamonds Are Forever.*

Technical Data

Calibre 40mm
Length Of Barrel 2.8m
Twist Of Rifling .... 1 in 46 to 1 in 27 cal.
Number of Grooves 16
Max. Gas Pressure .... 3,250kg / cm2
Weight Of Gun, Type A 5, 150kg
Number of Rounds in Racks 96
Number of Rounds in Loader 26
Rate of Fire .... Up to 300 rpm
Height of Axis of Bore, Travelling 1,335m
Max. Height, Travelling 2.35m

MAX. Length, Travelling, Tow Bar Up	7.07m
Width	2.225m
Ground Clearance	390m
Turning Radius	8m
Max. Towing Speed	32km / h
Elevation	-4 degrees to + 90 degrees
Traverse	360 degrees
Elevating Speed	45 degrees / s
Traversing Speed	85 degrees / s
Elevating Acceleration	135 degrees / s
Traversing Acceleration	127 degrees / s
Power Supply	220V, 50Hz.
Power Consumption	5 / 12 kw
Max. Horizontal Range	12,620m
Max. Effective Anti-Aircraft Range	3,000 – 4,000m

SOME INTERESTING WEAPONS USED AGAINST BOND

Oddjob's Hat	Auric Goldfinger's personal valet and chauffeur wore a black derby which embodied a brim with a razor-sharp edge. During the Goldfinger affair, Oddjob used this hat on several victims, throwing it like a boomerang.

Armalite Inc. of Costa Mesa, CA manufactured this AR-7 Survival Rifle. Bond carries this weapon in his special attack case on assignment in *From Russia With Love*. (Royal Ordnance, Nottingham, England)

This is the Swedish 40mm Bofors anti-aircraft gun that James Bond fired to shoot down Jack Spang's helicopter in the novel *Diamonds Are Forever.* (AB Bofors, Sweden)

Tee Hee's Claw Hand .... This hand of steel operated similar to a pruning sniper. It could crush a pistol, as it did with Bond's, or snip off a little finger. During the mission in *Live & Let Die,* Bond managed to disable Tee Hee's claw by snipping the cable that controlled the claw.

Yo-Yo Buzz Saw .... This novel little device operates on the same principle as your childhood yo-yo. It incorporates a table saw blade and power cells for energy. Kamal Khan's men used this insidious weapon to kill British agent Vijay in the film *Octopussy.*

OTHER WEAPONS USED AGAINST BOND

Mace .... *No Deals Mr. Bond*
Garrote Watch .... *From Russia With Love*
The Golden Gun .... *The Man With the Golden Gun*
Air Defense Missile .... *Octopussy*
Mirror Dart Gun .... *Live & Let Die*
Crossbow .... *For Your Eyes Only*

WOMEN IN BOND BOOKS

Casino Royale .... Vesper Lynd
Live & Let Die .... Solitaire
Moonraker .... Gala Brand
Diamonds Are Forever .... Tiffany Case
From Russia With Love .... Tatiana Romanova
Dr. No .... Honeychild Rider

Goldfinger .... Pussy Galore, Jill Masterson, Tilly Masterson
Thunderball .... Domino Vitali, Patricia Fearing
The Spy Who Loved Me .... Vivienne Michel
On Her Majesty's Secret Service .... Tracy di Vicenzo
You Only Live Twice .... Kissy Suzuki
The Man With The Golden Gun .... Mary Goodnight
Colonel Sun .... Ariadne Alexandrou
License Renewed .... Lavender Peacock, Ann Reilly
For Special Services .... Cedar Leiter, Ann Reilly, Nena Bismaquer
Icebreaker .... Paula Vacker, Rivke Ingber
Role Of Honor .... Percy Proud, Cindy Chalmer
Nobody Lives Forever .... Sukie Tempests, Nannie Norwich
No Deals Mr. Bond .... Ebbie Heritage, Heather Dare
Scorpius .... Harriet Horner
License To Kill .... Della Churchill, Pam Bouvier, Lupe Lamora
Win, Lose, Or Die .... Clover Pennington, Beatrice Da Ricci,
    Nikola Ratnikov.
Brokenclaw .... Wanda Man Song Hing Sue Chi - Ho
The Man From Barbarossa .... Nina Bibikova, Stephanie Adore
Death Is Forever .... Easy St. John
Never Send Flowers .... Fredericka Von Grusse
Seafire .... Fredericka Von Grusse
Cold Fall .... Sukie Tempesta, Toni Nicolletti,
    Giulliana Tempesta, Beatrice da Ricci
Goldeneye .... Xenia Onatopp, Natalya Simonova
Tomorrow Never Dies .... Wai Lin, Paris Carver
Zero Minus Ten .... Sunni Pei, Stephanie Lane
The Facts of Death .... Hera Volopoulos, Niki Mirakos, Dr. Ashley Anderson

WOMEN IN BOND SHORT STORIES

From A View To A Kill .... Mary Ann Russell
For Your Eyes Only .... Judy Havelock
Quantum of Solace .... Rhonda Llewellyn Masters
Risico .... Lisl Baum
The Hildebrand Rarity .... Liz Krest
Octopussy .... None
The Living Daylights .... Trigger
The Property of a Lady .... Maria Freudenstein
007 In New York .... So Lange

WOMEN IN BOND FILMS: aka "The Bond Girls"

Ursula Andress as Honey Ryder in *Doctor No*, 1962
Daniela Bianchi as Tatiana Romanova, *From Russia With Love*, 1963
Honor Blackman as Pussy Galore in *Goldfinger*, 1964
Claudine Auger as Domino in *Thunderball*, 1965
Mie Hama as Kissy Suzuki in *You Only Live Twice*, 1967
Diana Rigg as Tracy Vicenzo in *On Her Majesty's Secret Service*, 1969
Jill St. John as Tiffany Case in *Diamonds Are Forever*, 1971

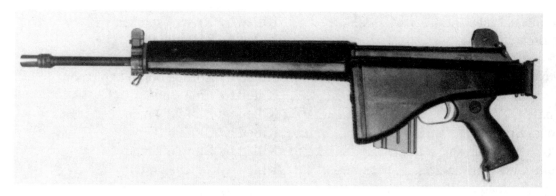

Armalite AR-18 Combat Rifle. This rifle was used by Bond on assignment in *For Special Services.* (Timberline Hawk)

Jane Seymour as Solitaire in *Live & Let Die*, 1973
Britt Eckland as Mary Goodnight; Maude Adams as Andrea, *The Man With The Golden Gun*, 1974
Barbara Bach as Major Anya Amasova in *The Spy Who Loved Me*, 1977
Lois Chiles as Holly Goodhead in *Moonraker*, 1979
Carole Bouquet as Melina Havelock in *For Your Eyes Only*, 1981
Maude Adams as Octopussy in *Octopussy*, 1983
Kim Basinger as Domino in *Never Say Never Again*, 1983
Tanya Roberts as Stacey Sutton in *A View To A Kill*, 1985
Maryam d'Abo as Kara Milovy in *The Living Daylights*, 1987
Carey Lowell as Pam Bouvier in *License To Kill*, 1989
Izabella Scorpuco as Natalya in *Goldeneye*, 1995
Michelle Yeoh as Wai Lin in *Tomorrow Never Dies*, 1997

WOMEN THAT BOND HAS NOT SLEPT WITH

Gala Brand, Tilly Masterson, Loelia Pononby, Maria Freudenstein, Mary Jane Mashkin, Rhonda Llewellyn Masters, Heather Dare, Miss Moneypenny, Clover Pennington.

WOMEN IN BOOK & FILM WHO DIED A VIOLENT DEATH [1]

Vesper Lynd	Suicide
Paula Caplan	Suicide
Nannie Norwich	Killed by Bond
Heather Dare	Killed by Bond
Irma Bunt	Killed by Bond
Fatima Blush	Killed by Bond
Naomi	Killed by Bond
Jill Masterson	Killed by Oddjob
Tilly Masterson	Killed by Oddjob
Mary Jane Mashkin	Killed by Franco
Emma Dupre	Drowned by Scorpius' men
Rivke Ingber	Killed by Paul Vecker
Harriet Horner	Died from snake bites
Mary Trueblood	Killed by Dr. No's men
Fiona Volpe	Killed by Largo's men
Stromberg's assistant	Killed by Stromberg
Corrine Dufour	Killed by Drax's dogs

Countess Lisl	Killed by Kristatos's men
Andrea	Killed by Scaramanga
Rosie Carver	Killed by Mr. Big's men
Mayday	Killed by Zorin's bomb explosion
Tracy di Vicenzo	Killed by Irma Bunt
Plenty O' Toole	Killed by Blofeld's men
Helga Brandt	Killed by Blofeld
Akiko Makabayshi	Killed by Blofeld's men
Della Churchill	Killed by Sanchez men
Nene Bismaquer Blofeld	Killed by giant snakes
Clover Pennington	Killed by Bast agent
Nikola Ratnikov	Killed by Bast agent
Nina Bibikona	Killed by Russian rocket launcher
Wanda Man Song Hing	Killed by Brokenclaw's men
Easy St. John	Killed by Wolfgang Weisen's men
Laura March	Killed by Dragonpol
Angela Shaw	Killed by Dragonpol
Christine Wright	Killed by Dragonpol
Jessie Styles	Killed by Dragonpol
Bridget Bellomy	Killed by Dragonpol
Betsy Sagar	Killed by Dragonpol
Janet Fellows	Killed by Dragonpol
Anne Frick	Killed by Dragonpol
Heather Barnabus	Killed by Dragonpol
Cathy and Anna	Killed by Maxwell Tarn
Heidi	Killed by Dodd
Beth	Killed by Bond
Paris Carver	Killed by Carver's hoods
Sukie Tempesta	Killed by General Clay
Toni Nicolletti	Killed by Tempesta brothers
Xenia Onatopp	Killed by Bond
Hera Volopoulos	Killed by Bond
Melina Papas	Killed by Bond
Two additional women unnamed	Killed by Bond

[1] On a previous assignment Bond had killed a woman Smersh agent in the Louvre in Paris.

WOMEN: IMPAIRMENTS / ODDITIES

Domino Vitali	One leg one inch shorter than the other
Gala Brand	Mole on curvature of left breast
Honey Rider	Broken nose
Pussy Galore	Lesbian
Simon Latrelle (Solitaire)	Telepathic
Tatiana Romanova	Excessive muscular development of the buttocks
Teresa Di Vicenzo	Obsessed with commiting suicide
Tiffany Case	Having been gang raped, no man could touch her
Nena Bismaquer Blofeld	One breast
Magda	Collects a photograph for her scrapbook of each man she has gone to bed with

Walther P88, 9mm in *License to Kill*. Bond used the Walther PPK 7.65, the P5, P88 and the 9mm signature rifle. (Carl Walther)

Xenia Onatopp .... Likes to crush her lover's chest and bites them after making love

WOMEN: AFTER THEY LEFT BOND

Honey Ryder married Dr. Wilder of Philadelphia, Pa. and has two children.
Gala Brand married Detective-Inspector Vivian of Scotland Yard, has three children and lives in Richmond, England.
Lavender Peacock attended a major agricultural college and studied estate management and is now successfully managing her Scottish castle and estate.
Tiffany Case married a Marine Corps Major attached to the Military Attache's Staff of the American Embassy and they returned to the states.
Ann Reilly (Qute) is still with 'Q' branch of M.I.6.
Loelia Ponsonby, Bond's first personal secretary, left to marry a rich member of the Baltic Exchange.
Lupe Lamora married Hector Lopez, former President of Isthmus.
Cedar Leiter, still with the CIA, but thinking of marrying the son of a wealthy oil man.

WOMEN BOND HAS SLAPPED ON THE SCREEN

From Russia With Love .... Tatiana Romanova
On Her Majesty's Secret Service .... La Comtesse Teresa di Vicenzo
The Man With the Golden Gun .... Andrea
Diamonds Are Forever .... Tiffany Case

ABOUT THE AUTHORS

HOYT L. BARBER is an authority on tax havens and international banking centers, and has worked with clients worldwide as a financial consultant.

Mr. Barber is author of numerous books including *How To Incorporate Your Business In Any State* (Tab Books), *Tax Freedom* (Tab Books), *Tax Havens: How To Bank, Invest, and Do Business Offshore and Tax Free* (McGraw-Hill), and *Protect Your Intellectual Property: An International Guide to Patents, Copyrights, and Trademarks* (Productive Publications).

Currently he is nearing completion on his first novel, an international financial thriller.

Authors, Hoyt and Harry Barber standing with Bacchus, a five year old gelding from the rare, old Trakehner breed bloodlines of Pelzjaeger and Gazal. Bacchus was recently imported from Germany and is presently training for the dressage grand prix circuit. (Steve Soulam)

HARRY L. BARBER began his advertising career with Young & Rubicam, Inc. where he worked on Hunt Foods, Union Oil, Capitol Records, Goodyear Tire, and other national accounts. Later, he established his own advertising agency in San Marino, California where he serviced industrial and financial clients.

For twenty years he served as Senior Vice President of Communications or advertising consultant to major corporations. His account activity experience includes film production, commodities, bio-chemicals, epoxy resins, food, franchising, petroleum, aviation, automotive, political, land development, and industrial equipment marketing.

In the past, Barber developed national advertising and public relations campaigns with screen and television personalities, Project Hope, The Breakfast Club, U.S. Astronauts and USAC racing. He authored *How To Steal a Million Dollars in Free Publicity* (1982) and is a World War II combat veteran.